Fidelity and Translation

Errata

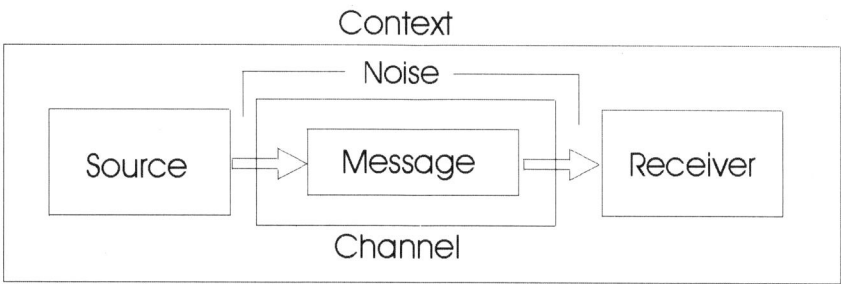

Figure 1: Transportation model of communication. (p. 220)

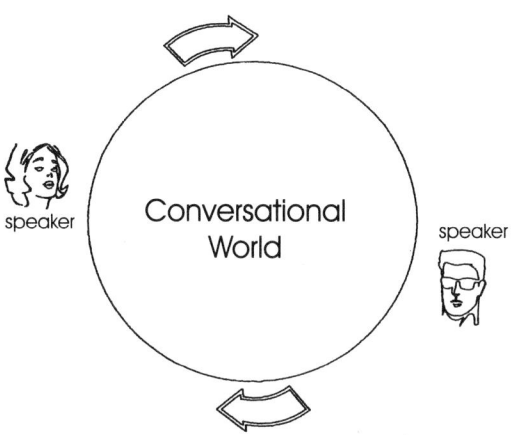

Figure 4: A conversational model of communication. (p. 229)

Fidelity and Translation

Communicating the Bible in New Media

*Edited by Paul A. Soukup
and
Robert Hodgson*

Co-published by

**Sheed & Ward
Franklin, Wisconsin**

**American Bible Society
New York**

As an apostolate of the Priests of the Sacred Heart, a Catholic religious order, the mission of Sheed & Ward is to publish books of contemporary impact and enduring merit in Catholic Christian thought and action. The books published, however, reflect the opinion of their authors and are not meant to represent the official position of the Priests of the Sacred Heart.

1999

Sheed & Ward
7373 South Lovers Lane Road
Franklin, Wisconsin 53132
1-800-558-0580

Copyright © 1999 by the American Bible Society

All rights reserved. No part of this book may be reproduced, stored in a retrieval system, or transmitted, in any form or by any means–electronic, mechanical, photocopying, recording or otherwise–without the written permission of Sheed & Ward.

Printed in the United States of America.

Library of Congress Cataloguing-in-Publication.
Fidelity and translation : communicating the Bible in new media / edited by Paul A. Soukup and Robert Hodgson.
   p. cm.
  Papers presented of two symposiums in New York, Sept. 1995 and Mérida, Mexico, May 1997 and other supporting material.
  Includes bibliographical references and index.
  ISBN 0-8267-0036-5
  1. Bible--Translating. 2. Bible--Hermeneutics. 3. Mass media--Religious aspects--Christainity. I. Soukup, Paul A. II. Hodgson, Robert, 1943- .
BS449.F53 1999
220.5--dc21   98-43462
                                                                                          CIP

This book was co-published with the American Bible Society (ISBN 1-58051-039-6) 1865 Broadway, New York, NY 10023. 1-800-322-4235.

1 2 3 4 5 / 02 01 00 99

Table of Contents

Acknowledgements vii
Preface ix
    Basil A. Rebera
Foreword. xiii
    David G. Burke

Section I: New Challenges to Fidelity in Translation 1

1. Faithfulness—A Wider Perspective. 7
    Euan McG. Fry
2. Anatomy of a Translation Process:
   A Case Study of *Out of the Tombs (Mark 5.1-20)* 29
    Fern Lee Hagedorn
3. Fidelity and Access:
   Reclaiming the Bible with Personal Media. 47
    Gary R. Rowe
4. The Historical Imagination 65
    Merle Worth
5. Designing Translation Exercises on CD-ROM:
   Pedagogical Principles and Theoretical Validity 75
    Mona Baker

Section II: Qualities of Texts 91

6. Fidelity and Literary Analysis 95
    Lydia Lebrón-Rivera
7. A New Voice in the Amphitheater:
   Full Fidelity in Translating. 101
    Bernard Brandon Scott
8. Multimedia Communication of the Biblical Message. 119
    Eugene A. Nida
9. The Imaged Word:
   Aesthetics, Fidelity, and New Media Translations. 133
    Gregor T. Goethals
10. Midrash: A Model for Fidelity in New Media Translation. . 173
    J. Ritter Werner

Section III: Seeking Fidelity: Theoretical Perspectives. . . . 199

11. Power and Interpretive Authority in Multimedia Translation 203
    Joy Sisley
12. Communication Models, Translation, and Fidelity 219
    Paul A. Soukup, SJ
13. Semiotics, Fidelity, and New Media Translation 233
    Robert Hodgson, Jr.
14. Peirce's Semiotics for Translation 249
    Ubaldo Stecconi

Reference List 263
Index 275
About the Authors 279

Acknowledgments

The editors of this volume would like to acknowledge the vision and leadership of the United Bible Societies (UBS) and the American Bible Society (ABS) for their role in sponsoring and planning the May, 1997 Mérida, Mexico Symposium which produced many of the essays gathered in this book. We especially want to thank then UBS General Secretary John D. Erickson, ABS President Eugene B. Habecker, ABS Vice-President Maria I. Martinez, ABS Associate Vice-President David G. Burke, then UBS Translation, Production, and Distribution Services Director Philip C. Stine, and UBS Translation Services Coordinator Basil A. Rebera.

Various publishers and copyright holders have graciously allowed us to reprint materials. We acknowledge them and offer thanks:

The American Bible Society for permission to reproduce images from their CD-ROMs, *Out of the Tombs, A Father and Two Sons,* and *The Visit,* and for permission to reproduce the images from the Sampler Bible on pages 155, 157, and 158.

Bantam Doubleday Dell Publishing Group, Inc., for permission to reprint, on pages 88-89, the entry "Issac Newton" from *A Brief History of Time: From the Big Bang to Black Holes*, by Stephen W. Hawking. Copyright ©1988 by Stephen W. Hawking. Used by permission of Bantam Books, a division of Bantam Doubleday Dell Publishing Group, Inc.

The Danish Bible Society for permission to reproduce the images of The Sermon on the Mount and The Last Supper by E. H. Kristensen from *Bibelen: Udvalgte fortaellinger*, on pages 163 and 165.

The Deutsche Bibelgesellschaft Stuttgart for permission to reproduce an image of the page containing John 20 (page 109), and the use of verses John 20.25-30 and Luke 10.30-31, from *The Greek New Testament*, 4th rev. ed., Editors B. Aland, K. Aland, et al. (Stuttgart: UBS and Deutsche Bibelgesellschaft, 1993). ©1993 Deutsche Bibelgesellschaft Stuttgart.

Kelly LaDuke/Gamma Liaison for permission to reproduce the photograph, a Wedding at Walt Disney World, page 48.

Routledge Publications for permission to reprint material from Mona Baker's *In Other Words: A Coursebook on Translation* , on pages 88-89.

The Scuola Superiore per Interpreti e Traduttori for permission to reprint Ubaldo Stecconi's essay, "Peirce's Semiotics for Translation." This appears as chapter 14.

The Board of Trinity College Dublin for permission to reproduce two illustrations from the Book of Kells, on pages 144 and 146.

The United Bible Societies for permission to reprint Euan Fry's essay, "Faithfulness–a Wider Perspective" (chapter 1) and Robert Hodgson's essay, "Semiotics, Fidelity, and New Media Translation" (chapter 13) from the *United Bible Societies Bulletin*, and for permission to reproduce the images from the UBS Scripture comics series on pages 166 and 168.

University Library, Utrecht for permission to reproduce two illustrations from the Utrecht Psalter, Psalm 57 and a detail of Psalm 57, Ms. 32, fol. 32r. These appear on pages 142 and 143.

The Vatican Library for permission to reproduce a page of the Codex Vaticanus, on page 108.

Merle Worth and Fred Berner Productions for permission to reprint parts of the script and to reproduce the images from their television production, *ABOUT US: The Dignity of Children*. These appear on pages 67-69.

Finally, we wish to thank the many colleagues who helped prepare the volume for publication: Ester B. Vargas-Machuca, Barbara A. Bernstengel, Christina A. Murphy, Chandra Mojaver, Anne Schabert, Deborah G. Atkinson, and many others of the ABS staff; Ingrid Murray and Connie Rice, of the Communication Department at Santa Clara University; and Jeremy Langford and Rebecca Luft at Sheed & Ward. We offer deep and special gratitude to Juliana C. Moseley of the American Bible Society's Research Center for Scripture and Media, who assisted the editors in more ways than we can count.

Paul A. Soukup, S.J.
Robert Hodgson, Jr.

Preface

Basil A. Rebera

When I think of the Indian subcontinent and Sri Lanka, with a population larger than China's, to say that TV and video is all the rage is not a journalistic banality. That medium is creating social and cultural transformations more rapid and more profound than centuries of earlier colonial rule.

I remember the concern of a Bible Society Auxiliary Secretary in one of the states of India at the havoc that TV and video were wreaking on the tradition of midweek evening Bible study and prayer groups in the Church in his state. Numbers dwindled and then groups became defunct, so that some parishes no longer scheduled midweek evening Bible study groups and prayer groups. Instead the faithful had gathered around the new icon—TV and video. It wasn't in jest that people said that street demonstrations ended where the evening TV programs began and that a government ploy to scuttle a demonstration was to stage a TV event.

The new media domination of communication is not a phenomenon peculiar to the United States of America or other western countries. In fact the peoples of the other nations are the more avid denizens of the new communication environment; the aural/visual media form the only channels of communication for the billions of non-literates and functional non-literates of the world. Books abound and ubiquitous newspapers and magazines, by their sheer volume, create an illusion of undiminished primacy of the pervasiveness, influence, and appeal of the print medium. But even in the mass print medium, visual images seem to entice. Even the new-look *New York Times* has a full color picture on the front page! In magazines one struggles to find where articles begin and run on in the labyrinth of glossy visual images that commandeer the attention of the peruser or browser. Newspapers had gossip before the creation of the tabloid, but perhaps it is the voyeurism that tabloid pictures create, more than print content, format, and price, that seduces the buyer.

So the illusory primacy of the print medium, and its tenacious prestige as an elite and erudite medium exclusively worthy as the medium of the divine utterance, perpetuates that medium as the norm for the dissemination of Sacred Scripture. Other media have been relegated as marginal, experimental, ancillary, and dispensable by the various Bible Societies as channels of communicating the Scriptures, and they have therefore elected to be on the fringes of the new communication environment. Also, Bible Societies measure achievement mainly by the volume of distribution of print products, not by the permeation of the message into the consciousness of audiences or by the transformations being effected by Scripture within individuals and societies.

But Bible Societies now recognize and acknowledge that the new media form—perhaps the most powerful and persuasive of the forces in the environment that shape people today and will continue to shape people into the future—is arguably the more effective communication medium for Scripture dissemination. Consequently Bible Societies have collectively made a commitment at the World Assembly in 1996 to make significant progress in the use of the new media for communicating Scripture to every audience.

For the Bible Societies to make a paradigm shift in media use, however, they, and the constituencies they serve, must define and understand the issue of faithfulness and scriptural authority.

Scholars have developed definitions of accuracy and faithfulness for translating from one language code to another, that is, from Hebrew and Greek to a modern language. The application of the theories of formal correspondence translation to the source text, or the use of theories of closest natural equivalents and functional equivalence in rendering the source text, have produced translations that people have judged as faithful; these have gained acceptance as Scripture. The key criteria here for judging what is Scripture and what has authority as sacred text have been and still remain code and medium. These criteria, for the present, remain immovably cast in the presuppositions that the divine revelation cannot be separated from the divine utterance in which it is encoded and that the sole authoritative repository of the utterance is the written text.

When the Bible Societies expanded into communicating Scripture in the audio media, the issue of faithfulness did not appear so acute because the message remained in a language code. The Societies developed principles and practical guidelines to ensure faithfulness to meet the expectations audiences had of the medium itself.

The Bible Societies now face the challenge to at least give parity of place to the new media in communicating the Scripture message to human populations now captive to them. The American Bible Society's (ABS) new media translation program has pioneered both in presenting Scripture in compelling video productions, of superlative quality, that have won the highest accolades from the new media industries, and in developing a theoretical framework for evaluating the faithfulness of a new media "translation" of Scripture.

Because the Scripture source exists in a written language code and because we must judge faithfulness in reference to that code, the definition of "translation" for the new media remains necessarily defined in terms of equivalence. One could achieve a faithful rendering of the source by an underlying word track, which is read, recited, or sung as lyric. But the more challenging task lies in achieving functional equivalence of other elements of the message of the source text through visual images and symbols.

The ABS new media team and United Bible Societies (UBS) colleagues have worked to develop principles of translation and practical guidelines for transferring the meaning of Scripture from one medium to another. Two symposia have explored the theme of faithfulness and worked to develop criteria for evaluating faithfulness. The ABS organized the first in New York in September 1995 and with the UBS Service Center organized the second in Mérida, Mexico on May 1997. Presentations at the first symposium were co-published in 1997 by ABS and Sheed & Ward under the title, *From One Medium To Another: Basic Issues for Communicating the Scriptures in New Media.* The theme of the second symposium in Mérida, Mexico was "Fidelity in New Media Translation." The presentations at that symposium and other supporting material appear in this volume.

Both these volumes offer major contributions to the development of a theoretical framework for defining the process of decoding, transferring, and encoding a message from one medium to another and establishing criteria for evaluating the fidelity of receptor medium to the source. They also stimulate the ongoing process of refinement of definitions and criteria and educate the Bible Societies and their constituencies in these new areas.

Foreword

David G. Burke

As a representative of the American Bible Society's (ABS) Translations Department, a host partner together with the United Bible Societies' (UBS) Translations Program in the 1997 Mérida Symposium, I am pleased to be able to make some introductory remarks. As we move incrementally toward the close of the 20th century, we are now beginning to see (at least in various places around the USA) electronic sign boards that already count down the years, days, and hours to the year 2000. We have only to look at modern communications to see that we now experience, throughout the world, a profound shift in communications technology and the resulting media environment. These days very few of us accept our information only in print without sound and visual dimensions.

We are now witnessing the movement of population segments to post-literacy. That is, we see segments of people that can and do read, but who prefer other forms of information transfer to those involving reading. New York University media critic Neil Postman has written:

> We have reached, I believe, a critical mass in that electronic media have decisively and irreversibly changed the character of our symbolic environment. We are now a culture whose information, ideas and epistemology are given form by television, not by the printed word. (1985, p. 28)

Some biblical scholars have foreseen enormous potential in this media shift—potential for communicating the Scriptures to pre-literate and non-literate population groups, as well as post-literate populations around the globe. In 1989, the ABS launched experimental and developmental research into the question of how to translate Scripture as Scripture into new media forms, under the leadership of Fern Lee Hagedorn. The experimental developments of this program targeted youth who are particularly inclined toward screen-centered media.

In the early to mid-1980s, the leadership of the UBS, particularly in directional statements issued from the Chiang Mai UBS World Assembly, issued a challenge that, in the process of producing new translations and relevant Scripture resources, Bible Societies dare not forget youth, the population segment from which the next generation's leaders will come. The challenge was to produce Scriptures in forms that would particularly communicate Scripture to youth. In the United States, this impetus, generated at Chiang Mai, led to both the innovative print translation, the Contemporary English Version (New Testament published in 1991) and the ABS project (1989-) involving new media Scripture translation and resource development. These projects have focused on youth in their teens, a cohort that tends especially to prefer words, sound, and images on screens to reading on pages.

All along, the ABS's new media translation program has aimed to explore ways within the emerging electronic technologies to share the Scriptures in the new language, as it were, of electronic media, to which youth especially are keenly attuned. An underlying assumption has been that the Bible, especially in its powerful stories and narratives, is not some mere conglomeration of interesting curiosities from the ancient past (like fossils), but rather a relevant resource for daily life in the real world of today. Its stories provide powerful guides for living, with meaning and purpose, amongst all of life's ambiguities and problems.

Many of the papers here arose from the 1997 Mérida Symposium exploring faithfulness in translating Scripture into new media forms. They, and others in this volume, represent an especially varied and stimulating collection that will enable the reader to listen and reflect, to engage and think through the issues involved from a wide range of angles. Again, as we move steadily into the newly unfolding communications environment of the 21st century, Bible Society translation programs will continue to find a basis in a thorough examination of the source texts—whether the target medium be print or non-print—as we seek to explore fresh and faithful ways of making the Scriptures accessible to those various audiences, whether centered on screen or page, who stand in need of the Word of God.

Section I

New Challenges to Fidelity in Translation

New Challenges to Fidelity in Translation

Notions of faithfulness in translation have changed over the years. Many people still hold for a literal (or formal) equivalence, where individual words in the source text match up with words in the translation. In fact, a recent commentary from the Vatican Working Group for the Final Revision of the *Lectionary for Mass* (1997) indicated a preference for this level of fidelity in biblical translation. Some scholars have argued for a goal of functional equivalence, where the sense of the translation matches the sense of the source text. This becomes particularly important in situations where a literal translation would mislead the reader, due to cultural or contextual factors. Bible Society translators, following Nida (1964), typically seek functional equivalence in their work. Finally, some hold that the very idea of fidelity in translation should be abandoned because of the inherent inability to map one language transparently onto another and the creativity required in translation (see Lambert, 1997, and Stecconi, this volume). A good translation is what the audience accepts as a translation.

All of these notions of fidelity in translation grow out of linguistic translation of texts and, to some extent, of oral translation. Each sense of translation—formal equivalence, functional equivalence and including the last-mentioned "non-equvalence"—do admit of a limit: No translation can disregard the source. Few would accept a treatise on nuclear physics as a "translation" of one of Baudelaire's poems. Few would accept a stand-up comedy routine as a "translation" of a speech to the United Nations Security Council. People presume that at some level translations will remain identifiable as such, even if we do not use the word "faithful." In a similar manner, people presume that some way to check a translation exists. In fact, whole branches of literary scholarship explore and compare translations, presumably working with commonly intelligible or objective measures.

What happens, though, when the translation does not follow linguistic lines, but seeks to move from one medium to another (Hodgson & Soukup, 1997)? Here the translator's task becomes "transmediazation," that is, putting words into dance or vice-versa, putting a text into a video format or producing a novel from a film treatment, or making a script into a film. All of these activities do take place and, on at least one level, they are translations, in the sense proposed by Lambert (1997) and Cattrysse (1992, 1997). How does this newer situation, made more relevant by the new media we experience, deal with the question of fidelity in translation? The question takes on more immediacy for the Bible Societies when the new media translation involves the text of the Bible.

This first section defines the situation that new media translators face. It begins with a 1987 essay by Euan Fry that formally introduced the idea of faithfulness in the contexts of the Bible and of new media. Because Fry's essay formed the starting point for the American Bible Society's New Media Translation Program and its affiliated Research Center for Scripture and Media, we begin with it in order to give a context to the reflections in this volume. Fry himself considered the Bible Societies' experience with Bible comics and looked to the possibility of dramatizations and audio recording of the Scriptures. His essay anticipates questions of media and audience and recognizes the dangers associated with the selection of texts and their necessary reconstruction. His concluding guidelines form touchstones still followed by the Bible Societies.

Fern Lee Hagedorn, who led the American Bible Society's New Media Translations Program through its first four multimedia translations, describes how the translators and the production group addressed questions of fidelity in their first project, a video translation of Mark 5.1-20, the story of the healing of the Gerasene demoniac. As well as providing a history of that project—a good narrative of theological reflection on communication in action—Hagedorn highlights the ways in which the video production followed the translation practices and procedures of the American Bible Society. As she notes, the production schedule and the exigencies of production demanded changes in the "script" in ways that the traditional Bible translator would not face. She outlines a very practical approach to fidelity, one that flows through the project from its inception through to its evaluation by the target audience. In her essay we begin to see what happens when the translation is not a text.

But what would happen if we were to stop thinking of the Bible as a book? Gary Rowe, a communication and new media consultant to the American Bible Society, ventures to answer that question. As the emerging digital world redefines the nature of communication, it challenges the print-based presuppositions about the Bible. Though scholars, clergy, and many Bible-study students know that the Bible began as oral expression, most still think of it as a book, complete with notions of fixed text and unchanging content, and sometimes with a canonical archaic language. These artifacts result as much from the characteristics of print and reproductive processes of the printing press as from the nature of the Bible. If the Bible appears in digital media, wider theories of fidelity come into play. To understand those, though, demands a deeper understanding of digital media. Rowe introduces the reader to the characteristics of new media in an attempt to "reclaim the Bible from its Gutenberg captivity."

Based on her career as a video editor, director, and producer, Merle Worth continues Rowe's exploration of fidelity in translating from one medium to another. Using a technique she terms "the historical imagination," she invites her viewers into the past—whether the past events of the Bible or the past events of our recent experience. Sound and image combine to evoke an interactive experience from each audience member. Fidelity only comes with personal engagement.

Like any translation project new media translation benefits from evaluation. The American Bible Society projects have included not only the translations themselves but also translation exercises and tools to help the video or CD-ROM users to better understand the translation process. Mona Baker, the director of Translation Studies at the University of Manchester Institute of Science and Technology, takes the reader through an evaluation of the CD-ROM products as a way of demonstrating the pedagogical principles involved in translating. In addition, she suggests a theoretical perspective that future new media translators can incorporate in their work. Because the American Bible Society entered on its New Media Translations Project as an experiment, exploring various media and genres (both biblical and contemporary), evaluation becomes an essential component. Such evaluation adds yet another element to the idea of fidelity. If Hagedorn shows how the translation group sought fidelity in their productions, Baker shows how to gauge that fidelity after the fact.

This section, then, sets the stage for a wider consideration of fidelity in translation. By narrowly focusing on the Bible, it invites reflection on an area long studied. And, as Fry points out, the question of faithfulness in new media calls for wider perspectives from biblical scholars. By demonstrating the process of transmediazation and the nature of the media, this section provides practical material for that process of reflection. Finally, it presents a model of evaluation and reflection. This section invites more people into the experience of new media and the Bible and, in doing so, invites wider participation in reflecting on fidelity.

1

Faithfulness—a Wider Perspective

Euan McG. Fry

What does it mean to be faithful to the Bible, and to the biblical author and his text, when we communicate a biblical message through a medium other than print?

> The prophet who has heard my message should proclaim that message faithfully. (Jer. 23.28)

Faithfulness to the text and message of the Bible is a matter of great importance to all who value the Bible as "the Word of God." It is natural therefore that the Bible Societies have a concern about faithfulness: It is an element in our raison d'être and in our ethos.

Being faithful to the biblical text is a matter of top priority for us in the field of translation. And not only in translation, but throughout our whole movement, it is regarded as something on which our very integrity as Bible Societies depends. In fact I think it is true to say that in many places our constituencies see the Bible Society in the role of a custodian of the pure text of the Bible; and that is a reputation which we want to preserve.

There have been a number of moves over recent years to grasp opportunities to present the Scriptures to wider audiences, through the use of media other than print. These moves have generally been seen in a positive light, but at the same time there have been concerns and fears on the part of people within the Bible Societies that, in the process of using other media, our standing and reputation for faithfulness to the Bible may be compromised. This paper has been prepared, at least in part, in response to some of the expressions of these concerns.

In the field of translation we define "accuracy" and make judgments about it in terms of our understanding of the principles of functional equivalence. We say that a translation is accurate, and therefore faithful, if the present-day receptor in his situation responds to it in the same way as the original receptor did in his situation, in terms of his understanding of the meaning and his feeling about the message. As translation consultants I

Originally published in the *United Bible Societies Bulletin, 148/149* (1987), pp. 41-60. Reprinted with permission.

think we believe that we have a sufficiently objective grasp of the principles, so that we can apply standards of faithfulness in our work checking and testing text, and advising translators.

When we move away from the medium of print, however, I think we soon find that our present concept of faithfulness is no longer fully adequate to cover or control what goes on in the presentation of the biblical text. This is because we have to move beyond the area of equivalence at the word, sentence, and paragraph level (although this still remains as a consideration), out into the area of wider discourse and communication factors which relate to the presentation of the message as a whole. In many cases we can no longer easily identify a presentation of the text as the "closest equivalent" of a unit of the source text.

I am not sure that we need a completely new definition of faithfulness to cover the presentation of Scripture in media other than print. What we need, in my view, is an extension of the application of the principles of functional equivalence to cover situations in which the receptors' apprehension of the message comes from a range of elements including (but not restricted to) words.

In doing this we may still make judgments about equivalence, as far as the elements of the source text are concerned, and how they are represented in the new presentation. But we will also need to concern ourselves with questions about the presentation as a whole, and how this accords with the overall message, perspective, and purpose of the biblical author.

What follows will be more a description of some of the aspects of faithfulness in a wider sense than a prescription to meet all situations and possibilities. The question to be answered is: What do we mean by faithfulness to the biblical text when we are referring to presentations of the text in media other than print? (And perhaps even, Can we continue to use the word "faithfulness" at all in any meaningful way for the other media?) Then in the light of answers to that question we may be able to suggest workable answers to the practical question: What should be the limits of Bible Society interest, involvement, and commitment in projects for presentation of the biblical/Christian message through media other than print?

A short list of the media other than straightforward print would include the following: radio, audio cassette, movie film, video, television, other audiovisual presentations, theater of various kinds, comics, posters, and other "different" print productions. The points that I make in this article may not all apply equally to all these different media, but in general terms I think the broad principles will mostly apply.

Selection of Text

The selection of text out of the biblical corpus, and publication of shorter or longer excerpts, is something we have become accustomed to in the print medium in recent years. The proliferation of "selections" is a fact of life in the United Bible Societies (UBS) today. In the media other than print also I would expect that a great deal of our output is likely to involve the use of excerpts of text rather than complete books.

Dangers in Selecting Passages

There are dangers in the very fact of selecting limited passages of text, as far as faithfulness to the message and intent of the biblical authors is concerned. We know this, I believe, but we often do not take it very seriously. The dangers arise in two rather different areas.

The first area, and the one that we generally focus on, has to do with the fact that a passage is lifted out of its wider context, in the immediate discourse setting, and in the whole book of which it is a part. That wider context often provides essential clues to the meaning of the passage, not only in the content of what precedes and what follows, but also through giving a better understanding of the setting and background of the book as a whole and the passage in particular. For those who are not very familiar with the Bible, an isolated passage may easily seem to say or mean something rather different from what it really says in its proper context. With a lack of understanding of the biblical setting, it may mean less to the receptor than it should; but when read in the light of the receptor's own situation and cultural presuppositions, it may also mean something very different or more than it should.

The other danger area has to do with the perception of the Bible as a whole that the receptor gets from a single excerpt or a limited range of short excerpts. Here again, for non-Christians, and even for Christians without first-hand familiarity with the Bible, the presentation of a very limited amount of text can all too easily convey a false view of the nature and content of the Bible overall. For instance a receptor who is first made aware of the Bible through a limited selection may very easily gain one or more of the following impressions:

"This is the main message of the Bible/the writer of this book."
"The whole of the Bible/this book is of this same genre."
"This is all that the Bible/this writer has to say on this topic."
"This is the only perspective on this topic in the Bible."

The observation may be made here that all this is nothing new: we have been aware of it in connection with the production of printed selections. But I would want to add a couple of comments to the observation.

Firstly, I do not think we have taken enough care to avoid the dangers with our printed selections, or given enough attention to dealing with potential problems. Trying to identify and think through these issues as they relate to the media other than print has made me much more aware of the sort of things that can and really do happen with our publications in print, especially those selections that are distributed widely to non-Christians, and all kinds of publications produced for situations where print is a new and unfamiliar medium. Our performance with printed Scriptures is not beyond reproach at all, as far as faithfulness to the Bible is concerned.

Secondly, and this is more to the point as far as the topic of this paper is concerned, I believe that the dangers inherent in the process of selection are more real and immediate in the case of the other media than they are for the print medium. In the programs or units of presentation in the other media, selected passages of text are less likely to be recognized as limited excerpts from a larger whole, because they will so often come in what is the normal and standard length and format of presentation in those media. In the audio and video media, for instance, a program running for anything from 10 minutes to 30 minutes will be perceived as a complete unit in the thinking and expectation of the audience. And even if a series of programs is presented, there is often such a time interval between episodes that little connection is made in the minds of the audience. Furthermore, with these particular media there is often the potential and the intention of reaching a very wide audience, including many non-Christians; and this raises the level of risk of wrong understanding on all counts.

Faithfulness to the Biblical Authors

Just from what has been discussed so far, there are certain basic requirements for ensuring faithfulness to the message and intent of the biblical authors in the matter of selection of text. The first requirement is that a clear identification should be given of the biblical material and its source. For some audiences this may need to include a statement about the Bible in general, as well as identification of the excerpt(s). It should also make it quite clear to the audience that the selected biblical passages are extracts from something much larger.

A second requirement, just as important as the first, is that everything possible must be done to ensure that, in the understanding of the intended audience, the essential theme and meaning of a selected passage as presented in the new medium is the same as what that passage has in its context in the written text of the Bible. In practice this will mean that the essential clues to the meaning of the passage that the Bible reader would draw from the wider context and the readers' helps must be provided along with the text for the audience in the new medium.

It should go without saying that the identification and information just referred to should be presented in a form that is appropriate in the medium which is being used. And this material should also be integrated with other elements in the overall presentation.

Choosing Complete Units of Text

The extent of passages of text selected out of their wider biblical setting is a matter that has concerned us ever since we began producing printed "selections." And in fact, we have a rather rough and ready guideline that goes some way towards reducing problems in this area: A selected passage should normally be not less than the material which occurs between successive section headings in the UBS scheme of headings.

The intention of this guideline is that a selected passage, or each passage in a series, should be a whole pericope or a "complete" recognizable unit of discourse from within the wider discourse setting in which it is found in the Bible. Without some sort of completeness or coherence in itself, a brief extract of text very easily assumes a meaning from the other elements with which it is linked in a presentation or production, and this meaning may be very different from the meaning of the extract in its biblical setting. The use of "snippets" and/or "proof texts" in developing and supporting a topic of our own definition is still one of our greatest problems.

The temptation or pressure to use very short extracts of text is often greater in the audio and visual media, where a "racy" style is supposed to be required, and where a rather short span of audience attention or concentration is assumed. At the same time the danger of a short extract of text being given a different meaning by other program elements with which it is combined is often greater in these media than in print, because of the role these other elements have to play in the overall presentation.

I think I want to insist here that, if we want to be able to make any sort of claim to faithfulness to the Bible when we present extracts of text, we must stick to the principle of using nothing less than a discourse unit which is recognizably complete in itself. And we should maintain this principle, even if the minimum discourse unit is not too easy to define for ourselves and our Bible Society colleagues, and even though it will require from us more careful study of discourse structure than we have undertaken so far.

While following this principle of using nothing less than a complete discourse unit, we should also note again one other principle. This calls for provision of clues for the audience from the wider context of the passage, to compensate for the loss of context when the passage is made to stand on its own.

Selecting Extracts from Longer Passages

A different issue, which also has to do with the extent of a selected passage, is the need to reduce the volume of text in a longer passage for certain types of presentation such as dramatization, whether audio or film/video or "live," and comics.

What is involved here is the selection of extracts of material out of a longer narrative or discourse. This will result in the omission of repetitions and of digressions from the theme or story line. It may also call for omission of the least important details in development of the theme or description of objects and events.

This type of procedure is not new to us, since we do already allow the omission of certain types of material from passages which are used in print selections. But for the types of presentation I am referring to here, a more extensive application of it may be called for.

I believe that faithfulness to the message and intent of the biblical author can be maintained through this process of selection of material. However this will require of us great care and skill in discourse analysis, to ensure that all the essential elements are expressed and that the overall perspective and thrust of the discourse is not distorted. In particular it will call for sensitivity regarding the elements of interpretation and evaluation by the author which are an essential part of the discourse.

The Part Represents the Whole

One last issue is related to faithfulness and the selection of text. This concerns the whole corpus of Scripture extracts that will be presented through a particular medium in an ongoing or large-scale project. This follows on from comments above.

With the exception of the reading of a whole Bible or Testament on audio cassette, the sum total of Scripture that will be presented through any one medium apart from print will amount to a fairly limited selection of extracts. Yet for some whole audiences, and larger or smaller parts of other audiences, that corpus of extracts will be the only part of the Bible they will know about—even if the whole Bible does exist in print in their language. So for those people, that corpus is "the Bible," and what we have created for them is in effect a canon of Scripture.

I believe that wherever this situation may possibly exist we have a responsibility, with the church(es), to try to be as faithful to the Bible as we can in what we present within the corpus of extracts overall. By this I mean that the passages we choose should be ones of major importance within the Bible, and that the range of passages included should be reasonably representative of the Bible as a whole. And the point made earlier about the need for clear identification of extracts as coming from the Bible will also apply in this kind of situation.

Who Has the Right to Choose?

This leads me to what I consider to be a very important question of principle. Whose right and responsibility is it to decide which passages from the Bible will be used in Scripture productions or presentations?

In selecting a particular passage or set of passages for presentation to a particular audience in a particular situation or environment, in any medium, we are making a judgment about the application of Scripture, which we do not make when we distribute whole Bibles and Testaments. Is it the role of the Bible Societies to make this kind of judgment? Many times over the years I have heard statements to the effect that we (in the Bible

Societies) supply the Scriptures, and it is the responsibility of the church(es) to use, interpret, and apply them. So should not the churche(es) have the responsibility to decide which extracts from that Bible will be used in presentations for particular audiences?

I do not want to put this forward as an absolute or purist position. I believe that the Bible Societies are in a sense part of the church, and I think we also have a part to play in informing and shaping the views of the church(es) regarding the nature and use of the Bible. But I still feel quite strongly that it is wrong for the Bible Societies to make decisions in this area without close and full consultation with the church(es). And I believe that this was the most important message for the Bible Societies coming from the meeting of the UBS Council at Chiang Mai in 1980.

Each national and regional situation is a different environment, in which a range of factors—social, linguistic, cultural, religious, political—are all at work. But in every case it is the church and Christian community who have to live and witness as the body of Christ in that situation. And whatever UBS leaders and consultants may feel, looking in from the outside, those people who are there will have their own well-grounded views as to what is appropriate and meaningful in their situation—both as regards the Scriptures to be used, and the ways in which those Scriptures should be communicated. If we are to take our role of serving and working with the churches seriously, we must respect the views of the Christian community in each situation, and work with people from the Christian community in producing the Scriptures and Scripture presentations which they want. It is they, after all, who will have to back up and communicate these to their fellows.

Restructuring

Two things happen when a Scripture text is communicated effectively through non-print media. Firstly, the text is incorporated and integrated into the framework of a program, whose format is natural to the medium being used. Then, secondly, the structure of the text itself is changed into a form that is appropriate to the medium. (This does not imply that there is only one appropriate format or only one appropriate form for the text; the choice of these, in the light of resources available, type of text, intended audience, and so on, is the creative responsibility of the "producers" of the presentation.)

This section of the article deals with restructuring the text. I take up questions related to the program in which text is presented in a later section.

Nonrestructuring

I should deal first with the option of not changing the structure of the printed text at all, since it is technically possible in almost all media to present a rendering of the text which matches the printed text word for word. I think that there are a lot of people who actually believe that this procedure is the best way or the only way to ensure that a presentation in one of the other media will be faithful to the Bible.

Because a change has been made from one medium with a certain set of characteristics to another medium with different characteristics, "nonrestructuring" is no guarantee of faithfulness at all. In fact it will almost certainly result in distortions of one kind or another for receptors who are not already familiar with the text in printed form.

Consider, for instance, the most common case of nonrestructuring: the reading of a printed text into a microphone for radio or cassette presentation. In the very act of reading aloud the text is changed from indirect to direct discourse. And, in addition, the text is interpreted for the listeners through the expression, emphasis, and tone of voice of the reader—this cannot be avoided, and if the reader does not give the right cues and clues to the proper meaning, then he gives the wrong ones, and distortion is the result.

The crux of the matter, however, is that oral discourse is naturally different from written discourse, both in structural features and in the choice of vocabulary and idiom. So what is appropriate, natural, and correct in the printed text will not always be the most appropriate, natural, and correct expression of the meaning in an oral text.

As an exception to what has been stated in general terms here, the "quoting" of a print text verbatim may be appropriate for some specific situations and audiences. These would be situations in which sacred texts are held in high respect and regularly quoted in the course of religious communication. And the quoting would need to be presented in the context of an appropriate overall format to make sure that its true meaning and emphasis were conveyed to the audience.

New Translations

Nonrestructuring should not be considered as an option if we are really concerned about faithfulness to the Bible, even though it has many devotees. What we need are new translations of the text (restructured forms of the text if you like), in the language and idiom that are appropriate to the medium to be used, and appropriate also for the intended audience.

Our well-known model of the translation process presents it as a three-stage process. (See Figure 1.) The three stages are analysis of the source text, transfer of meaning at near kernel level to the receptor language, and restructuring of the meaning into a new text in that language—a text which is not identical in form to the source text, but which is equivalent to it in meaning and impact for the intended audience.

In the restructuring phase the translator's goal is to produce a text which will communicate the message of the source text effectively and accurately to the audience. He/she must therefore have a good understanding of the audience and their situation, and use the form of language that they

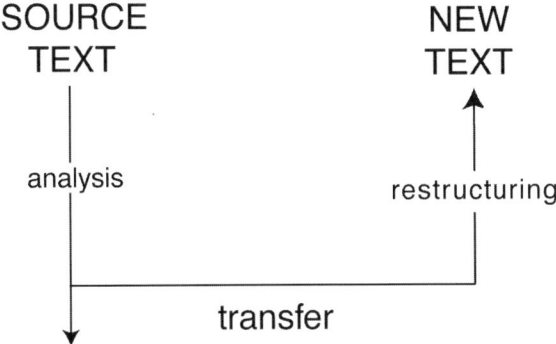

Figure 1: Three stages of analysis.

will understand and accept—so that they will have essentially the same understanding of the message, and the same feelings about it, as did the original receptors.

Generally in the past the whole process of translation has been thought of as relating to the print/writing medium. And in this context restructuring has meant the formation of a text in the literary form appropriate to print/writing, for the use of a particular (and often restricted) audience of people who are literate in their language or who may become literate in the future. The recently released book by de Waard and Nida (1986) continues in this tradition; and it is a pity, I think, that it does not discuss the role of the medium of communication, or give even a passing reference to the media other than print.

As soon as we start to engage in a little lateral thinking about what we are doing in the communication of the Scriptures through the print medium, important questions inevitably arise. We face many situations where the level of literacy is low and where the opportunity or motivation for acquiring literacy is also low or nonexistent. On purely pragmatic grounds we should consider the use of other media in these situations, in order to reach a potentially much larger audience overall. Then there are other situations in which the print medium itself and the business of acquiring and using literacy skills have certain values, which may actually be negative as far as some members and groups within the society and culture are concerned. And in bilingual or multilingual environments there are often pressures and expectations regarding how the various media will be used or not used for communication in the different languages. In these situations also there may be opportunities through the use of other media for a far more positive reception of the message than is gained by tying it to the print medium.

As we move away from the print medium, we find that we have to extend the application of our principles of functional equivalence to cover

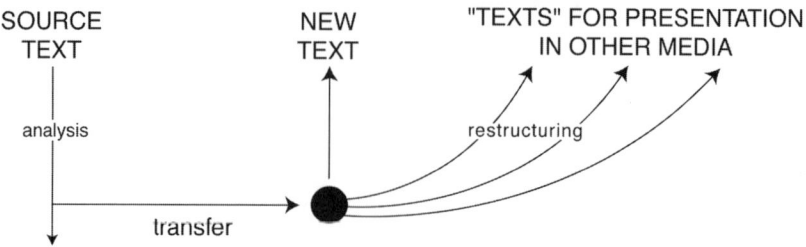

Figure 2: A modified model of the translation process

restructuring a message into a form of "text" which is appropriate for presentation in the particular medium chosen. In terms of our model of the translation process, this means modifying the model to provide a range of restructuring options. (See Figure 2.)

With this new model the principles and controls to be applied in restructuring would be essentially the same as before. But now they would be defined more broadly in terms of producing a new "text" or presentation of the message for reception by a given audience through a certain medium.

As I have suggested at the beginning of this section, presenting the Scriptures through media other than print really requires new translations of the text in the language and idiom appropriate to the medium to be used as well as for the intended audience. And a logical conclusion of this is that, in some languages at least, we may need a number of new translations: different ones for different media, and even for different types of presentation in the one medium. This may be the ideal, and desirable in any case if different audiences are being addressed. But practically it probably does not mean as much work as we might think at first, since we may be able fairly easily to develop from the existing text in print a base from which to make adaptations—particularly if it is itself a good common language translation.

Dramatization

I now want to move on to discuss restructuring at a fairly radical level, a recasting or adaptation of the text at the level of discourse into a different form, which is natural to one of the nonprint media and has the potential for communicating very effectively in it. There are numerous different possibilities for this sort of restructuring, but I want to refer mainly to dramatization, since this is a genre where some experimental work has already been done.

In dramatization a script is the equivalent of the text in a print production. But the script is in fact also the whole program for the presentation; and this means that other elements such as background information, text identification, and information from the wider context, which are required in most types of presentation, are actually integrated here with the Scripture text material.

Direct speech and dialogue are important features of drama and so, wherever possible, text will be restructured to produce these features. This will involve converting indirect speech and narration to dialogue. It may also mean giving names to characters not explicitly named in the original text, and developing characterization further than what is explicitly stated. New characters not even mentioned explicitly in the text may also need to be introduced.

While sound and voice "effects" may also be used in other types of presentation, they are an important feature of dramatization in particular, and they usually play their part in conveying both information and emotion in the overall presentation. In the restructuring of biblical text for drama, elements of the text may be converted to sound effects, such as crowd noise in place of the narrative statement "a crowd gathered." And emphasis or quality or expression of voice may take the place of statements in the text about the feelings or emotions of participants.

The Closest Natural Equivalent

The possibilities for restructuring of this kind are almost endless. But what can we say about the faithfulness to the original text of a presentation which involves such extensive restructuring?

I made the statement earlier that "nonrestructuring" is no guarantee of faithfulness at all when we move from the print medium to one of the other media. A corollary of that can now also be stated: Extensive restructuring, such as is involved in dramatization for instance, does not automatically result in a Scripture presentation being unfaithful to the biblical author and his text. I believe that it is possible to produce presentations of Scripture in which the biblical text is extensively restructured which meet a standard of faithfulness that we in the Bible Societies can accept and demand. (I say this in spite of the fact that many Bible dramatizations have been produced that either blatantly distort the author's meaning and intent or at least fail to convey it adequately.) And in support of my belief I would appeal to the widespread acceptance which has been gradually gained by our Asia Pacific Bible comic series, which are really just dramatizations in print.

There are two qualifications that should be added here. Firstly, it must be recognized and acknowledged that we are dealing with a category of presentation which is obviously quite different from a printed publication of the same biblical text. We cannot therefore expect to find the same order of equivalence with the source text as we would in a translation produced in the same medium as that source. I think that a number of us have already recognized this; and perhaps this is behind our desire to find an appropriate label (such as "adaptation" of the biblical text) for this type of presentation, which we can comfortably use to mark it off as "different."

The other qualification takes up again a point I have already made above. In order to maintain and to evaluate the level of faithfulness to the original text in this type of presentation, we will need to exercise great care and skill in discourse analysis—constantly checking that what is created in the new presentation is the "closest natural equivalent" in the new medium and genre to the essential elements of the source text, and that the overall perspective and thrust of the original discourse is not distorted. This is not a task for either the unskilled or the fainthearted!

Medium and Message

"The medium is the message." We do not have to agree with everything McLuhan has said to recognize that there is some truth in this statement. And as we make use of the various media, we have to recognize that, in the expectation and understanding of the audience, the use of a certain medium in itself conveys certain implications about the nature and content of the message that is being communicated. This is true of a given medium in general terms, and it is also true for the individual types or genres of presentation that are typical of that medium.

As an illustration of how the medium imposes its characteristics and requirements on what is communicated, consider the news genre in the television medium. Television typically features action and emotion and an element of immediacy in what it presents, and this leads to the shaping of a news bulletin both in what is presented and how it is presented. The actual items for inclusion, and the scenes and shots which make up each item, are selected not so much on the basis of what is "newsworthy" as for their contribution to spectacle and visual impact. And what is reported inevitably comes across as being more dramatic and impressive than what the audience normally encounter in their own real experience.

Media Norms and Audience Expectations

It is probably hardly necessary to dwell on the dangers inherent in communication of the Scriptures through the various nonprint media as far as faithfulness to the nature and status of the Bible and to the message and intent of the biblical authors are concerned. Wherever an audience has expectations about the nature and content of material communicated through a particular medium and genre, there is a potential conflict between this and the real nature and meaning of the biblical material that is presented. And in some extreme cases the only wise course of action may be to recognize that presentation of certain material, or even of any Scripture at all, in the particular medium or genre would be inappropriate and inadvisable. We already understand from the principles of functional equivalence that if an audience, for whatever good or bad reason, gets from a Scripture presentation an understanding and feeling about the message that is essentially different from what the original receptors got, then that presentation cannot be regarded as faithful to the Bible.

Leaving aside the extreme case, the pressure to conform to the expectations and characteristics of the medium can result in presentations of Scripture which do not meet an acceptable standard of faithfulness to the Bible original. On the one hand, adaptations may be made to the biblical material to make it conform to media norms and audience expectations, and the result is distortion of the message. On the other hand, the presentation may create a negative impression and have a low level of acceptance, if it falls short of audience standards and expectations of the medium, and again be less than faithful to the original. For all but the most dedicated Christian audiences, long periods of the reading of text by a single voice in the audio media, and programs which are nothing more than a "talking head" in the visual media, would be examples of the latter category.

Having said all this, I must now repeat that I do believe that Scripture presentations which maintain an acceptable standard of faithfulness to the Bible originals are possible in a great many situations—far more than we have tried to do anything in so far. But in order to succeed in any situation, positive action will be required to meet the potential dangers and problems that may arise.

In the first place, care must be exercised in the selection of the type of biblical material and the actual passages for presentation through the particular medium, so that there is not likely to be a wide variation between the actual nature and content of the material and the expectation of the audience regarding these. And the type or genre of presentation must also be such as the biblical material will fit comfortably into. We must recognize that there is a wide range of types of material in the Bible, and that not all types of material and subject matters lend themselves to presentation in each of the various nonprint media. Having in mind the situation and expectations of the intended audience, we should aim at a choice of text and the creative use of a type of presentation which are compatible with each other.

Secondly, recognizing that an audience may possibly not have at the outset much idea about the nature of the Bible or about the subject matter that will be presented, we may need to build clues and explanations into the presentation, by means of separate identification and within the actual program, that will help to create the proper expectation and understanding. The perspective and horizon of the audience may be able to be widened by this means, and the interest of the audience may also actually be increased in so doing.

In some situations it may also even be possible to actually create a new genre for Scripture presentation, different from the limited range of types of program with which an audience is already familiar in the particular medium, thus avoiding some of the dangers of a wrong expectation about the biblical material. But this approach should be seen, of course, as the opportunity for creative programming, proceeding with due understanding of both the audience and the medium, and not as an excuse for laziness.

There is another sort of audience expectation which we need to take account of as we consider Scripture presentations in the nonprint media. This is the complex of ideas and feelings that people have about "religious" texts in general and about the Bible in particular. There may, for instance, be strongly held views in the general community about the nature and place of religious texts, and about what are and what are not appropriate vehicles for rendering and communicating them. There may already be existing conventions about the appropriate ways of dealing with them in certain of the media.

When it comes to the Bible, we may find that the Christian community has strongly-held, and sometimes very narrow, views about the nature of "Holy Scripture" and what may and may not be allowed in presenting the Bible through media other than print. And even non-Christians may have similar views about the Bible, based on what they know and expect of the holy books of other major religions.

Should the Bible and extracts from it always be regarded as falling within the "religious" category as that is already defined in a given situation? And should the Bible only be presented in ways that are considered appropriate for this category of material? However we answer these questions, we should recognize the expectations that people have, and proceed with due caution if we decide to move Scripture presentations out of the recognized categories.

And should Scripture presentations through the nonprint media be restricted to what the Christian community or its leaders will allow? This too has a real bearing on faithfulness to the Bible, as those people see it, even if we in the UBS see it differently. And as we have already noted, we are pledged in principle to consult with the church(es) and to work with the church(es) in all that we do.

Music: Help or Hindrance to Understanding?

Thus far I have been referring mainly to the effect of a particular medium or type of presentation on the message that is being communicated. But there are certain features that may be used in the course of presentations in the various media which can also convey messages of their own to the audience and have an effect on the message which is supposed to be communicated. Music is a good example of such a feature.

While music may be used to provide interludes for the purpose of breaking up a program or linking different sections, it is hardly ever "neutral" in its impact. The use of music may itself imply something about mood or setting, and specific types of music can convey very specific messages to the audience. Different instruments or ensembles, different rhythms, different styles of composition or playing may all have different connotations. And certain melodies, to some of which there may be words, will have a very powerful impact. Different types of music can suggest different moods, or imply certain social settings, or even refer to particular themes.

The use of music in Scripture presentations can have a bearing on the faithfulness with which the biblical message is communicated, from a number of angles. Is it considered appropriate, for instance, for music to be used in connection with a religious text? And, if so, are all types of music appropriate, or only music which is recognized as religious? Then there is the possibility that the music which is chosen may suggest a mood, a theme, or a setting which conflicts with the actual mood, theme, or setting of the biblical passage. If words are either sung or known, they may conflict with or distract from the real message of the Scripture.

Music may be used very effectively in a presentation to support, reinforce, or reflect the message of the biblical text. But there are also potential dangers of distortion and unfaithfulness if it is not used with a great deal of care and sensitivity, having in mind the conventions and expectations of the intended audience.

The Total Presentation

In any of the media, a Scripture presentation consists of more than just a bare excerpt of text from the Bible. The biblical passage or passages are inevitably incorporated into the framework of a program, however minimal the other elements in the program may be.

A Scripture selection in the print medium is a good illustration of this. In addition to the biblical text we find such things as illustrations, headings, introductions and bridge passages, encouragement for readers to buy and read other Scriptures, credits and publisher's information, identification of the distributor, and so on. And all these elements are integrated into a single unit by the overall design of the selection.

For the nonprint media the nature and shape of the program framework is naturally different from what is appropriate in print, and there are also differences between the various media. But the fact of the framework in which biblical text is incorporated remains. And this has a large bearing on the faithfulness of the presentation to the source text.

Additional Elements of Non-print Scriptures

The elements which may be included in a program along with the actual biblical text are many and varied. They may be considered, however, as falling into three broad groups.

- *Formal elements* are those elements which provide identification and authorization of the whole presentation and certain elements or features of it. Included here would be the opening and closing

announcements identifying the program, the producers and/or sponsors of it, the biblical material (and if necessary the Bible), the topic or theme of the program, and calling for response or follow-up action.
- *Audience helps* are those elements which are required to enable the audience to get an adequate understanding of the message of the biblical text. They are the equivalent in the other media of what we call "helps for the reader" in the print medium, and provide a similar range of material to support the text. They may cover such things as historical background, geographical or cultural information, comments about the author, his audience, and their situation, and about the wider context of the selected passage(s) of text.
- *Application elements* are those elements designed to help the audience relate the message of the Scripture to their own situation. These elements may "start where they are" with comment or dialogue to gain their attention and interest. They may also provide comment or question to lead the audience to recognize the relevance of the theme or message of the biblical text to their own lives.

These various elements will not be separate or isolated, of course, but will be integrated into the "fabric" of the program. And the actual form they take will be what is appropriate in the medium and type of presentation. It is the relationship of these elements to the biblical text that is our concern as far as faithfulness of the presentation overall is concerned.

The Text Is the Central Element

I believe that, if a presentation is to be called a "Scripture presentation," the biblical text must be the central element in it, and the theme of the program must be the theme of the text. This is a matter both of focus and of weight. In the first place it should be the biblical passage which is highlighted in a program, to which the attention of the audience is drawn as the main element. And the other elements in the program should be organized and integrated in relation to this main element. If the attention of the audience is drawn primarily to some other element, either intentionally or unintentionally, then it seems to me that we would have to question the faithfulness of the presentation to the Bible.

The allocation of time or space within a program is also relevant here. If too little of the total time or space is allocated to the biblical text, it can hardly be said that the text is the focus of the program, and again I think that we must question the faithfulness of the presentation to the Bible.

There is an extreme case, of course, of the sort of program which includes some Scripture, but which ranges far more widely than the theme or message of that Scripture in particular. This should not be called a Scripture presentation, and it is really beyond the charter of the Bible Societies to commit time or resources to this type of production. But even where the intention is to present Scripture to an audience, I believe that, to be faithful to the Bible, the focus and weight within the overall program framework must be given to the biblical text.

Conflict of Context

The other area of concern in the relationship between the biblical text and other elements in the framework of a program is the potential for conflicts between the other elements and the text. A biblical passage is to be presented, which in itself, as seen in its original context, conveys a certain message and has a certain thrust. It is very possible, however, that other elements in the program will convey a different message, and in this situation the likelihood is that the message of the biblical passage will be distorted. The wrong mood or setting may be implied, or the other elements may make it appear that the theme of the passage is something different from what it is in its biblical context.

It is probably the application elements of the groups I have referred to above that pose the greatest danger to faithfulness as far as the biblical text is concerned. Because the audience relates readily to these elements, the message they convey will probably win out over the message of the text, if there is a conflict. The elements which are audience helps should actually reinforce the true message of the text and serve to eliminate some conflict—but the danger with them is that they can too easily be sacrificed from the program in favor of the application elements which are seen to have more audience appeal.

Besides the danger from conflict between other program elements and the biblical text, there is also a danger that the overall thrust of the program may be rather different from the thrust of the passage(s) chosen, in its original context and in the intention of the biblical author. This danger probably interacts with the danger of distortion from audience expectations of the medium and the type of presentation used.

There is a genre of jokes in Christian circles which involves the use of a quotation from the Bible in a particular situation such that the words have an entirely different meaning and application from what they have in their biblical context, often with a pun involved as well ("top not come down," "watch and pray," "the lot fell on Matthias," and so on). We know very well that the meaning of the Bible can be dramatically distorted when extracts are presented in new contexts of our own making. Yet this danger remains a very real one in our efforts in the nonprint media in particular.

Theological De-emphasis and Distortion

I made a brief reference earlier to the element of theological interpretation and evaluation which is an essential element of the biblical text. That reference was in relation to the selection of text, but it is also relevant to what may happen when text is incorporated into a program framework.

One tendency in producing a Scripture presentation for certain audiences is to "de-emphasize" the theological content, by not making any reference to it in the other elements of the program. Such de-emphasis is probably distortion, since the audience will automatically understand the biblical text in the light of their existing belief system, in the absence of any other interpretation. There may also be a tendency which deliberately allows the theological element to be colored (distorted, that is) by presenting it in terms which accommodate the attitudes or world view of the audience.

From the side of the Christian presenters of a program, there may also be a tendency to shift the theological content in a program from that which is a true element of the biblical passage(s) selected to something else which they would like to convey. In the extreme this tendency makes John 3.16 the theological content or message attached to every passage of Scripture. Another Christian tendency is to suggest more generally through the nontext elements in a program that the Bible is a book which contains the answer to every conceivable question or problem. ("The Bible has all the answers.") This conveys a false view of the essential nature and purpose of the Bible, of course.

Needless to say, I regard these last tendencies as seriously as those referred to in the earlier paragraph. Being faithful to the Bible is a matter of avoiding all possible distortions, and not of avoiding just those to which we object.

Conclusion

I should now restate what I said above with particular reference to dramatization. I believe that it is possible to produce presentations of Scripture in the various non-print media which meet a standard of faithfulness that we in the Bible Societies can accept and defend.

We must recognize, however, that not only where extensive restructuring is required, but in every non-print presentation, there will not be "equivalence" of the same order as we expect to find when we produce a new text which is in the same medium as the source text. So we probably should not use the term "accuracy" or attempt to define faithfulness in the same terms as for print medium productions. But if we have in mind what we understand to have taken place in the process of the shaping of the canonical biblical text we may be encouraged to believe that our standard is a worthy one.

It is my strong conviction that the Bible Societies ought to become involved, in consultation and cooperation with other organizations, in the presentation of Scripture through the nonprint media. Not only is this within our charter as distributors of Scripture, but we have a standing which others recognize in our concern for faithfulness to the Bible, and our involvement will give us the opportunity to play our part in setting and maintaining a standard of integrity to the biblical message in these other media.

In the body of this article I have made quite a number of suggestions for checking and ensuring faithfulness to the Bible in presentations of

Scripture in the various media. These suggestions relate to different areas of concern, but taken together they start to provide some sort of overall indication for a level or standard of faithfulness. The next section, then, presents a list of guidelines produced from the various suggestions made earlier.

In the list of guidelines each requirement would be essential. There could be no such thing as a "pass" for a proposed presentation if it met a majority of the requirements. The nature of the requirements is such that serious failure in respect of any one area would mean that the whole proposal would be unacceptable.

The application of many of the guidelines is a matter of judgment, of course. And different people may well have different views regarding the major theme, perspective, and thrust of a given biblical text. But this is not really so different from what we find as we check and assess functional equivalent translations in the print medium. In my opinion, if we believe that we are able to set and apply a consistent level or standard of faithfulness in what we are already doing in the field of translation, then we should be able to do the same in the field of Scripture presentation in media other than straight print.

Suggested Guidelines

1. Where presentations include biblical text selected out of its fuller and wider context, the essential theme and meaning of each selected passage as presented must be the same as for that passage in its context in the written text or the Bible.

In practice this will require the provision of essential clues to meaning from the wider context, and certain other helps to understanding for the receptors.

2. A clear identification of the biblical material and its source must be given as an element of each Scripture presentation.

For audiences not familiar with the Bible, this should include a statement about the Bible in general as well as identification of the excerpt(s) of text.

3. Each selected passage of biblical text must be a unit of discourse which is recognizably complete in itself.

Where more than one passage is selected, the material in any given program should be coherent, that is, the passages should be linked by a common theme or topic.

4. If a passage of text is compressed by the omission of repetitions, digressions, and/or unimportant details, the overall perspective and thrust of the discourse must be preserved, and all the essential elements of the text must be included.

5. Where a significant part of any audience, whether Christian or non-Christian, has no access to or familiarity with the Bible as a whole, the overall corpus of extracts selected for presentation must be reasonably

representative of the Bible as a whole, and the individual passages should be ones of major importance within the Bible.

6. In detail as well as in general, the integrity of the biblical text in its original setting must be respected in the restructuring of its various elements.

The meaning and intention of the biblical author are the base against which the faithfulness of a Scripture presentation is to be tested and measured at every point.

7. Extensive restructuring does not automatically result in a Scripture presentation being unfaithful to the biblical author and his text. But constant and careful checking must be applied to ensure that:

(a) what is created in the new presentation is the "closest natural equivalent" in the new medium and genre to the essential elements of the source text, and

(b) the overall perspective and thrust of the original discourse is not distorted.

8. The nature and content of biblical material selected for presentation must fall within the range of audience expectation for the particular medium used and the type or genre of presentation.

Where necessary, clues and explanations that will help to create the proper expectation and understanding should be built into the presentation, either by means of separate identification or within other elements of the program.

9. The biblical text must be the central element in every "Scripture presentation," and the theme of the overall program must be the same as the main theme of the biblical text.

This means that a significant allocation of time and/or space is given to the biblical text, and that other elements in the program are organized and integrated in relation to it.

10. All messages that other elements in a Scripture presentation convey, in themselves or by the fact of their use, must be in accord with the message and theme of the biblical text that is chosen.

11. The element of theological interpretation and evaluation which is found in the biblical text must be conveyed in every Scripture presentation and given an emphasis of the same order as it has in that text in its original setting.

It is already recognized that translation personnel have a role within the UBS family in maintaining faithfulness to the Bible in all our printed productions. As we become involved in presentations of Scripture in the other media, translation people must still accept and exercise this responsibility. As I have tried to suggest in the course of this article, the whole business of assessing and maintaining faithfulness is wider and more complex than for the print medium, and this can only mean that the involvement of people with understanding and skill in handling the biblical text is more necessary. I would hope that the role of translations personnel in the production of Scripture presentations in all media would be acknowledged, both on their own part and on the part of colleagues—not as "censors" waiting to kill good and creative ideas, but as "guides" seeking to assist in the working out of the ideas in a way that is faithful to the Bible, and to the biblical authors and their messages.

2

Anatomy of a Translation Process: A Case Study of *Out of the Tombs* (Mark 5.1-20)

Fern Lee Hagedorn

In 1991, the American Bible Society (ABS) completed an extraordinary nine-minute film and labeled it a video translation of Mark 5.1-20 (the story of Jesus and the Gerasene demoniac). The release of the translation evoked controversy from within both ABS and United Bible Society (UBS) circles, as well as in the secular media. Today, it still provides a source for heated discussions on the meaning of *translation*.

This chapter documents and analyzes why and how the ABS (which prior to the beginnings of this project in 1989 was basically a single-medium distributor of the Scriptures) thrust itself into the forefront of the creation and distribution of Scripture translations in new media. This chapter is deliberately entitled *Anatomy of a Translation Process* because none of the team who worked on this first prototype would claim this as the only way to translate and communicate the stories of the Bible into new media. The *Out of the Tombs* prototype included two parts: a video translation and an interactive software product. This chapter will describe in detail only the video translation side of the project. (Two additional prototypes were produced after *Out of the Tombs*. They are *A Father and Two Sons: Luke 15.11-32* and *The Visit: Luke 1.39-56*.)

Although the ABS historical records frequently have called the ABS program a "multimedia translations program," it has since been renamed "New Media Translations Program" in response to the problem that the word *multimedia* has become too easily a synonym for a single technology. "New media" more appropriately describes the task since that label includes the many formats available today and in the future.

Origins of the "Audiovisual Translations of the Bible" Project

David Burke, Director of the ABS Translations Department, invited me to begin a research project in 1989 entitled "Audiovisual Translations of the Bible." Burke arranged that I meet Maria Martinez, now ABS Vice-President for Scripture Publications, who expressed a deep concern that the research project dig into the issues of principles and guidelines for translation into audiovisual formats. The research project, I was told, should not consider production in the first year, but instead submit a final report with recommendations to the ABS by April, 1990.

Specifically, my "job description" stated the following regarding the preparation and compilation of research:

- reviews and outlines possibilities and processes for development;
- suggests guidelines and principles for proceeding in such development;
- delineates how best to handle all aspects of contexting in such development; and
- summarizes recommended future directions and next steps in general terms, as well as setting priorities among and steps for specific projects proposed. (American Bible Society Archives, 1989)

The project meant excavating and laying a foundation first for understanding how we understand the term *translation* in the context of images—**moving images!**—and sounds. It was an overwhelming assignment as my own field of expertise lay not in the theoretics of translation, but in the praxis side of film production and Christian education.

The reporting mechanisms included a monthly memorandum to Burke outlining what I did and questions that needed to be addressed. After a month of initial interviews with experts from a variety of disciplines, the first memorandum stated:

After having spent these initial 10 days on the project, several points need to be stressed:

There is a need to identify key audience(s) for this project, but more importantly, this project needs to undergird ABS's assessment of key audience(s) in its overall long-range goals.

1. There is a need to identify some general resultant goals of the project...this project needs to have ABS articulate its overall goals for the next years in order to be steered in the proper direction.

2. There is a general feeling from some respondents that computer resources need to be produced by ABS. This audiovisual related research needs to be in congruence with any ABS-wide computer research.

3. There is a general feeling from some of the respondents that children should be one of our key audiences in the audiovisual project.

4. It is important for ABS to do its own research, assessing its audience(s) to find out, for example, how people use the Bible, what helps they need, what age groups we are dealing with, what kinds of cultural, economic, social, etc., backgrounds do ABS audiences come from, and which audiences we haven't targeted that we would like to reach. This research would be independent of my research. There was a general

> consensus that the initial step taken by ABS in starting this project is
> much needed and exciting. (Hagedorn, 1989, pp. 1-2)

Therefore, we did not set out to produce *Out of the Tombs* but to lay the foundation for new media Scriptures.

In the process of laying this foundation, ABS acknowledges, and thanks, the fellowship of the UBS for its forward thinking on the subject which dates back, perhaps, to 1972, if not earlier. Patrick Cattrysse (1992) of the Catholic University in Brussels provided a helpful document which opened up a discussion on translation for non-biblical materials. The ABS used a paper by Euan Fry (1987, reprinted in this volume) as another basis for discussion. Fry opened his article with the question: "What does it mean to be faithful to the Bible, and to the biblical author and his text, when we communicate a biblical message through a medium other than print?" (p. 41). We circulated this article to a substantial number of scholars. In December, 1989, we convened an advisory group on audiovisual translations in New York to discuss Fry's article. This led the ABS research project to reflect not only on guidelines, but on some basic questions such as "What is the Bible?", "How can we ever know the original authors' intentions?", and "How can we recover the knowledge of the original receptor's responses?"

I synthesized the detailed responses into an article in 1990. In the conclusion of the article, I stated:

> The ultimate goal of the Fry article was to articulate a set of guiding principles for non-print translations of the Scriptures and in this realm, Fry has introduced the need to pursue much more research in audiovisual translations. Video as a technology and as a social institution keeps changing. Dramatization and narrative modes are effective, but how can they be utilized in biblical translation with integrity? There is the burgeoning field of multimedia technology combining computers with quality video images and sounds—what is the proper approach here? All of these compel and propel us into continuing research and exploration. (Hagedorn, 1990a, p. 9)

In addition to original papers delivered during its meeting, the advisory group reached a consensus concerning several key issues in relation to audiovisual translations. It drafted provisional guiding principles for "Audiovisual Translations" that were presented to the ABS Translations Subcommittee in December, 1989. Here are some excerpts from that document:

> Audiovisual translations of the Scriptures will seek a place in the long tradition of communication of the Scriptures through different languages, across cultural barriers, and in different communications media....The intention is not to produce **one** authoritative audiovisual translation for all time. An audiovisual translation will not **replace** the printed Bible. It is intended to be a series of **translations** available to the constituency. (Hagedorn, 1990b, p. 1)

Another excerpt:

> The term "audiovisual translations" catalyzes the articulation of controversial viewpoints. For example: (1) to place image and sound on a screen is already an interpretation of the text; (2) the problem of portraying God visually and orally; (3) the question of the propriety of modern media to convey meanings of sacred text.
>
> Another level of tensions is in the realm of the translations process: [i.e.] the need to be precise (in the "scientific" sense) and the responsibility to offer opportunities for meaning expansion. (p. 1)

One of the guiding principles which resulted from the meeting of the advisory group was the following: "Therefore each specific audiovisual translation project will deal appropriately and responsibly with the various tensions involved in translation from the original manuscript texts to an audiovisual version" (p. 1). The group drafted five additional guiding principles in the areas of context, fidelity, genres, elements, and selection. The meeting's articulation of principles formed a key event in beginning to understand the complexity of translating the Scriptures into new media.

After a year of research, I submitted a year-end report which contained the following unanswered questions:

> In the context of the present-day multimedia paradigm, what is (a) faithfulness to the Bible and (b) how is this measured?...are we talking about fidelity when we deal with contemporary media? Is this an appropriate question? Should we be asking, instead: In *presenting* biblical material in contemporary media, what factors contribute to the material's *functional equivalence* in the new media?
>
> Should we continue to use the term "translation"?
>
> How can "original meaning" (author) and "original impact" (receptor) be recovered for use in the present-day multimedia paradigm?
>
> Who are the "present-day" receptors in pluralistic USA?
>
> What are our long-range goals in dealing with text selection, audience selection, media selection?
>
> What is the role of the contemporary media translator? (Hagedorn, 1990c)

Although my work during that first year was to gain information and present preliminary findings, the resultant report, recommendations, and conclusions still apply today. We have come a long way since 1989, but we have not come at it fast enough to meet the growing needs of a world needing the Scriptures in visual and aural formats.

The Prototype: *Out of the Tombs*

The ABS's Board of Trustees' Program Committee boldly provided financial support in December, 1990 (see American Bible Society Board of Trustees, 1990) toward formation of a research team and the production of an experimental pilot video. The prototype had to be completed for presentation to the ABS Board of Trustees in December, 1991.

At that time Viggo Søgaard, audio and video consultant to the UBS, wrote the following to Kenneth Thomas, translations officer for the UBS, on the issue of guidelines:

> Who will establish the preliminary guidelines? It would seem necessary to try to establish some preliminary guidelines, carry out different experiments to produce programs/products, and then evaluate. In other words, there seems to be a need for a multistep process like the pilot projects carried out in the Asia-Pacific region. (personal communication, December, 1990)

Heeding Søgaard's advice, we were first equipped with the preliminary guidelines with the intention that through praxis we would have a better idea of the direction to set for audiovisual translations of the Scriptures.

As a first assignment we identified appropriate experts and scholars and tried to convince them to work with the ABS on this project. The original idea envisioned two teams: one that would deal with overall long-range issues and one that would concentrate on the specific project that had to be completed by December, 1991. The teams consisted mainly of biblical scholars but soon expanded to include music, art, and film experts.

Barclay Newman, senior ABS translations officer, helped us come up with the term *multimedia translation*, with the following definition:

> A multimedia translation combines a faithful functional equivalent rendering of the source text with supplementary audio-visual features that maximize the potential for both a proper understanding of and an appropriate response to the message of the source text. (Hagedorn, 1991, p. 22)

Newman observed that since the Bible Societies seek to create translations where the message of the biblical text has priority over the medium of presentation: "the full potential of the medium may be employed, but only to the extent that it enhances the possibility for a better understanding of and a more appropriate response to the message of the text" (p. 22). Newman's definition has formed the backbone of the program, that is, that the *message must drive the medium*. It also opened up a major area of potential conflict.

Given the diversity of the team needed to work on the prototype, real tensions surfaced regarding who was "driving" the translation process. These could be summarized as follows:

- From the biblical scholar camp: production people don't know the Bible. They will inevitably follow personal tastes and Hollywood norms.
- From the production team: biblical scholars are academics in ivory towers who don't know the meaning of deadlines and who keep changing their minds.
- From the marketing camp: how can other teams make decisions on genres and format when they don't know anything about the

marketplace? We're not in the artsy world nor the egghead world, but the real world.

These were real tensions that required discussion and action. In her role with the program as art director and art historian, Gregor Goethals has helped think through some previous models that seemed to apply to this project. In reflecting on historical models and processes that the church has used in relationships with artisans, she emphasized that the best creative work of any craftsperson or artist came from clear direction from the patron. In other words, much of what "drives" a project arises from who ultimately pays for it—in this case, the ABS. But as Goethals would emphasize, this should not constrain the artist, but give the artist a proper context within which to use his or her creativity and skill. Without it, the artist would sink in a sea of generalities.

In addition, the metaphor of the construction of a cathedral helped us to understand roles and processes. Goethals explained that the creation and construction of the cathedrals of the past—and she also described how cathedrals functioned in some ways as **translations** of the Scriptures—required a diverse team. These included artisans with expertise in stained glass, sculpture, painting, and construction, to name a few. Artisans had to execute each area in harmony with a larger whole—the cathedral structure itself—and to please the patron (the Church). This way also serves to describe producing a filmed translation: experts bringing their best skills to build a larger entity.

> The tension in the relationship between the research translation element and the production group was acknowledged. However, it was pointed out that the team, by virtue of its design, will be able to address this tension. It was also stated that, conceptually, the project is to be understood as a translation. It was also stated that the means of production will be an important element that can reshape the production process—from a one-person view/vision of reality to a collaborative, community-based project. (Multimedia Translations Research Team, March, 1991, p. 3)

This tension remained a constant during the project, and still forms an issue we must address. But it did not stop the project from going forward. However, we would need to utilize or create different models when a Bible Society is not the paying patron, or when other organizations co-fund a project.

The first team consisted mainly of biblical scholars (David Barr, Gilbert Bartholomew, Thomas Boomershine, John Ciampa, Joanna Dewey, Richard Harley, Ron Roschke). We added experts in the arts and media (Gregor Goethals, J. Ritter Werner, Gary Rowe) later. In its first job, the team grappled with the issue of selection of the biblical story we would use for the prototype. Many issues guided the selection of the range of stories we would need to cover for a long-term project: For example, the stories should reveal the life and teachings of Jesus; they should maximize existing research on orality of the Scriptures; and they should be relevant for teenagers, the target audience assigned to the project. Given these three needs, the team identified 10 stories from Mark. From the 10, we selected four as possibilities for the project: The Gerasene Demoniac: A Man with Evil Spirits (Mark 5.1-20); Bartimaeus: Jesus Heals Blind Bartimaeus (Mark 10.46-52); The Anointing at Bethany (Mark 14.3-9); and The Syro-Phoenician Woman: A Woman's Faith (Mark 7.24-30).

We tested these passages with audiences through focus groups. The ABS research team discussed the four stories based on the understandings of each text's elements of sound (going through the Greek text aurally/orally), strengths of the text, music, images—primary and secondary, target images/sounds, music video possibilities (Multimedia Translations Research Team, April, 1991). The audience testing through focus groups and the research team recommended Mark 5.1-20, the story of Jesus healing the Gerasene demoniac. The team understood that this video also would be incorporated within an interactive prototype.

Once it chose the passage, the team set to work on a "reinvestigation" of the source text by developing what we now call a textbase document—a series of articles covering the range of issues identified for understanding the ancient story. We also created a word track (new oral/aural English translation from the Greek). Armed with the word track and textbase—the source for all production work—the team was now ready to pursue the task of creating a translation for a target audience of teenagers in the target medium of music video. But we had to address two additional considerations: First, usic research, tradition, and direction (not as a cosmetic feature of embellishment, but enmeshed as an element of the translation, together with its cultural and multicultural implications); and second, image research, tradition, and direction (neither arbitrary nor fixed, but inviting of multiple images in the viewer's mind, again together with their cultural and multicultural issues).

The Production of the Prototype: *Out of the Tombs*

Pre-Production Begins: July, 1991

We started out with a film treatment featuring a story about a teenager who was cured of drug addiction after attending a storytelling workshop based on Mark 5.1-20. The team quickly made a decision that this treatment was more of an interpretation of the text rather than a translation of the text. Susan, the main character, was "healed" of drug addiction after having the text "explained" to her. This failed the "translation test" because it did not offer dynamic modern equivalents to the elements of the ancient story. The legion of demons, a powerful image in the biblical story, was reduced to drug addiction—an equivalent rejected by the team. The team rejected this proposal because drug addiction in modern society did not represent a close, natural equivalent to demon possession in the biblical world. In short, it was not faithful to the sense of the original.

While the work of textbase research and word track creation progressed, we began to look for a filmmaker who could share the vision of a collaborative endeavor. We identified Merle Worth who came with strong documentary filmmaking credentials, having done major productions for Turner Broadcasting and Public Television. She met twice with a small group of us in the summer of 1991. She participated in a research team meeting and, now armed with textbase material and key team members as resource people, she set to work on a conceptual treatment. In our first meeting together, Ms. Worth sensed that the team seemed to want a film that would be for many a first-time experience of this story, so that the people who watch the film would have a parallel reaction/response to the film as the audience did in Mark's time when he told it to live audiences.

During the collaborative process of scripting and casting, a number of new issues surfaced:

1. Good versus Evil: In western cinema, an evil character or storyline usually takes up more screen time, and in some ways, seems more "glamorous," while good is usually portrayed in a bland manner. How could we overcome some of the Hollywood conventions inherent in contemporary commercial cinema? In addition, how could we portray good without using overly-cosmetic vehicles such as the physical brute force so prevalent in the Hollywood movies of today?

2. Hollywood Jesus: Audiences have experienced Jesus portrayed usually within the context of historical dramatization. Thus, directors have cast Jesus with flowing robes, sandals, long hair, and a beard. Oftentimes, he has very European features. He tends to have a one- or two-dimensional character, and his physical movements reflect this flatness. Filmmakers present his supernaturalness through dramatic music and backlighting. How then could we handle Jesus, given the mythological dimensions created by Hollywood?

3. Genre and Audience Expectation: The Bible film genre reflected another part of the culture that the project would have to encounter. The project intended to produce a translation using contemporary images, sounds, and words. The project not only sought to create a video translation (a new concept) but also a different genre of Bible film—and a hybrid form of music video.

When the team finalized the word track, they gave it to the filmmaker for the narration, which had to be present in sound form within the film. This became non-negotiable since the research team deemed that, at this time, the words of the word track served as the historical continuity to the Scriptures being filmed that the images would lack. But, in another challenge for the team, the video translation had to visually break the one-to-one correspondence of words and images. We sought not a "formal equivalence" of the text, which supplies a modern word for each and every ancient word, or a modern image for each and every ancient image. Instead, we provided a functional equivalence, that is, we found equivalent meanings for whole ideas and concepts.

Some key decisions guided the whole production. For one, viewers would experience the story from the point of view of the possessed man. Therefore, they would see and hear all of the characters in the story from the perspective of the demoniac. For another, the television monitor would act as a device to help reveal the inner workings of the demoniac's mind. Additionally, the team determined that "Jesus" is the Jesus through the eyes of the demoniac; the power of Jesus in this story and throughout the New Testament appears not through grand gestures, but through his words; and, the theme that Jesus offers deliverance for those in deep trouble must come through the video. Finally, it was agreed that the video could not overly-personify demons.

The team decided to "house" both the video translation and the interactive material in a symbolic or metaphorical structure that would be faithful to the story. This choice helped drive the decision-making regarding many of the visual and sound elements of the project. The sea became the major metaphor we decided upon for both the video and the interactive material. In Mark 4, Jesus and his disciples crossed a stormy sea to the land of the Gerasenes. The sea and water imagery in terms of the theme for the Mark 5 story of "deliverance" pervades the Bible (the Exodus, Flood, Baptism). The story was also violent—a possessed man with the strength to break apart metal shackles, and 2,000 pigs hurling off a cliff into the sea.

We had to find equivalents for many key images. The pigs provide one example. The legion of pigs, for the original audience, stood for disgusting, filthy, animals that also conjured up images of an oppressive Roman army. This kind of meaning could not be conveyed by finding a modern equivalent animal. The video translation could only convey the idea of disgust and oppression in the scenes where the demoniac is in agony and when the evil spirit descends into the sea. An early treatment used a motorcycle gang turned into a pack of rats that swirled up into a tornado and died. We dropped this from the final script since it did not seem appropriate to categorize that group as a legion of demons. Due to the difficulty of replicating legion/uncleanness in one image, the film utilized the soundtrack—the squeals of pigs—as a component of an equivalent. The images of the demoniac in agony as well as the evil spirit's demise into the sea tried to convey the power of evil and the destruction of the legion of pigs. Another example dealt with the demoniac's "uncleanness" and the act of exorcism. Early on, someone suggested the idea of having the demoniac riddled with tattoos that disappear in the end. We decided against this imagery, again, because it did not seem appropriate to classify tattoos as unclean. Another solution involved having the demoniac pick off imaginary leeches from his body and spit out imaginary evil spirits.

We also needed visual equivalents for the legion of demons. During preproduction, we had engaged a group of Asian dancers to portray the legion of demons. As we neared the time for on-location shooting, the troupe canceled its involvement with ABS. The film finally employed the image of a single dancer (the Silver Apparition) to symbolize legion. Visual equivalents were also needed for the act of exorcism and the figure of Jesus. An early idea for showing the exorcism depicted it as the implosion of a building. We dropped this too, as it did not fit into the rest of the narrative. When the troupe of dancers canceled out, we considered the possibility of using a laser light show to illustrate the exorcism. Again, this device did not fit into the overall film. From the beginning we kept to the idea that the video translation would view Jesus from the demoniac's point of view. Therefore, the image of Jesus (or "the Welder" as he is named in the credits) would not be historical, but a likeness imagined by the demoniac. Lastly, the tombs, leg irons, and chains figured in our deliberations. The film utilizes two "equivalent" locations: a bunker or building where the demoniac lives and a cemetery. An actual set of chains was used on the "set" in the bunker.

The original script called for several flashbacks: the Calming of the Sea, the Raising of Jairus' Daughter, and the Temptation in the Desert. These flashbacks responded to the research that tried to contextualize this story into a larger frame. They, too, disappeared from the final script because the flashback idea did not have sufficient detail to satisfy the team.

The original script also called for an extremely happy ending, one scripted as a homecoming block-party. The healed man returns to his neighborhood, hugs his mother, and is hoisted up onto his neighbors' shoulders in celebration. This was rejected as it did not contribute to the overall understanding of the story.

In summary, we have detailed the beginnings of new media translation at ABS. Key steps included development of guidelines and principles, selection of a text, and development of a treatment and script, including crucial decisions about how to visualize on film the images of the text. Next came the actual production.

Production Begins: October, 1991

The issue of authority in the project surfaced again when shooting began. On location, the production company we hired to execute the approved script essentially took charge. The subcontractors all answered to the production company. Therefore, the detailed decisions achieved in preproduction became critical. However, once we arrived on location, how did the patron (the Bible Society) exercise control over content-fidelity in a production model? The positive aspects of the production process experience resulted from the close collaboration between ABS staff and consultants and the production company. For example, to keep the budget manageable, the production team occupied office space at ABS. This afforded daily contact regarding almost *every* issue that affected the production.

But, the production process placed me in roles that felt awkward. As the ABS person on location most of the time, I was referred to as "the client." Most of the crew did not know me or my role, so they did not know how to treat me. The fact that I represented the patron who commissioned the project did not matter to most crew members. However, it did matter to the director and her immediate staff who came to me for guidance and suggestions during the whole process. We learned how to handle this difficult situation during the production of the next two projects. First, there is strength in numbers, and perhaps having additional ABS colleagues present in the pre-production, production, and post-production phases could have alleviated the awkwardness I felt. The real solution lies however, in defining roles, especially on location. Second, even before that, we need to set up a model of accountabilities to reflect the goals and objectives of the "driver" of the project.

No matter how much preparation we accomplished during pre-production, numerous on-location decisions arose, which affected the outcome of the shooting and the faithfulness of the film. One decision had to do with location permissions. The cemetery could have stopped us on the day of the shoot. The name of ABS did not seem to make a difference to the owners of the cemetery. Another decision had to do with the actor portraying the welder ("Jesus"). He had difficulty moving smoothly. This limited the composition and length of each take. Then, on the Saturday when we had cast volunteers from ABS as extras, it rained. Corporate policy did not allow them to interrupt their work on Monday, when the crew finally shot the scene. There was a fire during production in the indoor studio. And, if that were not enough, the set director ran out of stage smoke and substituted military surplus smoke inside the bunker. This delayed the shooting when it was already close to midnight. During the on-location shooting, the composer, who normally would score the film after the director had edited it, was creating musical modules based on the script. We had a November deadline to complete the final film, and he was scheduled to leave for Europe for a major film scoring in two weeks' time.

These incidents are examples, perhaps, of the difficulty of defining fidelity as one fixed process. These are also examples of a translation process which is very different from producing print Bibles where the center of attention is words which can be changed more easily (and inexpensively) than a musical score or a scene in a film. A film script may have been scrutinized by biblical scholars and other experts to ensure fidelity, but once on location, we had to make determinations of whether certain scenes, if eliminated, or certain actions, if altered, were still within the fidelity arena. Realistically, some of that determination could only be made once we were in the editing room, during post-production. Certainly some of the lessons about fidelity that emerged out of this production were that fidelity requires a process of team decision making, and that fidelity reposes not just in words of a script, but in image, sound, film style, and all the other elements that constitute a new media translation project.

Post-Production Begins: October, 1991

Again, collaboration between the director and ABS proved critical during this period. A sample of the issues we addressed include the non-use of the demoniac's boyhood shots; the demoniac's finding a Bible in the pocket of the jacket he grabbed from the welder; the change from the overly-happy ending where the demoniac is reunited with his mother; minimizing the overly-happy ending with the crowd (we encased the footage in the monitor to try to minimize any superficial happy ending); and the decision to drop the chanted track as the primary track (listeners couldn't understand the words and the use of both the chant and spoken tracks confused the listeners).

The titles and credits also proved to be a major source of tension for the collaborative team. In the model of print translation the team remains anonymous. But, the model for cinema includes the display of individual credits. The Bible Society issue really had to do with the impression we would create if we followed the anonymous model. This would imply that the production company did all of the work. Therefore, in some way, the credits helped to establish ABS as not only the patron, but also the creators as well. In the second and third ABS video translations, we utilized two approaches: a non-credited version for ABS distribution and a fully-credited version for use by the production team. A more practical issue arose with how the video would display the title and credits, i.e., MTV style or film style. As we tested the possibilities with teenage focus groups, we discovered that when we utilized the phrase "American Bible Society presents" on the video, teenagers tended to be turned off by what they thought they would be seeing in a Bible product. We now use "ABS presents" at the beginning of the videos.

Testing and Evaluation: November, 1991 - February, 1992

ABS commissioned three formal studies, two of which involved focus groups of the target audience and leaders of the target groups. In the third, a group of 24 scholars completed a comprehensive questionnaire. A member of the ABS team, Ronald Roschke, took the 24 responses and compiled a report. He writes the following as an introduction:

> How does a person "re-view" something new? The task of criticism involves making comparisons between an object and a body of other objects which establish the standards and rules for interpretation—"the classics," if you will. If something genuinely new enters the horizon, no one (not even a scholar) is going to know initially how to judge it. At least in part this would explain the amazing variety of responses from scholars who watched The Gerasene Demoniac. At times it seemed almost as if the video was acting as an "electronic Rorschach" and that

what we are seeing through the reviewers' reviews has less to do with the video and more to do with the reviewers themselves. (1992, p. 1)

The discussion in the responses focused much on the term *translation*, and 10 areas stood out: the functional equivalence of the text; language of the translation; title; images; sound; the validity of video in biblical translation; the necessity of non-print translations; reaction to the theory used to create this translation; the development direction in video; and willingness to distribute in its present form. Of the 10 dimensions being tracked, only two received average scores in the "very positive" range: necessity of non-print translation and the validity of video in biblical translation. Three dimensions were in the "positive range": sound; development direction in video; and language of the translation. The remaining five had average responses in the "unsure range": theory used to create this translation; images; the functional equivalence of the text; the willingess to distribute in its present form; and title (pp. 2-3).

All respondents affirmed the need to move in the direction of electronic and visual presentations. At the same time:

> The "viable functional equivalent" issue was a key question to this group. The composite score here as "unsure" may not give a very accurate depiction. Only three of 20 responses in this category could be characterized as "unsure." However, 10 reviewers gave positive and seven gave negative reviews....The 10 reviewers who said The Gerasene Demoniac was a viable functional equivalent did so without a great deal of documentation as to what specifically made it such. Only two or three reviewers indicated that it might be difficult to know what "functional equivalence" for a non-print translation might mean. However...there is ample evidence to suggest that this is not at all easy for current traditional biblical scholars to ascertain. (Roschke, p. 8)

As noted earlier, we commissioned focus group tests with young people in peer groups, ages 16-22, in order to test for (1) understanding of the narrative, (2) the emotional impact, (3) the total effect, and (4) particular filmic elements. The executive summary notes:

> The video translation The Gerasene Demoniac is most appealing to teenagers who are church attendees familiar with the story. These individuals like the video for many reasons, particularly because they find it to be a relevant contemporization of a biblical story. Most executional elements comprising the video, especially the music and casting, are very appealing to these teenagers. The video maintains their interest throughout and communicates a very clear message of the positive power of Jesus' grace in saving someone in serious trouble. Some teens infer this message to reflect the need for humanity and caring in our troubled world and society. Finally, many teenagers also relate the video to the implication that Jesus' assistance is available if "in trouble you just ask."

Those teens primarily non church attendees not familiar with the story, who do not like the video say they find it to be very confusing. Their confusion directly stems from difficulty comprehending the symbolic elements and their disturbance with the concept that the visual action of the film is not replicating literally the spoken narration. (Vogt Marketing Services, 1992, p. 10)

The video has had a limited distribution since 1992, as has the CD-ROM version, which was completed in 1996. We still receive positive letters, however, about how the video moved youth groups, individuals, and young adults.

How do we measure the video's success? Why does it still evoke controversy? And is it a translation? The answers to these questions must be tentative since only time and testing of audience reaction will provide the data for conclusive responses. Still, we can say that our limited focus group testing showed a high level of interest in non-print Scriptures, particularly when they are set in contemporary dress. Controversy cannot be avoided, nor should it be. Out of the engagement of opposing views will come new insights and directions. Whether or not *Out of the Tombs* represents a translation will depend on our definition of a translation. If we limit a translation to print, then *Out of the Tombs* is not a translation. But, if we follow modern film and translation theory, with their insights about film adaptation as translation, and about the role of audiences in determining what a translation is, then there is sufficient reason to call *Out of the Tombs* a translation and to further test this hypothesis by additional research and prototype production.

Conclusion: What Did We Learn From the Project?

Whether the term "translation" is appropriate for *Out of the Tombs,* and the two additional prototypes which we have completed, remains an issue. We at ABS would argue that what we produced did go through a translation process, starting from a reinvestigation of the source text, to finding equivalents in image, sound, word, and music in the target genre. If *Out of the Tombs* is then a translation, what other issues remain debatable even among Bible Society translation colleagues? Some come immediately to mind: financial concerns, conflict with book culture, and lack of trained personnel.

Given the realities of the effectiveness and necessity of Scriptures in visual and oral delivery platforms, why do Bible Societies still organize themselves around one medium? A typical comment when someone proposes a film, video, or software project illustrates this: "It costs too much to produce," and, "We are not equipped to get it out on television and to the masses." Should we not organize the Bible Societies by content—the Scriptures—encompassing *all* media?

What are the financial realities of new media translation? In North America and Western Europe, it takes substantial amounts of money not only to produce films and television, but also to properly market and distribute these programs. The cost of doing one video in the United States may finance a whole Scripture program in South Asia. We need, then, to raise the question of partnership: All parts of the world need Scriptures in various media. How do the Bible Societies share resources—funds, assets, and talents—as a united front, to provide much-needed Scriptures in visual and aural formats globally?

Is new media translation *new*? Does everything have to be high tech? If only there were a term to encompass all visual and aural media in nature! Sadly, terms such as "new media" or even "multimedia" imply expensive technology in many people's minds. Eight years ago we grappled with finding the right term and I think we have come to that point again. Perhaps our time may be better spent in conceiving the task of Scripture translation and distribution as one major work, whatever the medium. Translators should conceptualize all works which attempt to serve as vehicles for the transmission of God's Word, whether three-dimensionally or from all media angles.

What role does a Bible Society play in a geographic location relative to new media Scriptures? The ABS serves church and parachurch organizations in the United States. Each of these organizations has a distinct identity and constituency and all have a mission to reach people with the saving Word of God, to change lives by conveying the depth and breadth of God's love for them. The ABS is not a church, but exists to provide affordable Holy Scriptures for every man, woman, and child. We all know that merely giving someone a print Bible or a video with no personal contact or follow up is not an effective way of evangelizing. However, we could explore some kind of model, or a division of labor, in the United States in which ABS provides the Scriptures—in all forms—and the churches use these Scriptures as part of a total program to make a difference in people's lives. As a Bible Society we are equipped to do this and to do it responsibly and with integrity. However, this model may not work in other areas. The Bible Society in another country may resemble a church in that it has to not only produce the Scriptures, but make the contact with individuals and directly share God's Good News with them. Whatever the role, the Scriptures we produce—in whatever format—must reflect the integrity, and the depth, of the Word of God in content and presentation.

What changes to the infrastructure does a non-print translation paradigm necessitate?

If Bible Societies don't take the production of new media Scriptures seriously, then other individuals and corporations will produce them for profit and without dedication to scholarship and fidelity. This is not new news. Multimedia CD-ROMs with biblical material appear frequently in the United States. It doesn't take too much time on the computer to discover how shallowly and stereotypically such programs treat the biblical material.

And if much of what we see on television or in the movies eventually ends up in our home communities, the colonialism of schlock—i.e., biblical films and software with no integrity—will also appear in other parts of the world.

Besides these, many other basic issues will require additional study as they relate to ABS, perhaps other Bible Societies, and the commitment of Bible Societies to new media Scripture projects. Some of these issues include perception and relevance of new media projects in relation to the total work of the Bible Society; the legal expertise needed for new media production, e.g., contractual issues with production firms; and financial realities of new media production: costs, payment schedules, rights, and royalties. One of the most difficult issues has to do with models of decision-making. New media translators are not a single-discipline group; given this reality, there is a real democratization of decision-making among biblical scholars, film experts, software designers, educators, and technologists. This can be threatening to certain segments of the translation world. New media translating is an extremely collaborative process that respects the expertise of many. There are also such issues as distribution of new media Scriptures with its different outlets, methods, and financial arrangements. Not to be overlooked are the physical and emotional pressures of engaging in new media Scripture production, the nature and costs of revising a new media Scripture portion, and the authority and integrity in the world of new media production.

Moreover new media projects call for ongoing work with theoretics, specifically the development of guidelines. Among the most recognized guidelines lies the idea that generally speaking, the message (the Scripture portion) must drive the medium, but as Marshall McLuhan (1964) argued, the medium also informs the message. Similarly both production and audience reception (Soukup, 1997) also affect the message. One might say that the old "Genesis project" (which drew its soundtrack word for word from the King James Version Bible or the Revised Standard Version Bible) was message driven, but ineffective because the medium of film did not inform it. The project did not employ the conventions of filmmaking which resulted in a strange end-product.

Additionally, research and development of the selected text, the audience, and the target medium must undergird and inform any production of new media Scriptures. This research and development, once completed, must be re-formed and communicated in a language understood by those who carry out the production. Practically speaking, research and development does not end, but continues as the production proceeds. A supervisory team must discuss and assign marketing, distribution, legalities, and financial roles and responsibilities prior to the actual production of a new media Scripture portion. Producing a portion that will never reach the hands of the intended audience makes no sense.

The key to the success of the process of new media Scripture production lies in collaboration by many experts, rather than the work of one individual. The project must allow each expert room for creativity yet acknowledge his/her accountability to the total project. In this kind of project, phases will no doubt overlap (e.g., research & development flows into production) with no clear hand-off. The sponsoring group needs to properly compensate the experts for working on new media Scripture projects. Given costs and deadlines, we cannot always depend solely on volunteerism; but we can depend on experts who are loyal to the Bible Society and faithful to the mission to translate the Scriptures with integrity.

We must develop a process that involves Bible Society entities and those whom the Bible Society will hire for the purpose of creating a common understanding of the Scripture product, the schedule for production, and approval processes. Bible Societies must realistically acknowledge production schedules, but they must also clearly articulate to non-Bible Society entities the need for expeditious approval cycles. A Bible Society must involve itself in the production of each specific new media Scripture portion on a daily basis. It cannot take any aspect of the production for granted, nor blindly hand-off responsibility to those who do not understand the issues of quality, integrity, and fidelity. The leadership of Bible Societies needs to provide moral support and proper financial compensation for persons who work in the area of new media Scripture production.

By continuing to do only book Bibles, national Bible Societies are wedding themselves to a single technology and allowing that technology to prevent millions from accessing the Word of God. For Bible Societies to be true to their mission to reach everyone with the Holy Scriptures, they must not force people to have to learn any single technology, whether it is to read a book or to operate a computer in order to experience the Bible. The New Media Translations Program at ABS represents an effort to use many media to communicate the Bible, and to do so with integrity and fidelity. The commitment of the New Media Program to treat its prototypes as translations means that translational guidelines and principles, together with translational and scholarly vigilance and respect for accuracy, direct every production. Such direction enables Bible Societies to go beyond printing the Word of God in book Bibles, to the communication of God's Word in screen and digital technologies.

3

Fidelity and Access: Reclaiming the Bible with Personal Media

Gary R. Rowe

What the Bible Might Be When It Isn't a Book

First, one need not read the Bible. The Bible can read itself. It can have its own soundtrack of vocal performance, dramatic narration, music. It can invite movement, so that its participants might even break out into dance. Second, one's eyes can feast on the Bible. Words come to life in images: those of the historical traditions in the fine arts, those derived from cultures worldwide, and those fabricated from the sights of the contemporary world. They also represent pictograms of the Bible's own historical and metaphorical worlds, and allow virtual journeys to those places.

Third, the Bible teaches as it goes. Its text yields assistance for a word, a reference, a place, a character, a connection. It invites thought and communicates the thoughts of many others. It opens itself according to interest and need and it engages communities of active participants with each other. Finally, if it can be "unbound" from the captivity of the printed page, the Bible can again become what it once was. If its keepers, its translators, take heed of the emerging ideas of a digital world, a world that erases the barriers and boundaries of the book, there is no telling of the centrality and power the Bible can have in the lives of humankind. To do that, though, challenges our notion of a faithful translation. If the Bible is not a book, then how do we measure its words? We cannot avoid the question, for contemporary American culture has changed our very understanding of media. Consider the challenge of the emerging digital world.

An Emerging Digital World: The Translation Challenge

A young bride in a wedding gown holds hands with her groom as they face a clergyman in a color photograph that graced a feature story in a recent edition of *USA Today*. An arch of stained glass frames the three in the picture. The telling point of this image, and a reason to give it our attention, is the total absence of any icon of faith. No religious art, no symbol of spiritual bonding, no story of the Bible nor artifact of the sacred graces this picture. At the focal center of the arch, and the photograph, stands Cinderella's castle. (See Figure 1.) It forms one set of images of "A wedding album from Walt Disney World" (Kelly & Wilson, 1997, p. 8D).

©Kelly LaDuke/Gamma Liaison, reprinted with permission
Figure 1: Wedding at Walt Disney World.

Certainly the slick marketers and image makers at Disney know enough to avoid sectarian symbols in an atmosphere designed to attract thousands of wedding ceremonies annually to what has become America's most popular honeymoon destination. But this representative triumph of fairy tale over sacrament should sound alarms to those trusted as keepers of faith traditions, of the Bible and its translations, and the transmissions of biblical faith to future generations.

In the modern American culture, secular stories have eclipsed Bible stories by their sheer numbers and by their audience penetration through modern media. A young couple approaching matrimony has grown up in a culture saturated with countless hours of stories that form a basis of belief and perspective about family life, child rearing, money, maturity, relationships, and romantic love. Most come from television. Comparatively few come from meaningful exposure to the stories of faith. Sunday school and Sunday sermons, let alone catechism or confirmation experiences, timidly compete with the secular media for formative influence among youth and throughout the culture at large.

Stories of action, adventure, heroism, fantasy, domestic comedy, horror, personal risk, sacrificial love, and lofty idealism fill the Bible. Modern media are filled with the same forms. Think about how many hours of exposure children get to such stories through television and video, comic books and interactive games, pop music and radio. But most of these stories never approach the valid touchstones of biblical experience. They celebrate, instead, a secular world without reference to the sacred, the transcendent, the divine. The ruling gradients of learning come, not from life considered authentically or from faithful presentations of the Bible's story, but life swept into a media tide of artificiality and commerce, most of it measured out in doses of passivity and social conformity.

The power of media conglomerates to appropriate the stories of our culture and tell them back to us through new filters appears nearly absolute. Disney provides a useful example. It is wholly capable of ingesting meaningful stories and massaging them until dramatic integrity is sacrificed to maximum entertainment values—sentimentality replacing honesty. It then cross-promotes each newly forged asset, turning movies into plastic toys and coffee mugs. Along the way there's time for a stopover in theme parks that idealize history, literature, and human aspiration in a bloodless pastiche of self-congratulation. Somewhere on this journey people are easily disconnected, not just from their money, but from a celebration of human experience filled with drama and joy.

It is always easy to critique media and the corporate producers who influence us so overwhelmingly. Among a thoughtful intelligentsia, such as the readers of this book, media-bashing takes on a delicious sense of revenge. But that should not be our purpose. Only now do we begin to see the profound significance of the media shift underway in our world. Only now do we begin to see what faithful presentation of Bible stories might mean for a culture defined in part by this media shift.

The beginning of something brand new in history—the technological bases for recording images and sounds—defines the progress of the 20th century. While the technologies that accomplish this may dazzle us, the media shift is not about transistors, airwaves, digits, and silicon chips. It is about the content.

The means to create mediated experiences in sight and sound gives us a new representation of reality, and a new opportunity to represent that reality in authentic ways. No humans have ever lived in this artificially mediated world before. Future generations will experience our own history in ways we cannot possibly experience the history prior to this century. The generations that succeed us will know us through our images, the sounds of our voices, our movements and actions. What happens when we can shift the time of the actual images and sounds of historic figures and events? Clearly, new forms supersede the culture once contained and objectified by bound text, and override the ways in which history was transmitted in the past. Who would think of studying the 20th century apart from the photographs, motion pictures, and video recordings that dramatize it in images and sounds?

But the 20th century may look, in the future, like a mere transition period between the Gutenberg world and a digital world now emerging. Television, the principal object of our thinking about media, has only now begun to mature. The possibilities of what television will become bear little resemblance to what we have already seen. A time span of 50 years marks the growth of television. That span measures television's infancy and is now coming to an end. A mature medium is only now evolving as television becomes a form of publishing and distributing information essential to human commerce and communications.

Up and down Sixth Avenue in New York City, the media empires represented by the traditional broadcast networks and their more recently formed cable cousins are led by executives who remain confident that we will all continue to use television in ways familiar and already established. A vast majority of Americans, the wisdom goes, will continue to spend hours in front of their television sets and consume the entertainment, news, and sports served up amid commercial clutter and breathless hype. Some hedge a few bets against the growth of the Internet and interactive media. But Wall Street's evaluation of these companies and their opportunities for continued growth and prosperity ignores the new sovereignty that will revolutionize media we know in favor of media we now only begin to discover.

If the ancient wisdom of the biblical canon is to last into a new millennium, we must take account of these swiftly moving currents of opportunity. As long as it stays captive to the printed page, the Bible stands at risk in a culture of electronic production, storage, and transmission. Moreover, the translation theory that supports printed modern language versions of ancient texts may prove inadequate for the requirements of new media forms. A new balance, indeed a fresh approach, is required in translation theory. The source-target paradigm will prove insufficient if its framework is narrowly defined by traditional notions of fidelity.

Bible translators must confront these questions of format and media because the opportunities of new media provoke questions about what we mean by fidelity in a world that has moved beyond printed texts. This means an aggressive expansion of our theories of fidelity will assure that Bible translation can be in the vanguard of connecting new media to its expectant audiences, especially if new solutions are affirmed that invite participation and interaction with information.

Who will define new media and its success? Unlike the standards of the past and the customs that drive traditional media, it will not be its producers; it will be its audiences, its users. The arguments that follow exhort us to take seriously new media forms and to renew and reclaim the Bible through a new understanding of the translation challenge.

The Television of the Book

Thinking about television remains stuck in the 1950s when most Americans had an extremely limited number of choices to make about television. In an economy based on spectrum scarcity, three network enterprises with roots in radio broadcasting came to dominate the use of television as a medium of entertainment and information. Educational television and a few UHF stations in large markets harvested roughly 10% of the available audience for alternative programming. Broadcast television represents the first of four major stages in the evolution of the medium—one characterized by highly structured centralized choices. A few people really did dictate, by and large, what American viewers could see on their screens. The scale of broadcast television gave rise to the concept of a mass audience. For viewers, this most resembled living in a tribal structure. Television worked for you as long as you were willing to belong to the tribe of fans who enjoyed *I Love Lucy* or the Cartwright's adventures in the untamed West or Walter Cronkite or the World Series.

The growth of cable television, a second stage of evolution, customized the broadcast schedule with its eclectic variety and carved it up into specialized channels. For the first time viewers could get news any time because news channels ran all the time; the same with weather, sports, movies, children's programming, comedy, and arts programming among many other choices. This "narrowcasting" fragmented the broadcast audiences and "disassembled" the programming of traditional broadcasters. Only the spectrum capacity of the cable system, not the available programming sources, confines the range of choices. A secondary benefit of cable came with marketing and management that moved sensitivities about the audience closer to the community marketplace and changed somewhat the New York and Los Angeles epicenters of the television industry.

A less obvious but most important third evolution of television occurred at the wall outlet. The "plug-in" channel offered by the connection of a VCR to a television set liberated any—or all—viewers from programming decisions made by others. New sources of programming available for rent or at retail put the average viewers in charge of their own personal "media castle" as a feature of domestic life. While the seemingly limitless choices allowed for the creation of a personally directed programming schedule, a residual notion also began to take hold in this new realm of choice: the notion of a video library. With the collection of videos in the household, much like a personal collection of books and periodicals, television began to take its rightful place as a medium of publishing.

The emerging digital evolution of television is the fourth stage; it requires radical redefinitions of the medium. To understand this transition, we must critically assess what we have believed and ask what in the traditional definition has limited us. Conventional wisdom correctly understands that a truly new medium of expression lives first in its antecedents. Early movies acted out stage plays before the camera; early television programs broadcast radio shows with pictures.

Traditional Television

A new critical analysis of traditional television needs to embrace a wider perspective. For 50 years, despite all the McLuhan-esque arguments marshalled to explain the glowing box, we have really watched a medium that has its strongest analogs in the Gutenberg technology of the printed, bound book. Like the logical sequences of books organized in chapters, television organizes time into artificial clock units. These act like programming containers, each discrete and limited. These units further divide through logic based on the demographics of the available viewers throughout the day and the night. Even the "all-the-same" narrowcasting channels of cable television establish patterns that march in lockstep with this rational division of time. (There are limited exceptions to television's rational time. These include baseball games, golf tournaments, awards programs, and breaking news reports. All of these drive programmers into agonies over allotments of advertising schedules, viewer tune-out problems, and the general mayhem caused by the uncontrollable demands of time measured by human needs instead of mathematics!)

Like the page flow of a book, traditional television moves in a linear fashion, from the macros that govern the clock of the broadcast schedule to the internal rhythms of plot structure and dramatic sequence within the programs. Television follows an Aristotelian logic. Whether a situation comedy or a newscast, a soap opera or a football game, we see standard formulas, predictable and reassuringly familiar. Like the limited boundaries of a book, not easily connected to other information, traditional television is a medium of reductionism. Driven by the clock and its dramatic formulas, it reduces nearly everything it contains to its own conventions. At times, this reduction overtakes reality with disastrous results: The trial of O. J. Simpson lost its way as a criminal proceeding and became a television program.

The sense of what matters in the world, if derived from traditional television, is often sadly out of synchronization with reality. Increasingly, the public controversies about television, the complaints that animate viewers who organize campaigns to protest violence or gratuitous sex on television, reveal a new dynamic that has something to contribute to a discussion of fidelity and to translation theory. Growing numbers of people in audiences do not want to let others make meaning for them in a one-way transaction because they know the power and persuasive influence of television in the culture. Television loses authority when people equate one-way with one-sided communication.

Traditional television has its basis in words and, ironically, practices an extensive distrust of icon and image. The very professionals who labor in the medium contradict the medium itself by insisting that fidelity is an issue of text, not image, not sound. Consider how journalists and sportscasters prattle on in endless descriptions of the pictures plainly evident to viewers. They impose an artificial distance between a viewer and the images as if the truth always requires words. The *Wall Street Journal* recently noted this distressing tendency in an editorial comment about the tragic death of Diana, Princess of Wales:

> We watch...for the images, because the information that cameras convey is powerful and unique. But to get this you must also endure logorrheac commentary of almost unimaginable falsity, coming from personalities thoughtful enough in person but on air unbelievably simplistic. You must watch human tragedy reduced to cheap melodrama and the human comedy reduced to slapstick. Despite some 50 years of daily effort, television news, at least in this country, seems to have rolled steadily downhill to its current resting place—a lukewarm muck of false sentiment and bathos. ("From O. J. to Diana," 1997)

Thus the truly abject practitioners of these narrations tell us how to feel about what we see.

An attempt to equate traditional television with the Gutenberg technology of the book may seem a radical misstatement, an assertion without connection to reality for those who comfortably live in the culture of the book, and an argument without meaning or context for the producers of television. But the book culture has always been a minority culture. And the culture of traditional television, as a culture of producer control, limits the unseen potential of this most iconic of media in similar ways. The book limits, reduces, and confines information divorced from the multi-sensory experience of human community. For all of its importance as a medium for the storage and transmission of thought, it creates information enclosure. It doesn't easily invite collaboration, connection, or action. Information bound in books, despite the efficiencies of transmitting text in this way, remains mute, motionless, and closed. Similarly, traditional television, for all its tribal connections to our psyches, remains bound by its own clock, its own logic, and its self-imposed limitations. All of it remains controlled, not by the audience, but by the programmer.

With instincts not even close to consciousness, audiences, given alternatives, will increasingly refuse to live in exile from the creation of meaning. Something truly dramatic is about to announce itself. Traditional television, with its uncritical beliefs in its market orientation, is on a suicidal mission of delusional self confidence. A new sovereign is about to appear.

Television That Belongs to Everyone

The new sovereign is an audience that expects translation into a common tongue. Only now the common tongue is "spoken" in the languages of sight and sound with expectations of interaction. Just as the monarchs of a previous age were challenged by the discontents of Luther, Jefferson, and Robespierre, new ideals about independent thought and community engagement invade the lofty comforts of those who believe the uses of media are somehow already settled. Fidelity is different for this new sovereign. It is about personal empowerment. Fidelity also exists in social settings where ordinary people have access to the broadband forms of information commonplace in a world woven together by wires and light.

Entrepreneurial innovators will find opportunity linked with the discontents of passive audiences anxious to move with them into new media possibilities. No longer do a handful of powerful executives act as gatekeepers to information. No longer do politicians enjoy popular support for making social rules that make government the central attention of life. There are fewer means at the hands of government to control access to communications through regulations. We see meaningful control of information of value passing from the ownership of the single enterprise to the shared wealth of enterprising collaborators.

For lack of an established name, call it personal television. Personal television, personal media, will grow explosively in the months ahead and utterly rearrange conventional thinking about television, what it is, and how it's used. This fourth evolution of television represents an epochal change in the media shift now underway. It also represents a unique opportunity to faithfully present Bible stories in compelling ways.

New digital work stations give anyone the power to look like NBC and to produce professional video! Just as the power of word processing and desktop publishing have altered the nature of these tasks and put enormous computational and creative power into the hands of individuals, inexpensive tools and desktop video processing now yield individual control of network quality television production. Some people might behold a video work station and think a technological miracle has occurred. But that view ignores the power of the individual to harness information and create from it powerful forms of media. That is the miracle. Budgets and the scale of costs associated with huge enterprises do not limit it; rather the modest means of traditional enterprises and the scale, not of money, but of imagination empower it. It democratizes the means of media production. Before long the work of a child can equal the technical standards of the professional. When that happens, who will control television?

The arrival of digitalization makes personal television possible. No longer a technology of the analog world, the zeros and ones of video merge seamlessly with the digits of the computer, of audio, of graphical images, of any kind of information that can be rendered in this way. The explosive growth of the World Wide Web is only the early weather vane of the radical change in communications underway. This convergence of media in the digital world is not simply a function of production technologies; it also provides the basis for the distribution systems that will make media ubiquitous. With digital convergence, a user can create any intersection desired among multiple sources of information and can manipulate these sources at the user's pleasure. This will be more like "tuning in" channels at a computer and "word processing" information on TV. The communications environment will move passive viewing into active using and create personal utilities that go beyond mere entertainment and distraction. Television, in this new sense, becomes a medium of reference, of learning, of participation, of interactivity, of publishing and communication with others. Fidelity will encompass more than a fixed text.

More than a technological evolution and more than a user-friendly information environment, the World Wide Web stands as a metaphor for how we humans understand communication, information, and transaction. It empowers the information user, not the information provider. Existing media empires run by Gerald Levin, Rupert Murdoch, Michael Eisner, Ted Turner, and Sumner Redstone rest on the premise that an audience will always prefer to sit passively and ingest information. (See Soukup, this volume, and 1997.) The power stays with the programmer. The Web creates a totally alien environment for that type of thinking. It fosters the very important and quite different expectation that "I get to decide; I get to use; I can interact and talk back...this is mine!" The power stays with the user.

The empowerment of the user underlies "personal television." This environment of image and sound has the look and feel of something controlled by preference, convenience, need, immediacy, convertibility, interaction, and connection to others. It is part of an electronic "neighborhood," a place that's familiar, friendly, and interesting. If the images and sounds delivered by television play a different, more personal role in the delivery of information, the network ideal for which the Web stands has a larger role to play in learning. The expectations that users place around television will increasingly include all forms of media. What this means is simple: Whatever users need—the text, the data, the graphical representation, the simulation, the software, even the book—will be available in a common environment of convenience and interaction.

Redefined in terms of emerging media, the Bible, removed from its confinement as a bound book, combines video, audio, text, data and graphics. Extensible and interconnected, it is available to anyone, anywhere. It is a personal learning network, an electronic community. With regard to the issue of fidelity, a digital, personal learning network creates an opportunity for individualized publishing and presentation of the biblical message. Faithful presentation of the Bible's stories will flow not only from the judgment of Bible experts and religious professionals, but from the insights and needs of anyone who has access to the new digital technology.

Publishing in the Bible Studio

The realm of personal television describes a different type of publishing enterprise than the factory-based system once common in print publishing, the hierarchical structure of traditional television, and the labor-management intensive organization in both. The ability to wire the digital machines together—to create a network—makes it possible to work in a highly collaborative way. This matters because the hierarchical structure of a factory system with managers and laborers gives way to a mutual enterprise of shared information, democratic decision-making, and common purpose. The new models for print publishing begin to resemble, then, not the factory but the studio in which the enterprise concerns the creative content, the design, not the means of production. Like the emerging realities of print publishing, the production of personal television requires great collaboration and takes into account the variable ways in which people might want to use the information. Its production occurs, too, in a creative studio guided by collaboration, not in a factory system guided by assembly line thinking. The requirements of the user govern the creative process. This system guides thinking about Bible translation and publishing. While Bible translation usually features collaborative work, new media options require translators to think beyond translating words of printed texts that is, to think on a larger scale of translation into the realm of new communications media as well. Translation does not end with text, it ends with delivery. The American Bible Society has a wide lead over most other publishing institutions in the culture by daring to open new horizons in biblical translation through its innovative new media translations project. As a prototype project truly on the frontiers of media, this formative venture heralds new opportunities and should be judged by how it has opened new thinking and not simply by its impact with audiences. In working with new media, most organizations merely try to adapt to new opportunities with a mindset bound by the past. Technology writer Denise Caruso observes:

> It is the conundrum of the electronic age: everything is changing at the speed of light, but few companies will risk the conceptual leaps that create new markets. So the risk-averse transform [the old]...into digital media, while a new generation of artists must find a way to survive...until some larger part of the world is ready for them. (1996, p. D9)

Until the 20th century, the printed word so dominated the culture that no one gave any real consideration or debate to *media* in the culture. People took for granted the transmission of information and knowledge through printed text. Today we gain little in thinking of publishing as an act of printing or to think of printing as only one of many forms of publishing. Information providers must think, plan, and produce in a multivalent way to capture all of the opportunities embodied in personal media.

Personal Television in Time and Space

The impact of personal media on Bible translations appears more clearly in the light of how students now study. Consider this one extended example. An archeologist for the National Park Service looks into the lens of a small, digital camcorder and invites her fellow travelers to follow her to the next dune to see what evidence of human history they can find in this isolated landscape. She stands a hundred yards from the Chuckchi Sea that bounds the northern edge of the Seward Peninsula just above the Arctic Circle. Numbering in the tens of thousands and dispersed in time and in space in middle school classrooms across North America, her fellow travelers watch this virtual travel experience organized around the combination of television and the Internet. Months after the archeologist has sorted through the pottery shards and the fragments of bone tools fashioned from whales and caribou, her attentive audience will experience her as a friendly guide to the hundred-year-old remains of an Inupiat settlement.

These students have taken an "electronic field trip," a newly minted way to organize a television program around specific curricular frameworks, text-based resources, scientific experiments, problem simulations, original source materials and extensive archives of information. While it cannot substitute for the real journey, it can dissolve the confining walls of the physical learning space of the classroom and vicariously include the wider world.

Electronic field trips as an information format seek to diminish the barrier of the television screen, if not eliminate it, by virtually combining the physical space of the conten—and its presentation—with the physical space of the learner through the medium of the World Wide Web. Using the Web, all of the resources of the location itself, the people, the scenery, the action, move virtually into the presence of the end-user, who lives, not in an audience, but among a peer group of participants.

Electronic field trips use the computer as an extension of the television screen, and the learners experience the images seen on it mirrored in Web-based materials that seamlessly tie the content "out there" with the content used and manipulated by themselves. Unlike the classic theories of communication that treat a receiver as the destination of the signal, the electronic field trip treats the learners as part of a circle that loops back to the originators and ties all participants into a Web-like communications network. The viewers/users have a "hands-on" experience of the information as something they can receive, appropriate, use, interact with, process, reproduce, contribute to, republish, and send to others.

The package also gives instructions for learners on how to produce their own related audio, video, or Web resources and how to share those resources with the program producer and with other participants in schools across the continent. In effect, the end-users finished the program. This format begins to deconstruct the old hierarchy of television production expertise. It invites the audience to become participants in the information, even to produce relevant information that the producer can place into the live telecast as learner contributions to other learners. Students do not read history. They explore it. They do not watch it, but do it. Television takes on the dimensions not of something that belongs to the people on the screen but something that belongs to "me, the participant." Participation becomes part of the television experience in electronic field trips because the program can actually begin months before the live telecast. With materials posted on the Web, learners can become intimately involved with the people they will meet in the telecast and the issues they will explore with those people. The electronic traffic that puts people on both sides in contact with each other blurs who's on which side of the glass. A learning neighborhood is launched around curricular components that form the building blocks of learning.

The practice of science, almost without exception, requires collaboration. Learning science should work the same way. Learning language, learning how to read, learning to multiply, all are social events. Shouldn't the appreciation of literature and the elegance of algebra live best in a circle of collaborators, joined by their common struggles and enjoyment? The semantics of learning pass from cults of experts to groups of committed learners.

Regard what the simple combination of television with the Web can mean. By deconstructing clock time and calendar time and passing control of time and content to the end-user, sovereignty has passed irrevocably from the producer to each person who participates in the mediated experience. While participation can move to the level of a single individual, the ultimate utility of participation is corporate. Through personal television, a new community is born. For thinking about the future of faithful Bible translation and communication, this energy of community will move us beyond the Gutenberg world to new creations.

A Wider Theory of Fidelity

The electronic field trip is a useful way to think about experiencing the Bible. Each time we open it, we should feel the embrace of language, of story, of learning. With new media, opening the Bible isn't about opening a binding and turning pages. It can mean, instead, plugging in, booting up, or turning on. Whatever the appliance, the Bible powers up as a multi-dimensional, personal experience.

The problem of fidelity in translation is redefined by these possibilities for personal interaction. Usually, "fidelity" refers to meanings defined, proscribed, and contained by a print-based understanding of the Bible. But this usual definition is inadequate to the media experience of the Bible. Its narrow meanings focus on accuracy and adherence to fact or detail. Even when we shift to audiovisual technologies, the meaning of fidelity remains unchanged: "the degree of accuracy with which sound or images are recorded or reproduced."

In the electronic field trip described, the end-users of the information are participants in the creation of meaning. Raised on Nintendo, remote controls, and personal computers, they bring to media the expectation that they can personally interact with it and interact on it. They participate in learning in ways that allow for massaging and customizing the information that is given by giving back information they publish themselves. Fidelity defined as accuracy does not reflect this learning community. Fidelity must include not only the needs of the end-user but also the validation that the user's interactions and contributions attach to meaning.

If end-users get to participate and contribute, they are not merely the target in the source-target theory of faithful translation. They join the source. They have a right to expect access to source messages such as the basis for a translation decision, the rendering of meaning in a particular way. Traditional source-target theory assumes passivity and compliance at the recipient end of the communications process. But the advent of personal media empowers the end-user. They expect active participation in and with information and thereby judge the very value of information. If there is no possibility to participate with the source, if there is no meaningful interaction, then the information has no fidelity.

Are there strong objections to a new understanding of fidelity? For those who must sanctify their own expertise and privately-held scholarly knowledge, yes. But, like the changes sweeping traditional television, these authorities are powerless to exercise one-way editorial power, control access, regulate use, and control ownership against the energy of the media shift.

The Grand Convergence and a New Media Bible

We have already begun to live in the experience of the fourth evolution of television. We have passed beyond the limited options of the mass audience and beyond the spectrum capacity of cable television and its specialized networks. We have passed beyond merely sitting in front of the television set. The ability of the user to become the publisher of his or her own information requires an openness on the part of translators and publishers to new ideas about how to make the Bible available. Fidelity in this culture involves access to the Bible, and an ongoing dialogue among all those who have access to the Bible.

Just as specialized networks and live television productions targeted to specific learners will transform educational media in schools, personal television can become the center of new communities of learners for Bible readers. Individuals can feel linked just like classroom communities through sharing common media and can communicate with peers using electronic mail. The publisher of the information can manage these links among people and can design these into the media to provide common purpose, connection, and excitement.

We live in a culture largely ignorant of the Bible at any reasonable level of understanding. When it comes to understanding the Bible, the communications link between the pulpit and the pew has not only lost any meaningful conversation, in many places it can't even be said to feature a dial tone! People want information about the Bible, and therefore have a critical need to harness the digital tools to serve them. The founders of the American Bible Society who wrote its statement of purpose could hardly know that their words would transcend a revolution in how to provide information "to every man, woman and child in a form each can readily understand." The grand convergence of all forms of media in the zeros and ones of the digital age define anew the "language and form each can readily understand," and the plummeting costs of appliances to take advantage of the information cornucopia sets "a price each can easily afford." At last, one can publish a Bible energized by scholarship and reignited by the images, sounds, and performances of its past. The opportunity to translate, publish and distribute the Bible in the realm of personal television, or personal media, can address at least three important goals:

- A new media Bible can motivate more people to spend more time with the Bible.
- It can make time spent with the Bible a richer experience with meaningful Scripture resources and study helps at hand.
- It can make time with the Bible more rewarding through easy interaction with others.

It can, in short, lead to a more faithful presentation of the Bible where faithfulness is defined, in part at least, as access. These goals resemble those of the electronic field trip, and show the way to bring remote information to life in an intimate encounter that takes on personal meaning through direct, personal involvement. They will lead translators to create an environment for the Bible that is friendly to inquiry and extensible to new communities of recipients. Such a Bible can cross boundaries of language as easily as it electronically crosses national boundaries without benefit of passport or import license! A Bible publisher can now put a television network in institutions of learning, in hospitals and care facilities, in prisons, in child care settings, in peoples' homes, on workplace desktops, or for use during discretionary time.

The specific goals for using electronic media do not focus on utility and speed but on personalization and information intimacy. The familiarity that can accrue between producer and user gives media an "information proximity" that print alone can't match. Organizational efforts to harness media opportunities should establish clear goals. Can media publishing lower costs or increase efficiencies over print publishing alone? Does it adapt easily to the needs of audience? Does it assure greater connectivity? Does it establish more reliance by constituents on the importance of the organization? Does it save time?

A Modular Bible

What forms and attributes might a new media Bible have? The chart below suggests one way to think about the organization and translation of information that surrounds a Bible in digital form. (See Figure 2.)

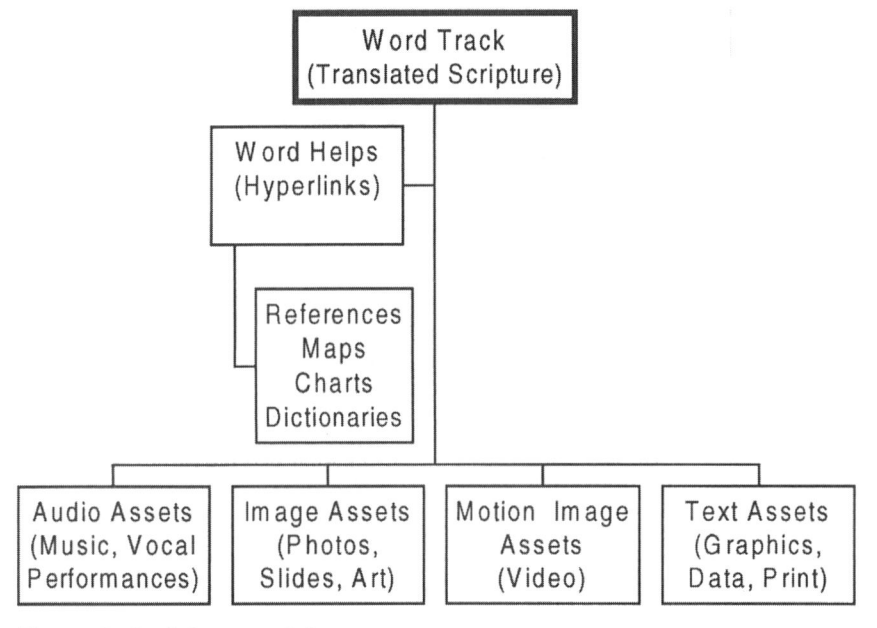

```
                    Word Track
                (Translated Scripture)
                          |
        ┌─────────────────┤
   Word Helps             |
   (Hyperlinks)           |
        |                 |
        ├──────── References
        |          Maps
        |          Charts
        |          Dictionaries
        |
   ┌────┼────────┬─────────┬──────────┐
Audio Assets  Image Assets  Motion Image  Text Assets
(Music, Vocal  (Photos,      Assets       (Graphics,
Performances)  Slides, Art)  (Video)      Data, Print)
```

Figure 2: Scripture module.

Recalling the ancient and still practical lectionary format of thinking about biblical information as modules makes it easy to conceive of producing modern discrete Scripture portions as a beginning point for making biblical information accessible in new ways. One module can easily link with another, or portions of modules with portions of other modules. In this way users can easily compare the texts of birth narratives in Luke and Matthew, hear scholarly opinions about the differences in the texts, access underlying information about the word tracks and translation issues in the narratives, see historical renderings of the stories in visual imagery, and command a host of other resources that once required access to an extensive and costly library of books.

Like the virtual travel in the format of the electronic field trip, biblical study can take people "into" the Bible's world through reconstructions of ancient sites. It can offer up the treasures of antiquities otherwise available only in remote museums. It can give a user a reliable three-dimensional sense of place. It can even create cultural context for travel in time. The modular approach also lends itself to scaling information to different age ranges and types of users. It allows scholars to customize the information uses in confirmation studies for young people, for college courses in religion, for adult Bible study in churches or homes, for use by individuals or groups, or for any other of the multiple ways to parse how people use or want to use biblical information.

Study resources, courseware, inspirational guidance, and mission outreach form only some of the applications for a new media Bible that can be more dynamic and powerful than a printed Bible alone. Publication can occur on the World Wide Web, certainly, but a more dynamic concept involves publishing in a web-like collaboration. The Visible Human Project at the National Library of Medicine provides digital imaging data of human anatomy taken from frozen cadavers. Funded by government, this public domain information is used by medical software companies to build proprietary information used in medical applications. Much like this public/private collaboration, a Bible translation can serve as a core of information for a wider collaboration. Sectarian religious publishing houses develop applications and extensions of the translation suitable to their own needs and constituencies. These production alliances might also include secular publishers and media networks.

If the Bible lives in a digital publishing house, it can become the point of origin for electronic services that can "push" information to users using the software technologies now growing on the Internet with news and information services that arrive at the desktop without the need for the user to go and get it. A daily devotional service, for example, can create a sense of shared community in the realm of cyberspace for individual subscribers. Using the Web to construct "membership" communities offers new ways to encourage Bible study with efficiencies unavailable in print publishing because of the point-to-multi-point interaction possible for users. These communities might organize around life's passages—birth, marriage, maturity—or religious sacraments, or struggles with daily problems or the celebrations that renew the human spirit. Imagine what might happen if a Web-site constructed especially for children promoted interesting ways to learn the characters of the Bible and to interact with peers about Bible stories.

Conclusion

The task of biblical translation, indeed, the work of faith communities, cannot ignore new media without risk of irrelevance and isolation. As the challenges arrive on our doorstep, so do the means to publish using the digital pathways of the emerging global information infrastructure. To do less is a betrayal of faith with the past and a denial of the future. Still, there is danger in the excessive enthusiasm about the promise of new technologies. We must temper the stampede towards high technology solutions by a more methodical gait and incremental steps. It is also important to remember that fidelity is not created by the technologies that dazzle us with new opportunities. Fidelity is a judgment levied by many people: scholars, translators, and faith communities. Fidelity however is related to access and purposes, each defined by personal uses and interactions. The clear focus for any endeavors in new media including Bible translation, must be the human interface and the human user. Those needs determine utility and value and, to the extent that those needs are met, they will contribute to that value judgment called fidelity.

It is time to reclaim the Bible from its Gutenberg captivity. We are, after all, the translators and communicators, not of God's book, but of God's Word.

4

The Historical Imagination

Merle Worth

Try as we may, we cannot return to the past. Nor can the past recreate itself for us. But we can *imagine* what the past was like and attempt to enter its bloodstream. Scholars imagine the past in one way; poets, in another; painters, in yet another. This chapter is an attempt to explore how, in collaboration with the American Bible Society (ABS), I tried to exercise my historical imagination to communicate biblical stories in the form of music videos. How to do so with integrity and faithfulness was the major challenge of the project.

To begin with, let me emphasize how aware I am of the power of image and sound to touch not viewers but real lives. Time and time again, I've seen a mere turn of phrase, an image, or a swell of music really alter one's sense of direction. At their best, the films that emerged from the ABS multimedia project are not so much educational tools but spiritual exercises. How did this remarkable collaboration evolve?

From my very first meeting with the ABS, we searched for a film style in which the events of long ago could feel like here and now. We asked ourselves, "How can history survive and revive in other contexts? And how do we pull the story through the recesses of time so that young people will be captured by the dilemmas of faith and transcendence?"

The critical element in the execution of these video translations was the application of historical imagination. But what, beyond the event itself, beyond the storytelling details, were we actually imagining? As a filmmaker, I was passionate to explore what it *felt* like—physically, morally, and spiritually—to be *in* that moment, to be humanly connected to our characters as real people, to make the complexities of their lives relevant to ours.

I had to make the distinction between what I call the *outside* of the action and the *inside* of the action, between the event and the *bloodstream* of the event. What might the reality have been for the Gerasene Demoniac as he ran along the edge of the sea, howling and beating himself with stones? What must have welled up in the heart of a father when, after years of estrangement, he first saw his Prodigal Son coming over that hill? The task I set for myself as a filmmaker was to use sound and image to immerse myself *deep inside* that moment—its sensation as well as attitudes, its emotions as well as events. William Faulkner's approach to time seems appropriate here. "The past is never dead," he wrote. "It's not even past" (*Requiem for a Nun*, 1959, Act I, scene 3, line 88).

Landscape painters who try to copy nature may think that they are reproducing in their own medium the actual shapes and colors of natural things; but however hard they try to do this, they are always selecting, simplifying, schematizing, leaving out what is unimportant and including what is essential. The artist, and not nature, bears responsibility for what goes into the picture. Similar principles apply to our videos. They are a web of imaginative construction stretched between certain fixed points. What a challenge—to distill the universality of a character, an atmosphere, a happening, to create an entity that has meaning for people at all times—yet remain true to the Scriptures and the premise of equivalent translation.

How do we hope to translate these concepts to film? Usually the greatest challenge for me is to first imagine the *emotional* line of development. Most film makers begin by asking: What does this story mean? I need to first imagine: How and *why* does this experience continue to reverberate? Only then can I address the actual meaning of it. Again, it is working from the inside out. Interpreting rather than illustrating, using the mind and spirit *simultaneously* so that the film gives birth to new ways of feeling, seeing and remembering.

Expressing Emotion

As a young woman, I lived in West Africa for some time and learned at the vulnerable age of 26 that American society has an undernourished view of what we call "information." It is usually defined as fact, as something quantifiable. But it took my African apprenticeship to teach me that *awe* can be just as great a source of information. Terror and rapture, despair and transcendence are deep wells of information too from which we draw the symbols and metaphors of our lives. I fervently hope that someday the full spectrum of human *emotion* will take its rightful and honored place in the process of historical imagination.

Some years ago, I made a film in Mississippi for Turner Broadcasting. I was interviewing a renowned blues player, Son Thomas, and *my* intention was to explore the roots of the blues. *Mr. Thomas's* intention, however, was to have the interview over with as soon as possible since he had a concert to perform later in the day. He was seated inside an abandoned box car and I knew we were headed nowhere. Clearly, he'd been asked all these questions before. Suddenly I noticed that each time he exhaled his cigarette smoke, he blew the most perfect rings into the air. Then, his gaze would follow them upward until they melted away.

Knowing that I had not moved past the exterior of Mr. Thomas's personality, I folded my notes, followed his gaze upward for awhile, and then felt compelled to ask him the strangest question, "Mr. Thomas," I said, "Do you believe in ghosts?" Somehow, on some deeply intuitive level, I had entered into his moment. The result was quite mysterious and often mystical—a truth of another kind. He spoke not about musicology but sociology, not about the blues but about a lifetime of blues.

And so I began to experiment with building sound and image in ways that reinforce how unbelievably layered our existence is. And what more exquisite instrument than film to create compressions of human experience. At our best, that's what we do. And when I'm eyeball to eyeball with other individuals on the screen, I'm forced to face my own fears and strengths over and over again, sending my responses back to the screen. I always try to find that moment of drama, that split-second intersection of subject and viewer in which we all rediscover yet another piece of ourselves.

ABOUT US: The Dignity of Children

For me, part of the mystery of compression, metaphor, and symbol is to create a heightened consciousness of my character's reality. I recently completed a two-hour special for the ABC network entitled *ABOUT US: The Dignity of Children* (1996). It features a true story of a boy named Tony who narrates part of the film. Tony's image is actually portrayed by an actor because Tony was too ill to appear on camera. I listened to dozens of hours of interviews, and I absorbed this boy's life as deeply as I could—his

©Merle Worth/ABC, reprinted with permission
Figure 1: Tony Reflects on his Childhood.

©Merle Worth/ABC, reprinted with perssmission
Figure 2: Tony Sharing Fantasies and Dreams.

trauma and despair, his fantasies and hopes—and imagined images that I believe were equivalent translations of his tale.

Figures 1, 2, and 3 are stills from the film. In one scene, Tony reflects on a childhood filled with trauma and despair:

> My name is Tony, and I was 13 years old when I was diagnosed with AIDS....I feel robbed of a lifetime that I think could have been a good one. I would never get married. I would never have a family. I'm angry that it happened to me....Childhood has got to be one of the most misunderstood eras in any person's life. It's so idealized with beauty and awe and wonder. The problem is, for many children that doesn't happen....There's an innocence involved in being a child. There's a lot of trust that goes into being a child. You need to trust the people around you. You need to believe that somebody, something in the universe, a person out there, is going to protect you at any cost....Emotionally kids feel as deeply as adults do. I know what it's like to feel joy. I know what it's like to be afraid so bad that I shake. I know what it's like to grieve, and to want, and to wish. (See Figure 1.)

In another scene, Tony shares fantasies and hopes:

> When you're told you're special, that means that there's something in you that has a potential to be a part of the world that you live in. It says that, there's something about you, that is worth saving, that is worth loving, that is worth just allowing to be part of the world. I think kids need more than that. They need an ear. Somebody to hear them when the world gets confusing and crazy. They want to know where God is when they're scared. They want to know what can get them through another day when it's a bad day. I think they want to know their place in

the whole universe. Good parents will never let the dignity of their children suffer. Dignity is like fingerprints. It's a different thing for each person, but ultimately it's the same thing. (See Figure 2.)

In Figure 3 we have an image of childhood, a childhood discussed by a teenage member of the Trinity Irish Dancers:

©Merle Worth/ABC, reprinted with permission

Figure 3: Image of Childhood.

I think grownups sometimes forget that kids are as smart as they are. They forget that we see things and we hear things and we feel things. And grownups sometimes forget that stuff that they do to you will always be there. Childhood is like what shapes you. That's what makes you who you are. And if somebody messes it up, it'll be messed up forever....I think that we can only really achieve perfection in groups. I don't think anyone ever does it by themselves. The pursuit of perfection can bring you more joy than you know. And the greatest moments that you achieve will always be with someone else's help.

A Father and Two Sons

I hoped to apply to the ABS new media translations project the same principles of experiential film making, of imagining the *whole* context, that I used in *ABOUT US: The Dignity of Children*. We could devote an entire book to the creative development of these videos, but allow me to focus on *A Father and Two Sons* to illustrate the intricate collaboration between film making, scholarship, and Scriptures. Here are just a few of the many challenging issues raised in the process of shaping this one scenario.

Music

Let us approach the music first. A key element in historical imagination is creating a relevant musicscape. After discussing many different styles, we felt that country blues would be an appropriate style. We listened to many different recordings and chose the talents of Rory Block whose voice resonates with sorrow and rapture. At first she found the task of setting Scriptures to music rather daunting. "The Scriptures were so ancient and formidable," she said, so Rory began by focusing on the relevancy of the text to her own life. Only three years before, she had lost her grown son in a tragic car accident. "Clearly," she said, "I was chosen for this task." (Interview with Rory Block, 1994).

At first, we approached the music not as one continuous piece but as a series of fragments. Rory broke down the Scriptures into separate sections, responded to the different moods, and wrote sketches inspired by the text—moments of anger, sadness, and forgiveness. She programmed a series of chord progressions that would be appropriate for the different emotions in the song. Once she developed the theme for *A Father and Two Sons*, she moved on to composing the verse and chorus. When that process was over, she stacked these elements together and listened for the flow and emotion of the text.

When it actually was time to record the song, she felt a sense of divine intervention, as if something larger than the sum of the parts had evolved. The story seemed to tell itself and the memory of her deceased son filled her with poignancy and informed the words, "He once was lost and now is found."

Film Structure

At the same time Rory was composing, I began developing the structure of the film. I was asked to create a story within the story and to explore a wide range of symbols for the characters. I had very specific direction from the ABS not to turn this story into an allegory, to create a piece of fiction rather than a sense that the event had actually occurred. I was also encouraged by the team to avoid wherever possible one-to-one correlations. The more we moved away from allegory into symbolic interpretation, the better.

In *A Father and Two Sons*, I needed to find a symbolic image for the father's wealth and decided on horse breeding. It was an image that carried a lot of potential for kinetic movement. The ABS confirmed that horses would indeed be an appropriate symbol for the story. The rationale was that the film needed an icon or functional equivalent to stand for the inheritance that the younger son would later squander. At the outset of the film, we decided that the horse would appear strong and vibrant, but as the story progressed and the inheritance consumed, the horse would disintegrate and eventually die.

Now the reality was that we were filming in Georgia at the peak of summer when neither man nor beast should have ventured out into the noonday sun. Needless to say, these horses were stars of great temperament, even greater than that of our film cast! In the original scenario, the father's prize horse was meant to die from the younger son's merciless floggings. We gave special care to choosing the proper horse. He needed to be aesthetically distinctive and, of course, trained to respond on command. But try as he did, his owner could not manage to get him to sink to the ground on cue. He simply refused! His trainer suggested we bring in a vet to tranquilize him for a short period of time but that idea really made us uncomfortable. So though the flogging was done in a series of swift cuts, the death had to be implied by an image of the horse fading from a positive to negative image.

Discussions were held about an appropriate icon or equivalent for the ruin of the younger son. I suggested a shabby carnival as a possible solution, and the team agreed. We built a carnival facade. And there we created the illusion of an ambiguous crime, placing the younger son in a police line-up to suggest his wayward life.

The script included a banquet scene that was to be shot as a great multicultural celebration. On the day of the shoot, a busload of African-American, Asian-American, and Latino extras was expected to arrive from Atlanta. Now the scripted banquet scene was to correspond to the biblical narrative which depicted a feast celebrating the homecoming of the repentant son. Our Bible scholars made clear to me that this feast was a symbol of the Kingdom of God and its heavenly banquet at which God welcomes all dispersed people home.

Of course, in typical film production fashion, the busload of extras did not show up, leaving only an all white cast for the scene. But ABS members on location intervened, pointing out that such an all white scene would flatly contradict the intent of the biblical story. Did we want to imply that only white people belonged in the Kingdom and at the banquet? It was an essential point and the production company arranged for a bus to go to a nearby town and transport a multi-cultural group of people to the site of the shoot.

I was particularly inspired by the decision to make the images more universal, to break away from the one-to-one correlation, and to open up the story to the whole human family. The montage of different family members holding up photos of missing loved ones was very stirring to me—the filming of it even more so. We had an open call arranged by a community center where people were asked to show up with photographs of loved ones. This idea was inspired by a news article I had read about the Seven Day War in which pictures of wounded and dead soldiers were routinely projected for people to identify missing members of their families.

When I held the casting call, all I asked of the extras was that they imagine that the loved one in their photograph was missing. One by one, they stepped up to the camera and were so profoundly stirred by that thought that some people actually filled up with tears, others waved, and a woman spontaneously blew kisses to the camera as if to a loved one. Time and time again I saw how immediate and palpable the Scriptures were to people's lives today.

Purpose, Courage, Conviction

I would like to share a personal memory with you now because this unique undertaking with the ABS led to some remarkable revelations about purpose, courage, and conviction. A number of years ago, I was traveling the Sahara Desert researching a film. We were a small caravan drifting through an infinite stretch of powdery dunes. About every half mile, I saw a stick marking a place in the sand. Dangling from it were eerie ribbons of red cloth fluttering in the desert air.

These streamers, I was told, were markers for an ancient caravan route. Nomads returning from their journey would fill their empty ostrich eggs with water, then bury them along the way for those travelers setting out into the desert. Very often, the guide told us, they'd wrap a note around the ostrich egg and place it beneath the sand. "The oasis is dry," it might say, or "Mano Dayak has a son," or "Greetings from a stranger who found the road but lost his way." Something crystallized for me in that moment. I suddenly longed for my films to be like those very notes beneath the desert floor. How could I ever imagine that the ABS would invite me to join a project that would point the way?

I would like to conclude by saying that I have worked my entire adulthood in the arts and have come to understand that the most beautiful paintings and sculptures, the greatest poetry, have *not* always been born from torment and bitterness. Often they spring from contemplation, from joy, from an instinct for wonder towards all things. And creating from joy, creating from wonder was for me the propelling spirit of this collaboration. It demanded discipline, vigilance, a sense of adventure, and great compassion...and a continual looking beyond...toward a greater spiritual reality. Such was our objective and perhaps our greatest achievement in creating these notes beneath the desert floor. I feel blessed to have been a part of this remarkable experiment.

5

Designing Translation Exercises on CD-ROM: Pedagogical Principles and Theoretical Validity

Mona Baker

Introduction

This chapter addresses issues in the design of pedagogical materials for translators, with particular reference to materials delivered through nonconventional media such as CD-ROM and the Internet. That an urgent need exists to develop such materials and deliver them through the new media has become self-evident in recent years. The changes that we continue to witness in education reflect not only the much-publicized constraints on time and cost worldwide, but also increased preference on the part of students everywhere for pedagogical models that allow them independent and flexible access to learning. The accelerated modularization of postgraduate courses in many parts of the world, for instance, constitutes one type of institutional response to the demand for flexibility. Needless to say, this type of response only partly addresses the demand for *flexible* access to education and does not even begin to address the demand for *independent* access to learning at any level.

In this context, it seems natural for national Bible Societies, who have traditionally pioneered the study of translation, to wish to be at the forefront of new developments in translation pedagogy. This chapter focuses on an attempt by the American Bible Society (ABS) to develop translation exercises specifically on CD-ROM. Although I may appear critical of what has been done so far in my attempt to suggest viable ways of moving forward with this material, I do recognize that I have the benefit of hindsight and that guidelines for good practice cannot be developed in a vacuum.

In the discussion that follows, I will attempt to outline some of my concerns with regards to the existing material and then move on to making a few suggestions about how we might in the future design more pedagogically useful and theoretically robust translation exercises in this medium. I will proceed from the assumption that we need at this stage to outline a general framework that can serve as a kind of blueprint for developing material

©American Bible Society, reprinted with permission
Figure 1: Screen from *The Visit* CD-ROM.

for different linguistic and cultural groups, rather than for developing material specifically in English, or only for specific episodes of the Bible. Indeed, I believe we should set our sights higher still and proceed to elaborate a framework that is not even restricted to Bible translation but can be used as a starting point for developing pedagogical materials for any kind of translation. Even within the context of Bible Societies, it is quite conceivable that our would-be translators will want to tackle a variety of religious texts and theological material of a scholarly nature, among other things.

But before proceeding to discuss some pedagogical principles that might help us refine our current models, I should perhaps begin by describing the main components of the current suite of study materials and the way they interact with each other and with the user.

Overview of Current Suite of Study Materials

Let us take the ABS's CD-ROM for *The Visit* (Luke 1.39-56) as an example of the way the user typically navigates through supporting study material, including a translation section, for any given episode of the Bible. The first set of options offered to the user is between MARY'S SONG and MARY'S WORLD, but there is also an OPTIONS menu with the following set of choices: EXIT, PRINT, REFERENCE SECTION, RESTART. (See Figure 1.) Clicking

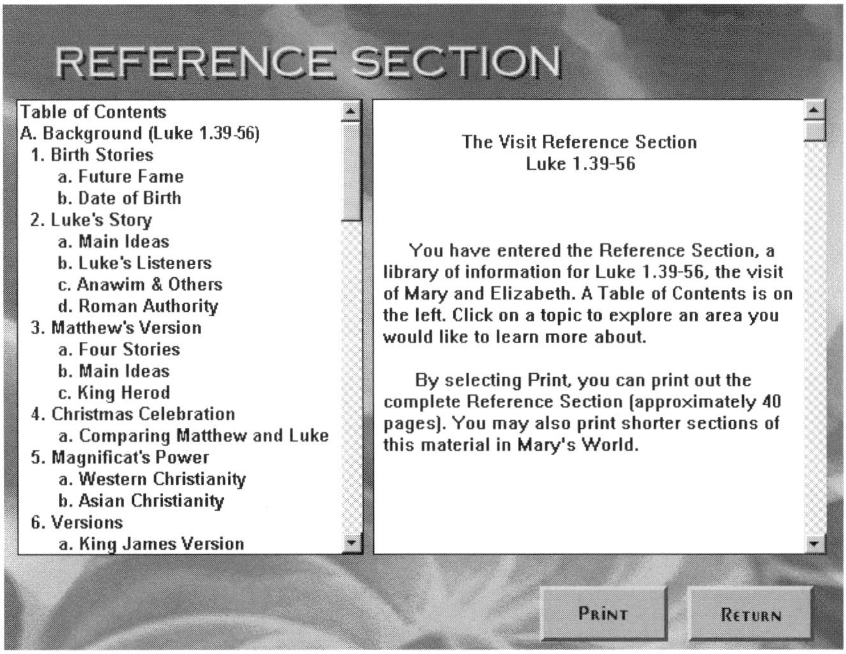
REFERENCE SECTION
Table of Contents
A. Background (Luke 1.39-56)
1. Birth Stories
a. Future Fame
b. Date of Birth
2. Luke's Story
a. Main Ideas
b. Luke's Listeners
c. Anawim & Others
d. Roman Authority
3. Matthew's Version
a. Four Stories
b. Main Ideas
c. King Herod
4. Christmas Celebration
a. Comparing Matthew and Luke
5. Magnificat's Power
a. Western Christianity
b. Asian Christianity
6. Versions
a. King James Version
The Visit Reference Section
Luke 1.39-56
You have entered the Reference Section, a library of information for Luke 1.39-56, the visit of Mary and Elizabeth. A Table of Contents is on the left. Click on a topic to explore an area you would like to learn more about.
By selecting Print, you can print out the complete Reference Section (approximately 40 pages). You may also print shorter sections of this material in Mary's World.
PRINT
RETURN

©American Bible Society, reprinted with permission

Figure 2: Screen from *The Visit* CD-ROM.

on REFERENCE SECTION gives the user access to a split screen: The righthand screen contains a brief statement of what the reference section provides and the way one can use it, and the lefthand screen shows a table of contents. (See Figure 2.) Clicking on any topic in the table of contents allows the user to access information (currently extremely brief, no more than a small screenful) on that topic. Topics range from types of stories in the Bible (e.g. birth stories) to specific versions of the text presented (e.g. King James Version [KJV], New Revised Standard Version [NRSV]), to background information on such things as geography and the status of women in biblical times.

I do not wish to digress too much into technical issues of design at this stage, but it strikes me as relevant to point out that an alternative way of navigating "by association" has already been very successfully implemented on the Web and may provide a suitable model here. Instead of—or in addition to—a table of contents, one can conceive of a more detailed, discursive overview of the text and its environment, in which keywords such as *status of women* and *versions* are highlighted and linked to separate pages of detailed information on the topic. These pages, in turn, would include highlighted keywords that can lead to further pages, and so on, with the option of clicking RETURN and tracing one's way back through the pages available at each stage. By clicking on any highlighted word, the user can access the relevant page and then return again to the discursive overview without

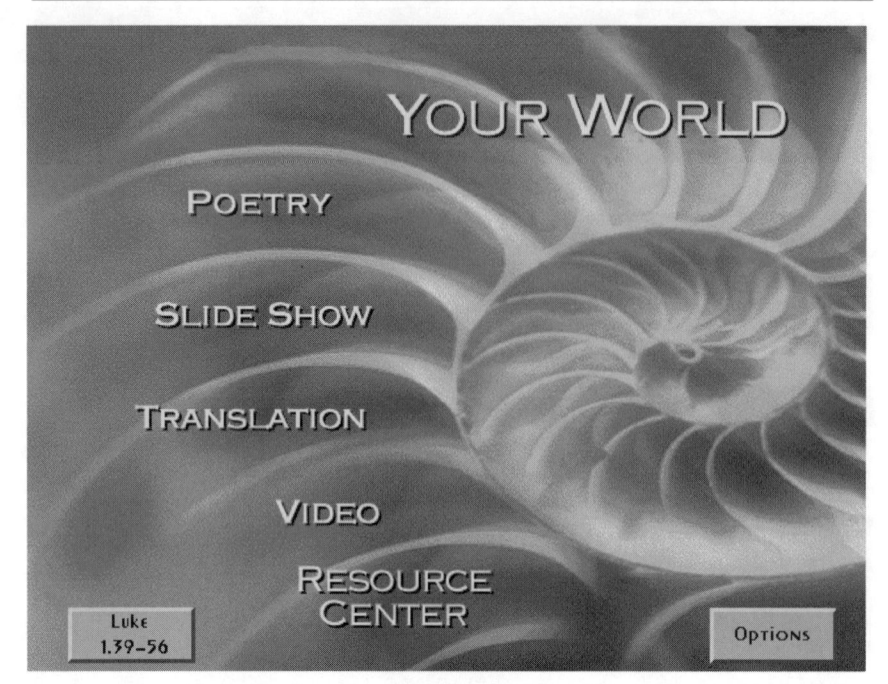

©American Bible Society, reprinted with permission
Figure 3: Screen from *The Visit* CD-ROM.

losing the overall thread of the presentation. This process supports a more flexible and independent learning style, where "free floating," "association," and "discovery" are recognized as valid learning techniques and at the same time complemented by a structured, coherent overview that holds the disparate associations together in a discursive framework.

So much for the REFERENCE SECTION. To access the section that contains translation exercises, one has to return to the previous screen and select MARY'S WORLD. From there, the user double clicks on a further option, YOUR WORLD, to select one of five sub-menus: POETRY, SLIDE SHOW, TRANSLATION, VIDEO, RESOURCE CENTER. (See Figure 3.)

The first screen that appears when one clicks on TRANSLATION offers a brief statement about the text, which will form the basis of the translation exercise, and informs the reader that this text was originally written in Greek and that it has been translated into many languages, including English. (See Figure 4.) Note first that this statement assumes that the user is not a translator: even the least experienced of translators will know this already. In fact, the statement suggests that the designers envisioned a fairly young user, with little or no exposure to translation of any kind. I will come back to this point shortly because it has important implications for the design and pedagogical value of the exercises.

The next screen (Figure 5) instructs the user to compare two verses from the text in two specific versions and then answer a set of questions that

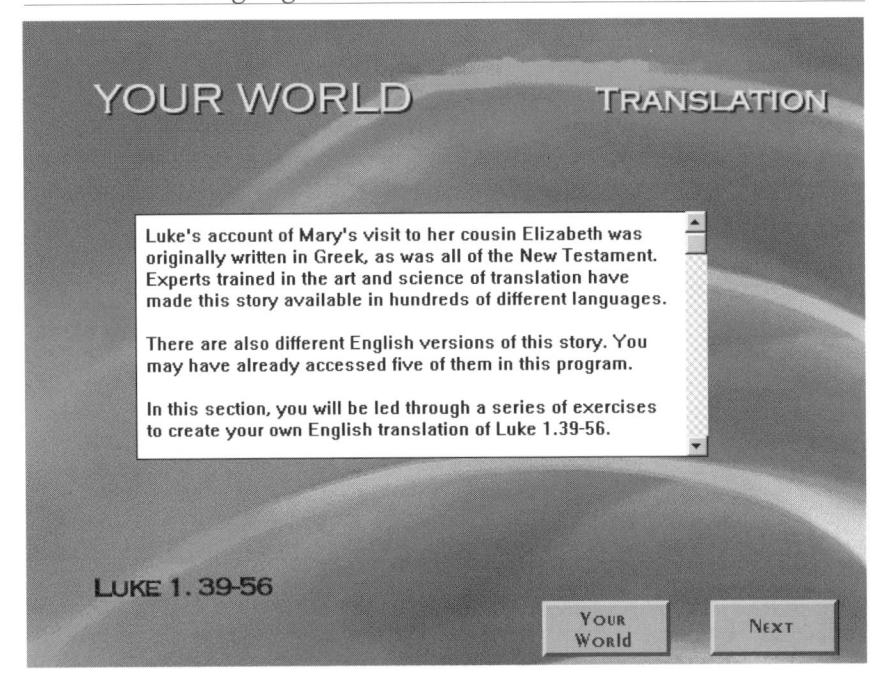

Designing Translation Exercises on CD-ROM 79

©American Bible Society, reprinted with permission
Figure 4: Screen from *The Visit* CD-ROM.

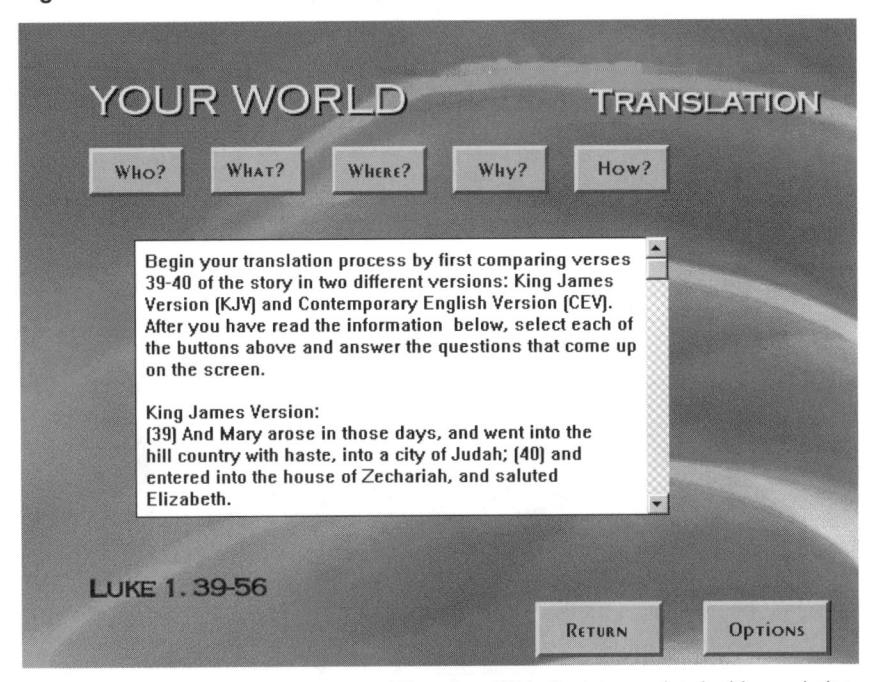

©American Bible Society, reprinted with permission
Figure 5: Screen from *The Visit* CD-ROM.

appear at the top of the screen: WHO?, WHAT?, WHERE?, WHY?, HOW?. By scrolling down this screen, the user can access not only the relevant versions of the verses but also a brief comment on the KJV and the Contemporary English Version (CEV) in general:

> The King James Version, first published in England in 1611, is a traditional and more literal translation. Such translations are sometimes called "formal equivalent" translations because they not only convey the meaning of a text, but try as far as possible to imitate the word order and sentence structure of the original Greek.
>
> The Contemporary English Version is a new translation which is based on the theory of "functional equivalence." According to this theory a translation should try to convey the meaning of the original Greek but not necessarily the word order and sentence structure of the Greek text.
>
> Using the King James Version as a base, you are now ready to create a new translation. After you have answered the Who, What, Where, Why, and How questions above, select Options, and then Next to access a Tool Kit to aid you further with your translation.

One might expect the user to base his/her own translation on the KJV, described as "traditional" and "literal," because this offers practice in producing a fluent, clear text from a literal rendering. I will come back in the following section to the rationale for the choice of version, and to the importance of explaining to learners why they are instructed to do things in a

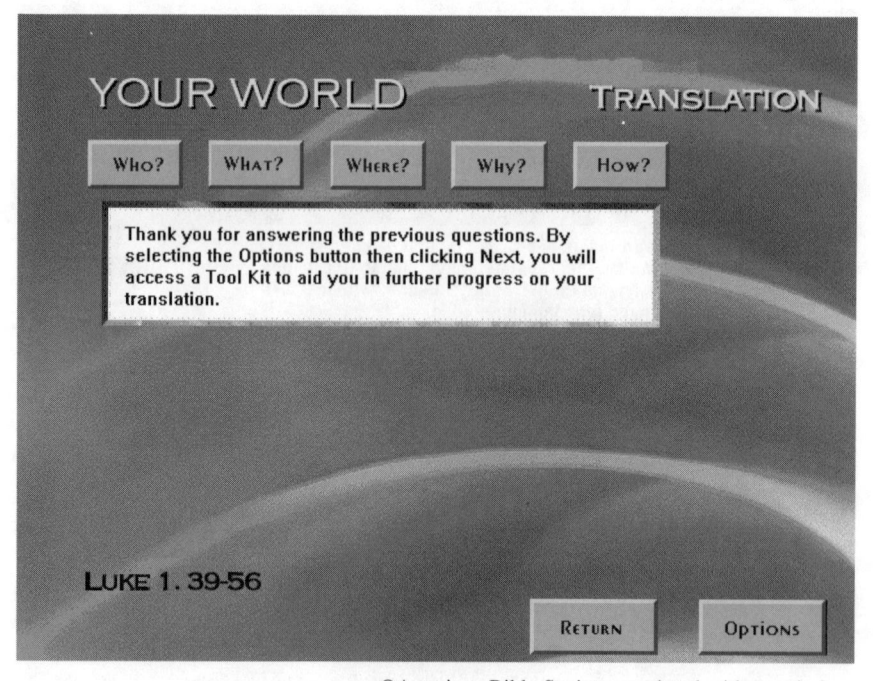

©American Bible Society, reprinted with permission

Figure 6: Screen from *The Visit* CD-ROM.

particular way. One should also note that the program instructs the user to proceed not from the original but from a translation of it, which means that this exercise features either paraphrasing/rewriting (if the user produces another English translation) or indirect translation (if the user produces a translation in another language). Both raise interesting theoretical and methodological issues that a designer can build into additional support material, which the user might want to access at this stage.

The rest of the translation exercise consists of clicking on each question and typing the answer to it in the screen provided before going on to produce the actual translation. The WHO? screen asks the question: "Who will be the audience for your new translation? Specify age range and English language proficiency." The WHAT? screen tells the user: "Print out the King James Version of Luke 1.39-56 as your base by selecting Options and clicking on the Print button." The WHERE? button asks: "Where will your new translation be used? in a church? in the home? What difference does the setting make?" And the WHY? button asks: "Why would your audience be motivated to use your new translation? What would make your translation different and more understandable for the audience you've chosen to target?"

As can be seen in Figure 6 (page 80), by clicking on HOW? the user can access a Tool Kit to help with the actual task of translation. The Tool Kit consists of six versions of the text to be translated, five English and one Spanish. (See Figure 7.) Each version highlights a number of lexical items.

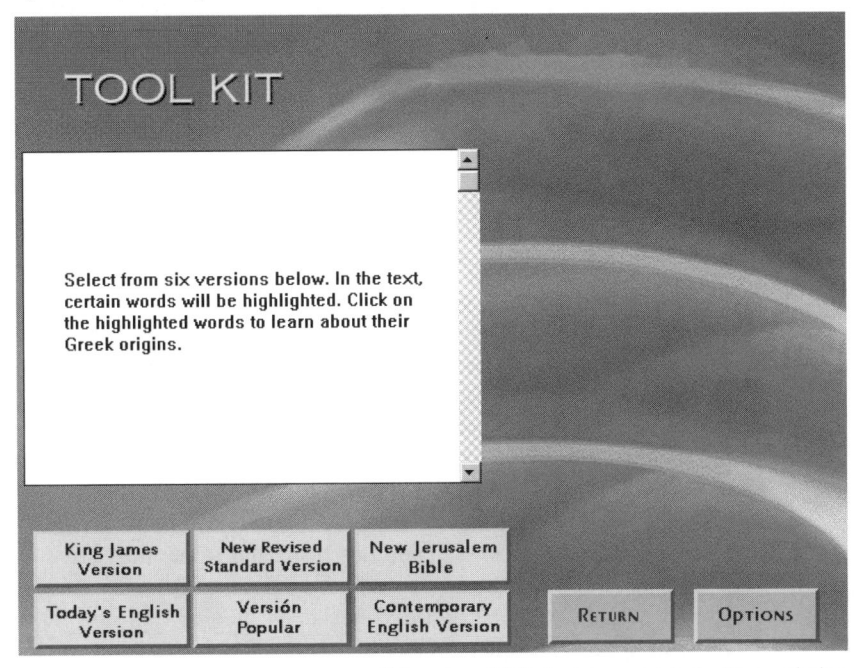

©American Bible Society, reprinted with permission

Figure 7: Screen from *The Visit* CD-ROM.

By clicking on a highlighted item, the user can access a definition of the lexical item, a list of "equivalent" items used in the six versions, as well as a demonstration of the way it is pronounced in Greek.

Finally, when the user has finished working with the Tool Kit, he/she clicks on OPTIONS and NEXT and receives the following message:

> You are ready to start work on a new translation. You should have a printout of the King James Version, your response to the questions, and information from the Tool Kit.
>
> You may wish to break the story down as follows:
>
> Verses 39-41
>
> Verses 42-45
>
> Verses 46-50
>
> Verses 51-56
>
> Click Create to begin writing.

A CREATE button appears at the top of this screen. Clicking on it twice brings up a blank screen for the user to type his/her translation.

Note that the same screen on another ABS CD-ROM disk (*A Father and Two Sons*) appears as BUILD TRANSLATION, an interesting metaphor that reflects the "building block" approach to learning which seems to inform the design of this particular set of exercises. We have here a set of discrete units that form learning steps along a pre-defined path. In the following section, I will argue that an inherent tension exists here between the power and versatility of the CD-ROM medium and the discreteness and rigidity of the learning model that informs the current design.

Some Basic Questions Raised by Existing Material

Let me sum up this quick overview of the material with a list of issues that require some attention at this stage:

- First, one must address the question of user definition or audience design, by which I mean that one must elaborate at the outset a sensible definition of the user who will want to do these exercises. Translation exercises differ from crossword puzzles or computer games—very few people will want to do them for fun. If one bothers to embark on a time-consuming and intellectually demanding exercise of this type at all, one almost always has a particular need to do so. Translation exercises, in other words, are inherently goal-oriented, even if the goal is sometimes restricted to passing a test or even showing off one's erudition. This suggests that translation exercises on CD-ROM must address the needs of viable groups such as trainees or professional translators. A realistic definition of the

user must inform the rest of this discussion and any translation material we develop in general, whether for CD-ROM or other media.
- Second, given the power and versatility of CD-ROM technology, the range of activities offered to the targeted group of users must be expanded considerably to justify the expense involved in developing it and the cost of buying it. Designers can build a great deal more into the Translation Section, including lexicographic activities, paraphrasing exercises, analyses of concordances, and much more.
- Third, arises the question of the depth (rather than range) of material offered and flexibility in navigating one's way around it. The prospective user must have sufficient incentive to use the technology. For one to bother to turn the computer on and put the CD-ROM in and wait for it to boot up, the new working environment must promise to offer something far more powerful, rich, flexible, and convenient than pen and paper or one's favorite word processor. As it stands, the translation section does not take the user very far, and ultimately only offers a blank screen for typing a translation. One can do this with any run-of-the-mill word processor. Moreover, the current components of the program stand alone, with no cross links between them. The user cannot, for instance, access the REFERENCE SECTION while preparing the translation, because the program forces one to get out of the translation section in order to check something in the REFERENCE SECTION, even though the REFERENCE SECTION contains information that the translator will almost definitely want to access at different stages of the exercise. If the CD-ROM environment does not allow the user easy access to a whole range of support material *while* he/she is translating (for example dictionaries, encyclopedias, spell checkers, examples of existing translations, or background information), then the user might as well get out of the program and use a word processor and a dictionary.

Needless to say, the above issues are all linked and demand careful thought in order to justify the use of the CD-ROM technology. But I want to deal with two issues more closely now: the pedagogical principles that inform the design of the exercises, and the need to draw on theoretical models in designing the tasks we set for any target group. Both issues are relevant whatever the medium being used, and they do require some attention in our current context. Because they relate closely to each other, I will try to deal with them together, rather than attempt to separate them artificially.

Pedagogical Principles & Theoretical Validity

Anyone with experience in education will know that there are different types of learners and different learning styles. Moreover, many learners like to be in control of what they learn and how they learn it, and indeed many educators believe in "empowering" the learner. Therefore we must design any translation exercises we develop to allow learners some control over what they do and how they do it. For example, the program I described in the previous section gives the user six versions of the same episode (Luke 1.39-56). The user can look at all of them, but when it comes to working on the actual translation, the user reads this instruction:

> Print out the King James Version of [X EPISODE] as your base by selecting Options and clicking on the Print button. ("What?" question above)

OR

> Begin your translation process by first comparing verses X-Y of the story in two different versions: King James Version (KJV) and Contemporary English Version (CEV). (See Figure 5.)

In other words, the current set of exercises predefine the resource and the task for learners: rather than allowing them a measure of control over what they do (or at least some element of choice), we tell them what we want them to do. This strategy does work with some learners, though usually not the brightest or most creative in a group. But it does work. In fact, some learners feel threatened by too much choice, especially in the initial stages of learning a new subject or skill. But this strategy can alienate some of the brighter, more independent and creative learners, who want to experiment on their own and make their own decisions—choose whatever version they want to work with, for instance. We need perhaps a format that offers the user the best of both worlds: independent choice if they want it, a default choice if they would rather let the program guide them through a particular exercise.

However, we still need to treat learners as intelligent adults and encourage them to develop a conscious and rational strategy of learning, even as we offer the default choice for those who feel unable to take control of their learning at a particular stage. We do this in part by making our own rationale and assumptions explicit, so that learners can understand why we advise them to proceed in a particular way. For instance, if we are going to advise the learner to use a particular version as a base or compare two specific versions, we might explain why these particular versions have been chosen. What is special about the KJV or the CEV, and how does our choice relate to the particular exercise we have set for the learner? Spelling out the educator's rationale and assumptions means that bright, independent learners will not lose their motivation, and all learners will get much more out of doing a particular exercise. After all, education is really about learning to think for oneself and developing the ability to make informed decisions, not about acquiring a particular piece of information *per se*.

Similarly, designers must carefully word any statements addressed to learners to avoid the kind of confusion that can result from lack of clarity about theoretical positions and assumptions. For example, the learner might wonder what is meant by the use of "translations, or versions" in the following statement (italics added):

> The story of a father and two sons was originally written in Greek. It has been translated into hundreds of modern languages. Six of these *translations, or versions,* are listed below. (Tool Kit screen from *A Father and Two Sons* CD-ROM)

What kind of theoretical assumptions lie hidden behind the use of expressions such as "translations," or "versions"? What is the difference between *translation* and *version*? Either we do not use the variation at all (settle for *translation* at this stage, to avoid confusing the learner) or we address the theoretical issue explicitly by, for instance, highlighting the two words and enabling the user to click on one or both to access a theoretical discussion of the terms.

Then what of the decision to include one foreign version (the Spanish version)? What has motivated this? Again, the user may well wonder what he/she is supposed to do with this foreign version, irrespective of whether he/she has access to Spanish.

The How and What of Learning

The most important thing that translation exercises can hope to achieve, in my view, is to teach learners the range of options and strategies they have at their disposal for a particular task, and the implications of using a particular strategy in a given context. This means that designers should pay more attention to the "how" of learning in general: What is the most effective way to ensure that learners learn the principles we are trying to teach them? How will they internalize the information the program offers them? How will they acquire the skills we want them to acquire? There is also the "how" of the particular task assigned in a given exercise: How might learners make rational decisions about what strategy to opt for at a particular point in a given exercise?

Take the basic information the learner receives at the start of the exercise included in *The Visit*. The information consists of two predefined translations of the same text (out of context) and a very brief comment on each translation, as cited in the previous section and repeated here for convenience:

> The King James Version, first published in England in 1611, is a traditional and more literal translation. Such translations are sometimes called "formal equivalent" translations because they not only convey the meaning of a text, but try as far as possible to imitate the word order and sentence structure of the original Greek.
>
> The Contemporary English Version is a new translation which is based on the theory of "functional equivalence." According to this theory a

translation should try to convey the meaning of the original Greek but not necessarily the word order and sentence structure of the Greek text.

This is arguably rather restricted information, too restricted to give the learner a model to follow in answering the five questions. Who produced either version? What circumstances surrounded the production of these translations? What were the aims of the translators? The presentation of this material suggests that the designer expects the learner to use the KJV or CEV only as an aid, without appreciating the relationship between the strategies used and the context and purpose of the translation.

Though important, I do not believe these issues have received enough attention yet. For instance, it seems strange that we currently take the learner through a series of questions like *How?* and *Why?* and *Who?* only to end up telling them to proceed in a particular predefined way, using a particular version as a base, irrespective of their answers to these questions. This limits the value of the exercise quite considerably as it makes the learner's answers to the various questions largely irrelevant.

If we will pose questions of this type to learners, and I think we should, then we have to acknowledge that the answers will have an impact on their choice of version to work with and on their choice of strategy to employ: The KJV may not offer them the best model for using a particular set of strategies. We should perhaps also prepare learners for the task by giving them some examples of how different answers to the questions posed have resulted in quite different approaches to translating the same episode, or the Bible in general, in different contexts. Learners need to see concrete examples of the link between the goal and the strategy (the *Why* and the *How* in the series of questions they have to tackle).

The questions themselves are in principle important and relevant, but the designers need to hold them together with some kind of theoretical framework, and make their relevance more clear: The designers need to give pedagogical value by clearly expressing, exemplifying, and verifying them in actual practice, and they need to link the questions to the implications of using particular strategies. But, how can we achieve this? Let us take the *Why?* question as an example.

As stated above, clicking on WHY? in the current program brings up the following screen question:

Why would your audience be motivated to use your new translation?
What would make your translation different and more understandable for the audience you've chosen to target?

Two things concern me here. First, the design shows a lack of attention to the learner's own reason for translating the text: Why the audience might be motivated to use this new translation bypasses the more immediate question of why does *the learner* want to produce this translation in the first place. Secondly, *Why?* in itself is pretty vague, but theoretical models exist that one can use to enrich this important question. Nord, among others, distinguishes between a number of different things which are collapsed here under the one simple heading WHY. For instance, she distinguishes between AIM and PURPOSE, aim being the final result that the translator wants to achieve and purpose being "a provisional stage in the process of attaining an aim" (1997, p. 28). These two notions are relative. So we might offer our learners an example such as this:

> Your aim is the ultimate result you want to achieve, for example to make the Word of God available to a new community. You can accomplish an aim by a number of means, including or excluding translation. For example, a literary translator might have as his/her aim introducing a particular Spanish author into the English-speaking world. This aim he/she could partly achieve by translating one or more of the author's texts into English, but may also perform complementary activities such as organizing tours for the author in the English-speaking world, publishing reviews of his/her work, and so on.
>
> You might also have several purposes in translating a given text: You might want to try out some new strategies of translation (purpose 1) in order to improve your translation skills overall (purpose 2) in order to become a professional Bible translator (purpose 3) in order to help make the Word of God available to more communities (purpose 4).

This is an important distinction to make in our current context because quite legitimately learners will approach these exercises with very specific, lower level aims (or purposes within this framework), such as learning a new strategy of translation.

The designer might also specifically offer examples of aims in religious translation to the learner, and note the complexity of such aims. For instance, religious and national aims often overlap, as in the following examples:

> Uilliam Ó Domhnaill (William Daniel) translated the New Testament into Irish in 1603. In his translation he aimed to "rescue the Gaelic Irish from the intolerable darkness of their ignorance and superstition so that they would no longer be in the shadow of spiritual death" and "to restore Irish Christianity to its former glory." (based on Cronin, 1996, p. 54, 56)
>
> Tadhg Ó Conaill translated a number of devotional texts in the second half of the 18th century because he wanted "to remedy the widespread ignorance of the principles of Catholic teaching that is the result of religious oppression" in Ireland at the time. This explains, for instance, the relative absence of gallicisms in his translation and his tendency to expand on the original texts he translated (to add explanatory material). (based on Cronin, 1996, p. 81)

The aim during some historical periods might have even included supporting the use of a particular language, such as Irish, in religious services.

These aims and purposes then need to link to the strategies one might opt for, or the HOW in the current model. Providing a context for the learner, even an imaginary one, might help bring these two elements together and allow the learner to select strategies in a rational way. In other words, the program may instruct the learner to work to a particular, realistic scenario. Moreover, the designer could make the point of the exercise clear to ensure that the learner knows what to focus on and can assess his/her own success in learning a given skill. Baker (1992) provides this example, which illustrates how to design goal-oriented exercises of this type:

> Stephen Hawking's popular science book, *A Brief History of Time: From the Big Bang to Black Holes* (1988) includes a number of appendices, each giving an insight into the life and personality of a famous scientist. This is one of them:
>
> *Isaac Newton*
> Isaac Newton was not a pleasant man. His relations with other academics were notorious, with most of his later life spent embroiled in heated disputes. Following publication of *Principia Mathematica*—surely the most influential book ever written in physics—Newton had risen rapidly into public prominence. He was appointed president of the Royal Society and became the first scientist ever to be knighted.
>
> Newton soon clashed with the Astronomer Royal, John Flamsteed, who had earlier provided Newton with much needed data for *Principia*, but was now withholding information that Newton wanted. Newton would not take no for an answer; he had himself appointed to the governing body of the Royal Observatory and then tried to force immediate publication of the data. Eventually he arranged for Flamsteed's work to be seized and prepared for publication by Flamsteed's mortal enemy, Edmond Halley. But Flamsteed took the case to court and, in the nick of time, won a court order preventing distribution of the stolen work. Newton was incensed and sought his revenge by systematically deleting all references to Flamsteed in later editions of *Principia*.
>
> A more serious dispute arose with the German philosopher Gottfried Leibniz. Both Leibniz and Newton had independently developed a branch of mathematics called calculus, which underlies most of modern physics. Although we now know that Newton discovered calculus years before Leibniz, he published his work much later. A major row ensued over who had been first, with scientists vigorously defending both contenders. It is remarkable, however, that most of the articles appearing in defense of Newton were originally written by his own hand—and only published in the name of friends! As the row grew, Leibniz made the mistake of appealing to the Royal Society to resolve the dispute. Newton, as president, appointed an "impartial" committee to investigate, coincidentally consisting entirely of Newton's friends! But that was not all: Newton then wrote the committee's report himself and had the Royal Society publish it, officially accusing Leibniz of plagiarism. Still unsatisfied, he then wrote an anonymous review of the report in the Royal Society's own periodical. Following the death of Leibniz, Newton is re-

ported to have declared that he had taken great satisfaction in "breaking Leibniz's heart."

During the period of these two disputes, Newton had already left Cambridge and academe. He had been active in anti-Catholic politics at Cambridge, and later in Parliament, and was rewarded eventually with the lucrative post of Warden of the Royal Mint. Here he used his talents for deviousness and vitriol in a more socially acceptable way, successfully conducting a major campaign against counterfeiting, even sending several men to their death on the gallows.[1]

Imagine that you have been asked to translate the above appendix into your target language. Your translated version is to be included in a portfolio of light-hearted but factual background material for science students in secondary education, designed to stimulate their interest in the world of science at large.

Comment on the strategies you decide to use to convey Hawking's implied meanings to your target audience. For instance, do you transfer typographic signals such as exclamation marks and the inverted quotes around *impartial* (third paragraph), or are there better ways of signalling similar meanings in your target language? Does the text, as it stands, convey the same image of Newton in your target language as it does in English, or do you have to make adjustments to accommodate your target reader's cultural background? (pp. 256-258)

This exercise attemps to engage learners by contextualizing the task they are asked to undertake and by spelling out those features of the text they are expected to focus on. Note that the restrictions of the printed medium do not allow the designer to make the exercise more interactive, a feature that can be enhanced considerably in a CD-ROM environment and even more so on the Web.

Conclusion

A powerful range of technology can now deliver education to various groups of learners in a flexible and highly versatile environment. Given the current state of the art in translation studies, especially in the field of translation pedagogy, it will probably take some time before we can develop viable models of instruction that can make maximum use of the power and versatility of the new technology, for it is probably fair to say that translation pedagogy remains a seriously under-developed field even in the traditional context of classroom instruction.

---

[1] From *A Brief History of Time* by Stephen W. Hawking. Copyright ©1988 by Stephen W. Hawking. Used by permission of Bantam Books, a division of Bantam Doubleday Dell Publishing Group, Inc.

Viable pedagogical models cannot be developed in a vacuum. They have to emerge gradually from the interplay between the requirements of a given learner group, the constraints and strengths of a given learning environment, and our cumulative experience of learning styles and effective methods of delivering education in general. The ABS has started the ball rolling with the experimental CD-ROM material now available. Designers of the next generation of translation study material on CD-ROM will undoubtedly benefit from this experience, even as they point out its limitations.

Section II

Qualities of Texts

Qualities of texts

The question of fidelity raised by new media translation directs attention not only to the translation produced but also to the source material. By looking to meet the needs of digital media (sounds, images, hypertext links, and so on), new media Bible translators have come to see the Bible in a different way: The Bible itself appears as more than a text.

Given the oral heritage of a great deal of the Bible, it is not surprising to recognize the rhetorical qualities of the Bible, nor the echoes of its oral performance. Certainly parts of the Bible—the Psalms, the Song of Songs, canticles, poetic sections, for example—were intended to be sung, performed, or recited rather than to be read. Indeed silent reading develops rather late in the history of literacy. Therefore we may well misunderstand the Bible if we regard it only as a literate enterprise or if we divorce it from its wider context in the assembly. Similarly, the Bible contains a lot of what we might call interactive material; we have long recognized that the Bible engages even its reader in ways that other literature does not. If we regard the Bible only as literature, we may again misunderstand it, to the detriment of any translation.

The essays in this section examine the biblical text from the perspective of the new media. Each author seeks to enlarge our understanding of the biblical text by calling attention to things that we see more clearly from an experience of other media.

Lydia Lebrón-Rivera uses the tools of literary analysis to better understand the dynamics of storytelling in the book of Genesis. The play of the Hebrew text calls attention to the relationships within the narrative; in addition, the choice of words in the text connects this narrative to legal, narrative, and wisdom literature throughout the Hebrew Bible. Fidelity, then, demands more than a rendering of the text, more than a rendering of the sense, but an appreciation for the full quality of the source.

The printed Bible reduced the experience of the Bible. Bernard Brandon Scott argues that vernacular translations produced by the early explosion of printing led to the privatization of the Bible. These translations removed the experience of the Bible from the assembly, allowing individuals to read the Bible on their own; simultaneously the vernaculars made the Bible more opaque by hiding from the reader the scholarly tools used by the translator and the printer, cutting the reader off yet again from the experience of the Bible. Scott further argues that the Greek New Testament, for example, contains oral cues that puzzle print translators, but make perfect sense when the Bible is performed. He invites the reader and the translator to learn to "see sound" in order to free the Bible from a prison unintentionally erected by Gutenberg and his heirs.

Eugene Nida reminds us that the use of symbol systems other than printed texts for biblical material did not begin in the 20th century. In addition to singing and chanting, even printed texts marked material with different typefaces and different colored inks. Biblical illustrations added yet another symbol system to the printed text. As important as these elements are for the new media translator, Nida argues that any translator must also take cultural and contextual material into account. Because of this, new media translation projects should follow a dozen guidelines that serve to ground their work in the biblical text as well as in the new media. These include the selection of biblical material, the setting, additions to the biblical material, and the nature of the translation.

As we have seen already, the biblical text has long found an alliance with the imaged word. From early in their history, Christians expressed the scriptural message in representations, ranging from church decor to illustrated manuscripts. Gregor Goethals, the art director for the American Bible Society's New Media Translations Program, reviews the history and aesthetics of biblical representation. She examines mosaics, manuscripts, reformation symbolism, and 19th and 20th century biblical art in an attempt to discern how artistic practices of fidelity related to the Bible. As we might expect, the visualization of the Bible draws as much from biblical material as from artistic style contemporary to it. Sadly, artists of our own period have drawn on an aesthetic of religious art rooted in the past and have often limited their work to stereotypes. Goethals shows how the longer visual tradition both calls attention to past practice and directs the work of contemporary multimedia translation. A careful examination of that tradition can enlarge the bounds for the translator by showing the Bible in a new light.

The last essay in this section examines the musical qualities of the biblical text. Like the artistic tradition, the musical one dates to earliest Christianity. J. Ritter Werner, the music director of the New Media Translations Program, roots his discussion of biblical music in a wider theoretical paradigm–that of midrash, arguing that this "dialogue with the biblical text" provides a model for translation and a touchstone for evaluations of fidelity. To illustrate the process, he provides a history of church music and a detailed case study of the settings of the Lord's Prayer. The key steps in his midrash take us through a linguistic analysis of the text of Matthew 6.9-13, a paralinguistic analysis of the text, and an extralinguistic analysis. From this basis, he examines several examples of the music of the Lord's Prayer and then, to complete the midrashic process, offers his own musical setting.

By calling attention to the biblical text, this section argues that the question of fidelity must begin with the original rather than with the translation. Multimedia translation does not add to the text so much as manifest what is already present in it and in the Christian tradition's use of the Bible.

6

Fidelity and Literary Analysis

Lydia Lebrón-Rivera

Introduction

The way that one tells a story makes the story as provocative and engaging as the story itself. The opportunity and challenge for the "new media" are to discover ways to tell a story in such a compelling manner. To meet this challenge, the translator must identify the images, sounds, dimensions, structures, and patterns that emerge from the biblical narrative so as to weave correspondences between the text and its broader biblical and canonical context.

In this chapter I propose to show how the literary approach to the biblical text can elucidate meanings embedded in the text and texture of a biblical story. The literary approach to the biblical narrative in general begins and ends with the text. In paying attention to the formal articulations (patterns) of scene, dialogue, report, symmetry, repetitions, etc., we enter into the text's own articulation of meanings. We give particular attention to (1) the interaction of the forms to convey information; (2) the elements of the narrative introduced in the story by cultural traditions; (3) language: the use of words and emphasis on words and particular phrases; and (4) other categories of plot, structure, character, message, and style. Furthermore, I will illustrate how this type of reading/translation illuminates dimensions and nuances of the text that resonate with a contemporary context and may be faithfully conveyed in the new media.

In the following pages I will present a case study in a literary and rhetorical reading of a biblical narrative: Genesis 4.1-16, the story of Cain and Abel. From Philo to Luther to Boesak, the story of Cain and Abel has been interpreted within strikingly different contexts with similarly strikingly differing meanings. In the literary approach that I employ, the contrasts embedded in the text are revealed as a theme of the story, and meanings emerge from the text itself.

The Text: Genesis 4.1-16

This translation is rendered in order to provide the English reader with a sense of the structure, flow, and nuances of the Hebrew text in so far as is possible. Text in italics represents dialogue. Non-italicized text is narrative material:

> And Adam knew Eve his wife and she conceived and bore Cain and she said: *I have created a man, Yahweh.* She bore again his brother Abel and Abel became keeper of sheep and Cain became tiller of the soil. And it happened that in the course of the days Cain brought from the fruit of the soil an offering to Yahweh. And Abel brought, he also, the first born of the cattle and their fat, and Yahweh favored Abel and his offering. But Cain and his offering he did not favor. And Cain was very angry and his countenance fell. And Yahweh said to Cain: *Why are you angry and why has your expression fallen? Is it not true that when you do good, there is uplifting, and when you do not do good, sin is a lurking one at the door and to you is his desire? You are the one who must master him.* And Cain spoke to Abel his brother, and while they were in the field, Cain rose up against Abel his brother and killed him. And Yahweh said to Cain: *Where is Abel your brother?* And he said: *I do not know. Am I the keeper of my brother?* He said: *What have you done? The blood of your brother cries out to me from the ground. Now, cursed are you from the ground that has opened its mouth to take the blood of your brother from your hand. From when you till the soil it will not give of its strength to you. A fugitive and a wanderer you will become in the land.* Cain said to Yahweh: *My punishment is greater than I can bear. You have driven me out this day from the face of the ground, and from your face I will be hidden and I will be a fugitive and a wanderer on the earth and it will happen that all who find me will kill me.* And Yahweh said to him: *Not so! Any one killing Cain, seven times will be avenged.* And Yahweh put a mark on Cain so that no one who came to him would kill him. And Cain went out from the presence of Yahweh and dwelled in the land of Nod, east of Eden.

Retelling the Story

The story begins on a genealogical note (cf. Genesis 4.17; 5.1) with a narrator relating that Adam and Eve had sexual intercourse, that Eve conceived and bore Cain. An exclamation by Eve follows the announcement bringing together Cain's name, by assonance, with the name for the divine in the same sentence—the Hebrew phrase reads *qaniti ish et adonai*. (See Cassuto, 1978, pp. 199-201; van Wolde, 1991, pp. 27-28.) The story then moves to the birth of Abel. Abel is referred to only indirectly as the brother of Cain and the meaning of his name—breath, vapor, nothingness—defines his identity and his life. Like the meaning of his name, Abel is characterized by elusiveness. A carefully constructed parallel structure, ABA'B', sets both brothers alongside each other and attests simultaneously to their fixed identities:

And Abel became	A
keeper of sheep	B
And Cain became	A'
tiller of the soil, (the *adamah*).	B'

With this rather subtle notion of "basic distinctiveness," (White, 1991, p. 155) the narrator sets the scenario for a story of contrasts.

A temporal note, "And it happened that in the passing of the days..." and a grammatical mark, "disjunctive *waw*," delineate the contours of a new scene: the presentations of the brothers' respective offerings to Yahweh. The narrator's open-ended description of the passage of time builds suspense. We learn that Cain is first in presenting his offering, fruit of the soil, to Yahweh. The text gives an unqualified description of Cain and of the content of his offering. In the case of Abel, the text emphasizes his person as the one making the offering: "And Abel, even he (*gam hu*)." A parallel structure further emphasizes the contrast between the two:

And Cain brought	A
from the fruit of the soil (*adamah*)	B
And Abel brought	A'
from the first born of the flock and their fat.	B'

With no indication of God's means of acknowledgment of the offering, we are told that:

Yahweh favored	A
Abel and his offering, but	B
Cain and his offering	B'
He (YHWH) did not.	A'

A chiasm centers the action. On the inside, both structure and content center the brothers in perfect symmetry. On the outside, YHWH's actions lead to a reversal. What the structure proclaims, YHWH's actions subvert (Trible, 1994).

In the intimacy of the scene, Cain burns with anger. But what the narrator veils, Yahweh discloses. A switch from the narrative flow to the more elevated style of poetry in the next three verses reveals the tension of the moment: The story has reached its climax. Yahweh's words cut through the tension of the moment. In a new scene, God twice interrogates Cain:

> Why are you angry?
> and why has your countenance fallen?
> Is it not true that when you do good, there is uplifting?
> and when you do not do good, sin is a lurking one at the door
> and to you is his desire
> and you are the one who must master him.

For differing approaches in the rendering of this verse, see Leibowitz (1974, p. 41); Wenham (1987, p. 104); Brueggemann (1982, p. 58); Westermann (1984, pp. 299-300); Speiser (1964, p. 31); and van Wolde (1991, pp. 30-32).

Cain's inner emotions become the subject of Yahweh's rhetorical questions. Once again the image of a "lurking one" elicits connections with the paradise story. In this light, the last verse resonates with the curse on the woman: the same root for "desire" is used here. As in the woman's story, silence from the one questioned follows.

The narrator then moves us back again to the sphere of the brothers: Cain is found with his brother Abel. Cain speaks to his brother. The grammatical construction typifies the form introducing a speech: *vayomer*. Nevertheless, the words are missing. Poignantly, this is the first time in the story that reports a conversation between the brothers and it results in murder (White, 1991, p. 160; van Wolde, 1991, p. 35). The sounds of Cain's quick killing can be heard by pronouncing the phrase that describes the murder: *vayakam cayin vayejargeju*. The action of murder stands apart in the story as an almost isolated act.

Following the scene of the murder, as it were, God addresses Cain a second time. But now, God's words follow Cain's most drastic unleashing of rage, the murder of his brother: "Where is your brother?" The rhetoric of the question brings into the picture the echo of a similar one asked in the context of the first fall: "Where are you?" In the previous account, Adam and Eve are hiding themselves from God, and God's question prompts their confession of their new found fears. But here, Cain's response to God's question about his brother reveals no fear. For the first time Cain breaks the silence. Significantly, this is the first time that his brother is referred to in the second person in relation to him. He in turn refers to him as "my brother," but for the purpose of disavowing any responsibility towards him. In Cain's answer ("Am I the keeper of my brother"), the use of the root *smr* for "keeper" is an ironic response to YHWH and means, Does a keeper need a keeper? This translation comes from the double use of *smr* as "kept" and "shepherd" (Wenham, 1987, p. 106).

Again God addresses Cain "What have you done? The blood of your brother is crying out to me from the *adamah*." The metaphor of the blood crying brings other voices into the story (cf. Genesis 18.20, Deuteronomy 22.24; 2 Kings 8.3; Job 16.18f; Genesis 41.55; Exodus 14.10; Exodus 22.22; Judges 4.3), appealing for legal protection: the desperate cry of men without food expecting to die, the scream for help from a raped woman, the plea to God from the victims of injustice and those oppressed by their enemies. The cries from the above images become one with the sounds that the mourning of the ground and the choking of the blood elicit—the alliteration: *demi ahika min adamah, min adamah, demi ahuka*.

God's final question to Cain is followed by a curse: "You are cursed from the *adamah*." Again the wording of the curse on Cain invites comparison with the curse of Adam in the fall story:

"Cursed is the *adamah* because of you" Gen. 3.17

"You are cursed from the *adamah*" Gen. 4.11

Here the curse is uttered directly against Cain. The *adamah* which he had tilled, whose fruits he had offered, mirror back to him punishment. A well crafted chiasm structures God's words to Cain:

A	B
Your brother's blood	the *adamah*
B'	A'
the *adamah*	your brother's blood
C	
from your hand	

Abel's blood and the *adamah* had come together as equals to accuse Cain. The phrase "from your hand" reminds us that Cain's hand, instrument of his occupation, was the instrument that murdered his brother. The phrase, standing alone at the center of the chiastic structure strongly dramatizes Cain's isolation. The chiastic structure, in design, previews both the rupture of Cain's relationship with humankind and with the source of his livelihood, the *adamah*.

The conclusion of the story takes on a distinctively ironical character. In the context of curse, the divine mentions the *adamah*. Cain, the one who lived by the *adamah*, will now be cursed by it. The *adamah* will negate Cain's strength. From then on he will be a "fugitive and a wanderer" through the earth. The strong character of this new given identity is indicated by the doubling *Na Vanad*.

Cain's final words dramatically bring to a culmination the chief irony of the story: the one who lived by the *adamah*, became the defender of the *adamah*, is finally expelled from it. To be uprooted from the face of the *adamah* is to be hidden from God's face. God's words to him become his own: "I am a fugitive and a wanderer on the earth." Cain internalizes his new fate. Ironically, the murderer faces murder.

The story ends by resonating with the account of the fall in regard to Adam and Eve's expulsion from the garden. Cain will settle "east of Eden," precisely where the cherubim stands banning access to the tree of life. As it is so eloquently phrased: Cain's journey ends "in the direction from which there can be no return to paradise and the presence of God" (White, 1991, p. 168).

Conclusion

A faithful new media translation will convey the narrative structure complete with its own rhythm and contours that shape the story. It will pay attention to the rhetorical features that nuance the story, and it will accentuate the literary genre particular to the text and its function in contributing meaning. It will also facilitate, for the reader, resonances with other biblical texts which the style, content, and rhetorical devices of the text themselves invite.

Attention should also be given to narrative style: the manner and timing with which narrative switches from prose to poetry and the function which sudden changes in voice and person play to alternately heighten and de-escalate the tension of the plot. The character development of particular figures projects broader themes and anticipates future developments in the narrative. The use of particular images and words that evoke a resonance with other biblical accounts needs to be brought into the context of the story. Finally, alliteration, onomatopoeia, and other literary devices add dimension and interest and engage the audience with the story.

From a literary perspective, the Cain and Abel story belongs to the genre of irony. Therefore, it will be necessary to faithfully portray the story genre as well as story content so that the full character of the message be uncovered. Embedded in the composition of the story are the seeds of rivalry and subversion. What begins as a story of equals is consistently subverted by the rhetorical constructions. There is a striking incongruity between the characters' actions and their consequences. In the case of Cain, for example, his own identity and all his efforts towards an identification with the divine culminate in a relationship with God that is veiled to him. The one who exercised his vocation as a farmer of the soil is expelled forever from it. And the one who raised his hand and became his brother's killer fears at the end of the story that he will be, in the end, one who is killed. The irony of the story is most acutely portrayed in the ultimate reversal of fate of both Cain and Abel. The divine protection that is afforded or not afforded is turned upside down. Abel, the one who pleases God, ends up murdered and clamoring for vengeance; Cain, who did not enjoy divine favor, receives God's mark that no one might kill him. In this story the structure itself serves to communicate the irony.

This story also takes its own internal clues from its wider literary context which includes, most strikingly, the account of the fall of Adam and Eve and their expulsion from paradise. A faithful translation will present a story which invites dialogue with a wider tradition.

In general, attention to the literary character of a text opens and invites a variety of possibilities for interpretation. Generating meaning is not an end unto itself, but rather should be seen as an avenue which opens encounters with not only the text at hand, but also its larger context. A new media translation which is faithful to the context, genre, narrative structure, shape, and rhetorical devices of the text itself opens to its audience new opportunities to engage with the story and plumb new depths of understanding.

7

A New Voice in the Amphitheater: Full Fidelity in Translating

Bernard Brandon Scott

Plato's Illusion

We hear all too often a cliché that we are in a new age. The upcoming turn of the millennium marks a trivial yet obvious sign of a new age since it simply denotes a chronological shift. Deeper shifts, at times harder to identify, are obviously at work. In some profound sense the modern age has ended and we have now entered a postmodern age. That we call it "postmodern" indicates the difficulty in identifying exactly what constitutes this post-modernity, this new age.

For translators, people bound to texts as the dominant medium, the most profound shift now underway moves from print to an environment in which a variety of media both compete and combine into seemingly endless permutations. To avoid confusion I will term this environment vari-media, indicating its variety. The medium in which we perform contains hermeneutical assumptions. This is what is meant by the aphorisms "form follows function" and Marshal McLuhan's famous "The medium is the message" (McLuhan, 1967). Neil Postman long has warned that every "medium contains an ideological bias" (Postman, 1992, p. 16). Even more, every medium has an implicit epistemology (Postman, 1985, ch. 2). The media we employ are not neutral tools massaging the content. Rather medium is the form in which the translation content takes place and that content is always affected, even changed, by the medium. For too long we have sought the illusion of a pure Platonic essence, that unchangeable inner core hidden beneath the various media we employed.

Gutenberg Galaxy

We are so accustomed to the medium of print that we are not always aware of its hermeneutical assumptions and tend at times to universalize those assumptions, assuming that they have always been true. Print has had a radical impact on the Bible in the West. Martin Luther is reported to have referred to printing as "God's highest and extremist act of grace, whereby the business of the Gospel is driven forward" (Black, 1963, p. 432, with no citation; Eisenstein, 1979, 1:304 citing Black, with no citation; Holborn, 1942, p. 137; and Dickens, 1974, p. 109). Print made the Bible widely available in cheap editions and shifted printing from imitating manuscripts to developing new forms (Edwards, 1994). The Bible became, because of the printing press, the first mass product.

Besides making the Bible widely available for the first time, the printing press led to several important shifts that have critically affected our understanding of the Bible. Print led to the privatization of the Bible. Whereas previously the Bible had primarily been a public text, publicly performed and corporately understood, it now became the possession of the private individual who owned a printed text. This privatization, which continues unabated to this day, has had several important outcomes.

The printing press gave rise to the distinctive doctrine of the Reformation and Protestantism: private interpretation. When there were few Bibles in existence, most often in the hands of the clergy, and even then frequently in the form of missals, interpretation was ecclesially dominated and determined. But when individuals had their own Bibles, their own private copies, then interpretation inevitably fragmented and became private.

Along with private possession of the Bible came silent reading. In the ancient world, reading was normally out loud and it was not until late medieval times that silent reading became the normal way to read. (See below on silent reading in the ancient world.) Even then, the Bible was normally read, or primarily read, in public proclamation. The dynamics of silent reading are very different from those of public, out loud, reading. As Michael Stubbs has pointed out, "listeners have to understand in real time" (1980, p. 33). They do not have the luxury of re-reading, stopping, reflecting, and looking back. Silent reading leads to the interiorization of meaning and the understanding of meaning as taking place primarily at the level of the abstract concept, what Saussure termed the signified (Saussure, 1959). The sound vehicle of communication, the signifier, is neglected and even set aside. Saussure stressed that a sign was made up of two parts, a signifier and a signified. (See Figure 1.) One can see the logical outcome of this neglect of the signifier in some forms of modern poetry where the poetry must be seen abstractly arranged on the printed page.

The dominant metaphor for communication in a print culture is the container metaphor expressed formally in the transportation model. (See the

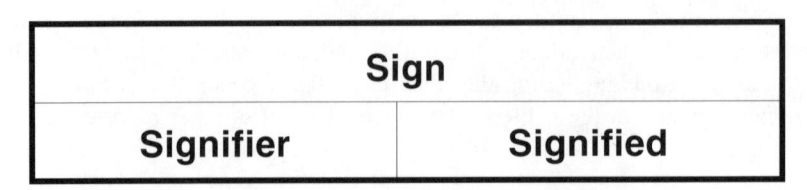

Sign	
Signifier	**Signified**

Figure 1: Two parts of a sign, according to Saussure.

essay by Soukup in this volume.) We envision communication as taking place in a container (Lakoff & Johnson, 1980, p. 10). The sender sends a message to a receiver through a channel. Thus the telephone is the ideal model of communication. The caller sends a message through the channel, the telephone, to a receiver. This model of communication fits our new technologies, since the book, the wire, and the airways, are simply seen as channels and do not radically affect the message. The message is transferred from one brain to another and language is understood as the container for the message. Thus reading is often compared to knowing or engaging an author's mind.

Vernacular translations facilitated this privatization of the Bible in two important ways (Eisenstein, 1979, 1, ch. 4). First, vernacular translations made the Bible widely available to the faithful without the need of learning the sacred languages, although the continued importance of the King James translation indicates the need for a "sacred language" even in a vernacular translation. Vernacular translations created a transparent relation between the Bible and the contemporary reader. Since the Bible was in the reader's own language, translations created the appearance that the Bible was addressing the reader directly. Thus the better the translation, the less the need a reader believes he or she has for an interpreter to serve as an intermediary. The Bible becomes a contemporary, and not an historical, text. On the other hand, the printer needed the scholar to develop the tools necessary to produce critical editions of the Bible and translations. These very tools made the Bible appear opaque, its meaning less and less obvious in a contemporary context. Ironically, the division between the academy and the pew, a division that plagues the Christian churches to this day, originated in the print shop (Scott, 1994, pp. 35-37).

The container metaphor impoverishes the biblical text, reducing it to a signified, an abstract concept, a message. Thus translation models conceived within the hermeneutics and epistemology of print deal only with one dimension of the composition. From the point of view of the semiotic model, they translate only half of the composition, the silent half. Eugene Nida brought a great sophistication to the science of translating. Even though he advocates a very dynamic view of translation, in the end, it is the message that dominates the translation. For example, he notes five elements in communication important for translation: subject matter; participants in the communication; the speech act or act of writing; the code used, i.e., the language; and finally the message. But in the end the message is primary: "Though the actual process of communication in any specific instance may be described on the basis of these five phases, it is also possible to treat communication as a procedure by which source and receptor are related through the instrument of a message" (Nida, 1964, p. 120).

A Kodak Moment

Clearly we are experiencing a media shift comparable to the invention of the printing press. This transition may well have begun with the invention of photography and the telegraph. These two inventions created a speed and immediacy of communication not before possible. The photograph allowed people to see with clarity and realism what a painting or etching could not approach, and the telegraph made communication almost instantaneous, cutting the trip for a message across the continent from days to seconds. However, this communications revolution has greatly accelerated with television and now the computer and shows no signs of slowing as these two media begin to merge. Marshall McLuhan was one of the first to try to name this new age. He termed it the global village, because he understood the world to be wired together. Others have suggested the "Graphic Age" or the "Electronic Age." Both of these have their advantages. "Graphic" emphasizes the pictorial, image-based character of communication today. "Electronic" indicates the environment in which communication more and more occurs today.

From the point of view of the question of fidelity in translation, it is important to accent that today's medium is media, and it is vari-media. The signifier is no longer single, but multiple. One can no longer refer to communication as taking place in speech or writing, as though those two media exhausted the repertoire. Now communication increasingly takes place in a vari-media environment. Even print today is more visual. Compare, for example, the *New York Times* with *USA Today* to see at a glance the impact of the new media on the old medium.

This new electronic, vari-media age, has three characteristics that will affect our understanding of the Bible and translation. First, electronic media are fluid or plastic. Their forms are indefinite, changeable, unlike print which images the world as solid, as fixed. Gradually, perhaps rapidly, the sense of solidity and permanence that print has bequeathed us is disappearing. In its place will come a sense of fluidity, plasticity, transitoriness. What is written is not permanent, but can change with a key stroke. Even the photograph, which drew its persuasive power from its apparent ability to depict what was really there, can now be manipulated by the computer so that we can no longer tell what was really there. The movie *Forrest Gump* exploited this manipulative, plastic ability of the new media to make the impossible look ordinary.

Secondly, electronic communication greatly enriches the communication process, primarily by enriching the signifier, the vehicle of communication. Thus many more signifiers become available to us with which to communicate and often times now these various media can be combined into a vari-media environment. Print, graphics, image, and sound all integrate now in the communication process. Users increasingly expect a vari-media experience, as witness the shift from the columns of print format of most newspapers a few years ago to the graphics of a modern newspaper.

As lines between newspaper, television, and computer begin to blur, so also the line between news and entertainment blurs.

Finally, electronic media are user driven and not author driven. Communication has traditionally been understood as one active person, a sender, communicating to a passive receiver. This simple model was never really true, but now it is under increasing attack (Soukup, 1997, pp. 91-107; also his essay in this volume; Iser, 1974; Iser, 1978; Tompkins, 1980). The hypertext model of communication allows users to navigate through a text following their own interests, not those dictated by an author. Print has a strong beginning and end, a canonical direction—straight through from beginning to end. But hypertext allows a user to skip around, to jump from here to there, to rearrange and reorder the experience as they wish (Bolter, 1991). The combining of various media into a single presentation will change the way readers read. In the future, they will demand books that interact with them, that offer them more than just the text of the book.

All the World Is a Stage

If the metaphorical model for print is the silent message in a container, and for the electronic age the model is the user-friendly vari-media, how was communication understood in the New Testament period? I am separating the Greek New Testament from the Hebrew Bible, not because I think the evidence or situation is substantially all that different, but because the evidence for the Greek situation is so much clearer and developed. The Greeks were sophisticated thinkers about their media, as witness their development of grammar, rhetoric, and literary criticism.

We might assume that the manuscript in the ancient world paralleled in function the printed book in a print culture. But the manuscript functioned only as the penultimate medium, because the ultimate medium was the human voice. The environment for communication in the ancient world was sound. The ancients read out loud and the human voice performed on a stage, for this was a rhetorical culture (Robbins, 1993, p. 110), where the point of communication is persuasion (Kennedy, 1963).

Silent Reading in the Ancient World

While clearly some ancients could read silently, examples of silent reading are very rare. Much more common are references to reading aloud. The evidence for reading out loud is, in fact, so overwhelming that there has been in the literature an overstatement of the case. Josef Balogh (1926), in "Voces Paginarum," the classic reference on this issue, was accused by Knox of setting the "standard doctrine that silent reading (and writing) was, if not completely unknown in the ancient world, at least so rare that whenever it was observed, it aroused astonishment, even suspicion" (Knox, 1968,

p. 421). Even accounting for Balogh's overstatement of evidence, his case was well made, as all subsequent commentators have acknowledged: the ancients normally read out loud. Even those critical of Balogh admit that "ancient texts were most often read aloud" (Gilliard, 1993, p. 691). Significant essays supporting Balogh include: Stanford (1967), Hendrickson (1929-30), Clark (1930-31), and Achtemeier (1990). Critical of Balogh is Knox (1968). Critical of Achtemeier's uncritical acceptance of Balogh is Gilliard (1993).

There are three principal reasons why the ancients normally read out loud: schooling, economics, and literacy. All three of these elements intertwine to produce reading out loud as the normal way of reading.

Greek education stressed recitation and memory. The student recited his lessons and large sections of the poets were memorized. Grammar stressed sounds, and students learned all the sounds of the letters, and possible syllable combinations, before learning to read (Dean, 1996, p. 54). Students learned to write not from written texts, as modern students do, but from taking dictation. Aristotle shows the dominance of speech in reading: "Generally speaking, that which is written should be easy to read or easy to utter, which is the same thing" (*Rhetoric* 3.5.6). Even in the philosophical schools, reading aloud was the normal practice and one wrote so that it could be read aloud (Lentz, 1989, pp. 100-102). Not only did education assume reading out loud, but importantly students were not taught to read silently. Anyone who observes the modern teaching of reading quickly realizes that students do not naturally read silently, but must be taught to read silently. Many students never fully master it, but continue to mumble their words.

The economics were against silent, private reading. As Lentz notes, "The simplest practical explanation for this absence [of silent reading] is the high cost of papyrus and the expense of having copies written upon it. Making multiple copies of discourses—for each member of a group, for example—would be prohibitively expensive" (Lentz, 1989, p. 102). Furthermore it is clear that literacy was not in the interest of the empire and so it failed to support education (Harris, 1989, pp. 15-17, 333).

Finally, only a small portion of the population at any time could read and write. Reading tended to be a phenomenon of the elite and reinforced the values of the elite. As Botha has noticed, there were few incentives in the ancient world for learning to read (Botha, 1992, p. 202). So low was the literacy rate that publication in the ancient world consists of oral declamation. The success of an author frequently depended on the fame of the declaimer (Hadas, 1954, pp. 60-64). William Harris has concluded that never more than 15% of the adult population in an urban area like Athens could read, and more likely only 10% were really literate, able to read with real facility. Furthermore he notes that of the general population, including women and slaves, the number probably never exceeded 5% (Harris, 1989, p. 328).

The evidence for silent reading is actually very limited. (For the most optimistic case see Knox, 1968). For example, in all of Greek plays there are only two examples of people reading silently. In one case it is an oracle that is read, while in the other it is a letter. In both cases these are short readings, not extended reading (Lentz, 1989, pp. 159-160). There are on the other hand many examples of characters reading aloud or being overheard (see, for example, the famous example from St. Augustine's *Confessions*, where Augustine hears the voice of the young man reading aloud). Frank Gilliard, in a recent excellent survey article, adduces other evidence of people being able to read short letters or oracles (Gilliard, 1993, pp. 689-691). Thus it is beyond doubt that people could read silently, at least short texts.

Mary Carruthers reviewed the famous text of Augustine observing Ambrose reading silently (*Confessions*, 6.3). She notes that silence in this period does not have the same meaning as it does when we speak of silent reading. Silent reading is connected with *meditatio* and *memoria*. It need not be "silent" i.e., without noise. She quotes the example of the *Rule of St. Benedict* that when reading silently monks should take care not to disturb other monks, i.e., they are making noise. Likewise in medieval libraries, silent reading produced less noise than in the monastic cell (Carruthers, 1990, pp. 170-172; 329, note 58).

Schooling, economics, and literacy were against the development of widespread silent reading. For writing to communicate, it had to be read out loud.

Amphitheater as a Model for Communications

The amphitheater forms the best and most appropriate model for envisioning communication in the ancient world. The public, performative character of the Bible has largely gone unheard since the invention of the printing press which has converted the Bible into a private, interior experience. A simple comparison between a page of a codex (Figure 2, page 108) and the United Bible Society (UBS) Greek New Testament (Figure 3, page 109) will quickly indicate that manuscript and printed page do not play the same role in communication.

The most immediate difference between the printed page of the UBS edition and Codex Vaticanus is that print provides a vast number of typographical clues for segmentation, organization, and interpretation. One of the first things that printers did was develop conventions of typography that eased the interpretative burden for the reader (Eisenstein, 1979, vol. 1, p. 52). Readers, reciters, and declaimers had to prepare in the ancient world because reading was not an easy task. Chirography provided few clues to its interpretation. This indicates the primary difference between the manuscript and the book. The book is the object of interpretation and so it must provide its own interpretative clues. In the ancient world "writing was a means of

Reprinted with permission of Vatican Library

Figure 2: A leaf from Codex Vaticanus

recording and preserving the spoken word" (Lentz, 1989, p. 47). It is always subject to the spoken word and this held true well into the Middle Ages. Writing supported memory and a well-trained memory was viewed as more accurate than a professional copyist (Carruthers, 1990, pp. 156, 161-162). Since papyrus and copying were expensive, and since at best never more than 10% of the population could read and write (Harris, 1989, p. 328-329), writing could never be a mass medium.

In the ancient world, the medium of interpretation is sound. Typography leads to silent reading, internalization, and privatization of interpretation. Reading in the ancient world takes place out loud, takes place in public. For the ancients, grammar is the science of sound (Dean, 1996). Aristotle defines grammar as the science that "studies all articulate sounds" (*Metaphysics*, 1003B). For him, grammar deals with sound and writing. Likewise Plato has Socrates saying: "but knowing that of which the number and quality of sounds consists, this it is that makes each of us grammarians" (*Philebus*, 17B). Plutarch makes the explicit connection to memory when he defines grammar as "an art useful for the production of sounds and storing up sounds by letters for their recollections" (*On Music*, 1131D). George Kennedy makes the telling observation that this dominance of speech "may

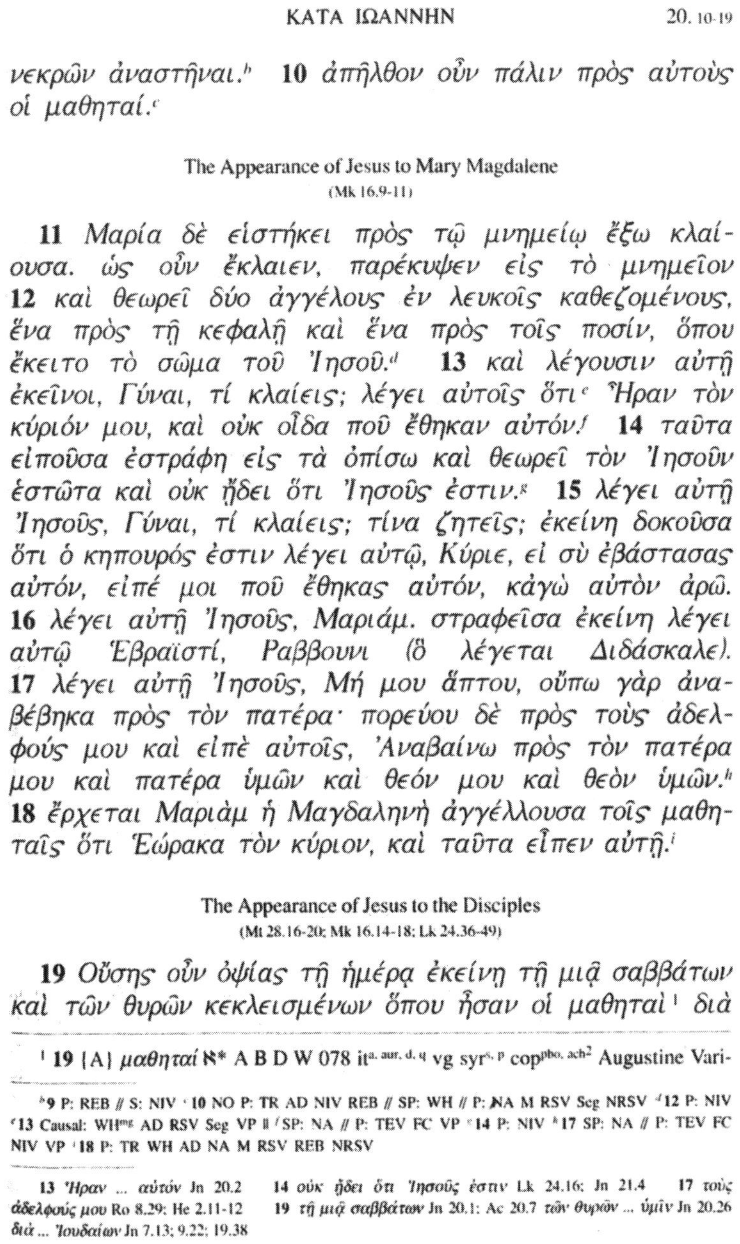

ΚΑΤΑ ΙΩΑΝΝΗΝ 20. 10-19

νεκρῶν ἀναστῆναι.[h] 10 ἀπῆλθον οὖν πάλιν πρὸς αὐτοὺς οἱ μαθηταί.[c]

The Appearance of Jesus to Mary Magdalene
(Mk 16.9-11)

11 Μαρία δὲ εἱστήκει πρὸς τῷ μνημείῳ ἔξω κλαίουσα. ὡς οὖν ἔκλαιεν, παρέκυψεν εἰς τὸ μνημεῖον 12 καὶ θεωρεῖ δύο ἀγγέλους ἐν λευκοῖς καθεζομένους, ἕνα πρὸς τῇ κεφαλῇ καὶ ἕνα πρὸς τοῖς ποσίν, ὅπου ἔκειτο τὸ σῶμα τοῦ Ἰησοῦ.[d] 13 καὶ λέγουσιν αὐτῇ ἐκεῖνοι, Γύναι, τί κλαίεις; λέγει αὐτοῖς ὅτι[e] Ἦραν τὸν κύριόν μου, καὶ οὐκ οἶδα ποῦ ἔθηκαν αὐτόν.[f] 14 ταῦτα εἰποῦσα ἐστράφη εἰς τὰ ὀπίσω καὶ θεωρεῖ τὸν Ἰησοῦν ἑστῶτα καὶ οὐκ ᾔδει ὅτι Ἰησοῦς ἐστιν.[g] 15 λέγει αὐτῇ Ἰησοῦς, Γύναι, τί κλαίεις; τίνα ζητεῖς; ἐκείνη δοκοῦσα ὅτι ὁ κηπουρός ἐστιν λέγει αὐτῷ, Κύριε, εἰ σὺ ἐβάστασας αὐτόν, εἰπέ μοι ποῦ ἔθηκας αὐτόν, κἀγὼ αὐτὸν ἀρῶ. 16 λέγει αὐτῇ Ἰησοῦς, Μαριάμ. στραφεῖσα ἐκείνη λέγει αὐτῷ Ἑβραϊστί, Ραββουνι (ὃ λέγεται Διδάσκαλε). 17 λέγει αὐτῇ Ἰησοῦς, Μή μου ἅπτου, οὔπω γὰρ ἀναβέβηκα πρὸς τὸν πατέρα· πορεύου δὲ πρὸς τοὺς ἀδελφούς μου καὶ εἰπὲ αὐτοῖς, Ἀναβαίνω πρὸς τὸν πατέρα μου καὶ πατέρα ὑμῶν καὶ θεόν μου καὶ θεὸν ὑμῶν.[h] 18 ἔρχεται Μαριὰμ ἡ Μαγδαληνὴ ἀγγέλλουσα τοῖς μαθηταῖς ὅτι Ἑώρακα τὸν κύριον, καὶ ταῦτα εἶπεν αὐτῇ.[i]

The Appearance of Jesus to the Disciples
(Mt 28.16-20; Mk 16.14-18; Lk 24.36-49)

19 Οὔσης οὖν ὀψίας τῇ ἡμέρᾳ ἐκείνῃ τῇ μιᾷ σαββάτων καὶ τῶν θυρῶν κεκλεισμένων ὅπου ἦσαν οἱ μαθηταὶ[1] διὰ

[1] 19 {A} μαθηταί ℵ* A B D W 078 it[a. aur. d. q] vg syr[s. p] cop[pbo. ach2] Augustine Vari-

[b]9 P: REB // S: NIV [c]10 NO P: TR AD NIV REB // SP: WH // P: NA M RSV Seg NRSV [d]12 P: NIV [e]13 Causal: WH[mg] AD RSV Seg VP II / SP: NA // P: TEV FC VP [f]14 P: NIV [h]17 SP: NA // P: TEV FC NIV VP [i]18 P: TR WH AD NA M RSV REB NRSV

13 Ἦραν ... αὐτόν Jn 20.2   14 οὐκ ᾔδει ὅτι Ἰησοῦς ἐστιν Lk 24.16; Jn 21.4   17 τοὺς ἀδελφούς μου Ro 8.29; He 2.11-12   19 τῇ μιᾷ σαββάτων Jn 20.1; Ac 20.7 τῶν θυρῶν ... ὑμῖν Jn 20.26 διὰ ... Ἰουδαίων Jn 7.13; 9.22; 19.38

©1993 Deutsche Bibelgesellschaft Stuttgart, reprinted with permission

Figure 3: A page from the UBS Greek New Testament.

even be one of the reasons why the critical faculty was not highly developed in antiquity. Poetry and prose were ordinarily read aloud, even in private, and appreciation took precedence over analysis" (Kennedy, 1969, p. 102).

If the amphitheater forms the primary metaphor for communication in the ancient world and sound is the medium of communication, then what are the implications for translation? The communications model of the ancient world lies closer to the vari-media model of modern communications. From the point of view of the communications model, print has impoverished the Bible as communication by translating only a part of the communication event. It has reduced translation to the level of the signified, to the message abstractly understood. Thus full fidelity in translation should now involve opening the translation process to other dimensions of the communications event besides the signified. We must now begin to envision translation from amphitheater to the vari-media environment of modern technology. Nida in his listing of basic factors in communication has listed four others besides the message. It is now time to pay attention to those other factors and how those other factors affect the message.

In order to expand this enriched view of translation, we need a two pronged research task. How did the ancient world, both Greek and Hebrew, understand the communication event? And at the same time what are the possibilities in vari-media communication? Without intense investigation into both of these areas, the ancient and the modern, and also research that combines these two areas, we will have no way of knowing whether a translation in a vari-media environment is faithful to the original. We will unfortunately be thrown back upon the utilitarian criteria of "if it works do it" or, even worse, "if we can do it, do it." With an enriched understanding of the biblical composition, primarily at the level of signifier, we can develop an enriched understanding of the possibilities of translation as well as the criteria for what full fidelity in translation means. To put it more provocatively, does the Bible provide the necessary clues for its performance as the first step in its interpretation?

Performance Directions

Since an ancient manuscript offers no chirographic clues, much less typographic clues, to its interpretation, the clues must be found in its very sounding out. In their idiom, an author composes and a reader declaims or performs. The evidence indicates that a Greek reader could not recognize a word until it was sounded out loud. Since sound is the first vehicle of communication, we must view the sound as communicating more than just the signified.

Let me offer a very simple example. In the parable of the Good Samaritan (Luke 10.25-37), the activity of the priest and Levite are set in parallel, although not identical phrases.

10.31 κατὰ συγκυρίαν δὲ ἱερεύς τις κατέβαινεν ἐν τῇ ὁδῷ ἐκείνῃ καὶ ἰδὼν αὐτὸν ἀντιπαρῆλθεν

10.32 ὁμοίως δὲ καὶ   Λευίτης [γενόμενος] κατὰ τὸν τόπον
ἐλθὼν καὶ ἰδὼν ἀντιπαρῆλθεν.

> 10.31 Now by chance   a priest was going down   on that road;
> and when he saw him, he passed by on the other side.
>
> 10.32 So likewise   a Levite, [happening] to the place
> when he came and saw him, passed by on the other side.

The careful balancing of the phrases lends emphasis to the final word ἀντιπαρῆλθεν (*antiparelthen*), usually translated "He passed by on the other side." Such is a perfectly faithful translation of the signified of the Greek, but fails to translate the signifier. If "passing by" was all that was to be conveyed, why the double preposition? παρῆλθεν (*parelthen*) would be sufficient for such a meaning. The signifier gives instructions to the reader/performer as to how to perform the composition. *Anti* has the sense of "over and against" and *para* of "beside." This word is an instruction in body language. The reader-actor would initially push away and then slip by: ἀντι (*anti*/pushing away) παρ (*par*/sliding beside) ἦλθεν (*elthen*/going on). This word paints a picture that no silent translation in print can capture. It calls for a vari-media translation.

Sound Mapping

In the first step we must pay close attention to the clues the Greek offers for its performative translation. One can view this aspect of a Greek composition as offering stage directions for its performance on the stage of an amphitheater.

In this connection, a basic foundation for analysis is to print the Greek and probably also some English translations in the form of the Greek cola instead of in the form of printed sentences. The compositional element of Greek is not the sentence but the colon. And we should print the text in a colometeric form so we can see how Greeks heard it.

Because we can no longer hear what the ancients heard, I have proposed the metaphor of mapping. Sound mapping is an effort to discover and display those clues the composition provides for its performative interpretation. Ideally these clues would provide a basis for a real vari-media translation which would include minimally not only a visual mapping but an oral performance. Since the Bible arose in a rhetorical culture, it was never meant to be read silently but orally performed.

The Greeks view what we have taken recently to calling "the text" as a composition (in Greek σύνθεσις *synthesis* "a putting together"; likewise in Latin, *compositio* "placed together"). So the composition is a thing-put-together. So what do they think they are putting together? Not words as we think, but cola (Dean, 1996; Foley, 1995, pp. 2-6). So then, the first element in a sound map is the division of the composition (the put-together-thing) into cola and then periods. The effort of a modern interpreter to discover the colometric structure of a composition engages the interpreter in hearing in the units in which the ancients would have heard the composition.

Aristotle summarizes the oft-repeated common wisdom that the difference between poetry and prose is meter. "Wherefore prose must be rhythmical, but not metrical, otherwise it will be a poem" (Aristotle, *Art of Rhetoric*, 3.8.3). Underlying this common sense difference between poetry and prose is the Greek assumption that both poetry and prose are *in lines*. While the poetic line has meter and the prose line has rhythm, they both are heard as a line. The basic analogy for all composition is the metric line (3.9.4). Demetrius begins *On Style* with this basic analogy: "Just as poetry is organized by metres (such as half-lines, hexameters, and the like), so too prose is organized and divided by what are called clauses (κῶλα)" (*On Style*, 1). Thus the colon is the basic "line" of prose. This undoubtedly had to do with the way in which Greeks were taught to read and write and the view of Homer as the educator of all Greeks (Jaeger, 1986, pp. 35-39).

As the Greek word κῶλον suggests, a colon is a member, a limb. The period is the whole and the colon is the member or part. A period is made up (σύνθεσις, *compositio*) of cola. Aristotle approaches its definition not formally, but pragmatically: "It is what can be said in a breath" (*Art of Rhetoric*, 3.9.5).

The Greek word for period, περίοδος (*periodos*), suggests a circular path. Aristotle defines a period as "an expression (λέξις) having a beginning and an end in itself and a magnitude easily taken in at a glance" (*Art of Rhetoric*, 3.9.3; Kennedy, 1991, p. 240). Demetrius quotes Aristotle's definition with approval and elaborates on the circular metaphor implied in Aristotle: "For the very use of the word 'period' implies that it has had a beginning at one point, will end at another, and is speeding towards a definite goal, like runners sprinting from the starting place." (*On Style*, 11). The period is roughly equivalent to the English sentence, and it has a grammatical, analogical, and metaphorical meaning. Grammatically it is a complete thought; analogically it is like a metric line; metaphorically it is a circuit.

Employing these pragmatic definitions of period and colon, the first task of sound mapping is to discover the basic auditory units of a composition. Thus we can begin to see, or graphically represent, the skeleton of σύνθεσις "the putting-together." As the cola and periods begin to emerge, how the sound of the composition segments, organizes, and selects data for interpretation becomes evident.

Seeing Sound

What follows is the last section of the resurrection story from John 20.24-30, the story of Thomas, arranged into cola and periods. The cola are the short lines, which are organized into 8 periods. Three of the periods have a very strong and distinctive form, periods 4.3, 4.5 and 4.8.

4.1
    Θωμᾶς δὲ εἷς ἐκ τῶν δώδεκα,   24
       ὁ λεγόμενος Δίδυμος,
    οὐκ ἦν μετ' αὐτῶν ὅτε ἦλθεν Ἰησοῦς.

4.2
    ἔλεγον οὖν αὐτῷ οἱ ἄλλοι μαθηταί,   25
    Ἑωράκαμεν τὸν κύριον.

4.3
    ὁ δὲ εἶπεν αὐτοῖς,
    Ἐὰν μὴ ἴδ<u>ω</u> ἐν ταῖς <u>χερσὶν</u> αὐτοῦ <u>τὸν τύπον τῶν ἥλων</u>
    καὶ βάλ<u>ω</u> τὸν δάκτυλόν μ<u>ου</u> <u>εἰς</u> <u>τὸν τύπον τῶν ἥλων</u>
    καὶ βάλ<u>ω</u> μου τὴν <u>χεῖρα</u> <u>εἰς</u> τὴν πλευρὰν αὐτοῦ,
    οὐ μὴ πιστεύσ<u>ω</u>.

4.4
    Καὶ μεθ' ἡμέρας ὀκτὼ   26
    πάλιν ἦσαν ἔσω οἱ μαθηταὶ αὐτοῦ
    καὶ Θωμᾶς μετ' αὐτῶν.
    ἔρχεται ὁ Ἰησοῦς τῶν θυρῶν κεκλεισμένων
    καὶ ἔστη εἰς τὸ μέσον
    καὶ εἶπεν,
    Εἰρήνη ὑμῖν.

4.5
    εἶτα <u>λέγει</u> τῷ Θωμᾷ,   27
    Φέρε τὸν δάκτυλόν σ<u>ου</u> ὧδε
    καὶ ἴδε τὰς χεῖράς μ<u>ου</u>,
    καὶ φέρε τὴν χεῖρά σ<u>ου</u>
    καὶ βάλε εἰς τὴν πλευράν μ<u>ου</u>,
    καὶ μὴ γίν<u>ου</u> ἄπιστος ἀλλὰ πιστός.

4.6
    ἀπεκρίθη Θωμᾶς καὶ εἶπεν αὐτῷ,   28
    Ὁ κύριός μου καὶ ὁ θεός μου.

4.7
    λέγει αὐτῷ ὁ Ἰησοῦς,   29
    Ὅτι ἑώρακάς με πεπίστευκας,
    μακάριοι οἱ μὴ ἰδόντες καὶ πιστεύσαντες.

4.8
    Πολλὰ μὲν οὖν καὶ ἄλλα σημεῖα ἐποίησεν ὁ Ἰησοῦς ἐνώπιον
    τῶν   μαθητῶν [αὐτοῦ]   30
      ἃ οὐκ ἔστιν γεγραμμένα ἐν τῷ βιβλίῳ τούτῳ·
    ταῦτα δὲ γέγραπται   31
        ἵνα πιστεύσητε ὅτι
            Ἰησοῦς ἐστιν ὁ Χριστὸς

ὁ υἱὸς τοῦ θεοῦ,
καὶ ἵνα πιστεύοντες
ζωὴν ἔχητε ἐν τῷ ὀνόματι αὐτοῦ.

4.1
 But Thomas one of the twelve 24
 who's nicknamed the Twin
 wasn't there with them when Jesus came.

4.2
 So the other disciples were saying to him, 25
 "We have seen the Lord."

4.3
 But he said to them,
 "Unless I see in his <u>hands</u> the <u>nail holes</u>,
 and unless I stick my <u>finger</u> into the <u>nail holes</u>,
 and unless I stick my <u>hand</u> into his side
 there's no way I'll ever believe!"

4.4
 And a week later 26
 his disciples are again inside
 and Thomas with them.
 Jesus comes through the locked doors
 and stands among them
 and said,
 "Peace be with you."

4.5
 Then he says to Thomas, 27
 "Please, put your finger here
 and look at my hands,
 and now take your hand
 and stick into my side,
 and don't be faithless but faithful."

4.6
 Then Thomas answered and said to him, 28
 "My Lord and my God."

4.7
 Jesus says to him, 29
 "You think that because you've seen me, you really believe?
 Well, blessed are those who haven't seen and yet still believe."

4.8
 Many other signs also Jesus did in the presence of his disciples, 30
 which are not written in this book;
 But these are being written
 so that you might believe that
 Jesus is the Messiah

the son of God,
and so that continuing to believe,
you may have life in his name.

Periodic Style

Thomas's response in 4.3 to the disciples' declaration "We have seen the Master," is a carefully constructed period with many long vowel sounds. The aorist (he said) introduction gives the impression of a carefully worked out position, a completed, stable position. The repetition of "mark of the nails" and the sandwiching of hand/finger/hand tie the first three cola of his speech together. The strong negatives in the first and final cola give an overall negative cast to the whole speech and create the rounding favored in the definition of a period. The οὐ μή "there's no way" with the aorist subjunctive, a classical form, emphasizes an emphatic negative in the future: "Never ever will I." The shortness of this final colon in comparison with the other cola in this period draws attention to this negative declaration creating an abrupt ending. The long o-sound ("I") of the verbs ties all four cola together and provides the final climax of the period. This period is in the style that ancient grammarians termed archaic and its purpose is to indicate authority. The sound of the Greek indicates that Thomas is making the strongest possible negative claim. He is usurping authority for himself.

Jesus' reply to Thomas in 4.5 sounds very different from Thomas's demand in 4.3. Thomas's speech was introduced with an aorist, εἶπεν "he said," indicating its fixed position; Jesus' response is introduced by λέγει "he says," a present tense, which moves Jesus' speech center stage. While Thomas's speech was bounded in its first and final cola with strong, negative sounds ("Unless", "never"/ἐὰν μή, οὐ μή) and dominated by strong long vowel sounds, Jesus' command leads with short vowel sounds and the final negative is softened ("and do not"/καὶ μή). Jesus' speech consists of five cola. The first contains a soft rhyme: *phere...hode*/φέρε...ὧδε "Bring... here." The rhyme bounds and defines the entire activity between Jesus and Thomas. The next three cola in paratactic form repeat the imperative with its short "e" sound but the lines end with the same sound, "ou." This sound is picked up from the "*sou*" of the first colon creating an ABAB pattern of *sou, mou, sou, mou.* (you, me, you, me). This "ou" sound is then repeated in the final imperative γίνου (*ginou*, "don't be") tying all five cola of his speech together. This final colon is constructed with refinement and balance in comparison to the final colon of Thomas's speech, whose final colon was strongly negative and abrupt with a harsh ending. Jesus' final colon rounds off his period with the final contrast "be not unfaithful but faithful" (ἄπιστος ἀλλὰ πιστός). This rounding effect gives Jesus' speech elegance and refinement. His speech pictures Jesus not as commanding, but as pleading, so, "Please bring your finger, and please look at my hands," might be a better translation. The elegant style of Jesus contrasts with the harsh authoritative style of Thomas. Ironically, the one with real authority does not speak in an authoritative style.

Seeing Tenses

One of the real advances in Greek grammar in recent years concerns verbal aspect. Grammarians long have understood that the Greek tenses do not function primarily as temporal markers, as tense does in English and other modern languages. This difference has recently been clearly formulated in terms of verbal aspect (Fanning, 1990; Porter, 1989). "[A] speaker or writer grammaticalizes...a perspective on an action by the selection of a particular tense-form in the verbal system" (Porter, 1989, p. 21). The aorist, the default tense in Greek, views an action as completed. It provides the least semantic force and as the default tense is the one that is used when there is no other reason to use another tense. The present tense views an action as in process and the perfect views an action as reflecting a given, often complex, state of affairs. The aorist indicates what is stable and does not change, while the present depicts action against the aorist backdrop and the perfect is selected action. A less abstract way to understand these differences employs the metaphor of a stage, which is very appropriate to a rhetorical culture like the first century. The background or scenery is the aorist. The foreground or center stage is the present, while that action selected to move to the stage's apron, the frontground, is the perfect. Verbal aspect is one of the ways sound initiates visualization on an audience's part. We can view the tenses selected as stage directions to an audience as they construct their image of the narration.

By the careful use of the present, aorist, and perfect tenses, the narrative of John 21 has foregrounded and backgrounded various activities and speeches. This gives the story a strong sense of presence. Verbal aspect constructs a stage on which the audience can view and locate the action. In 4.6 both verbs are in the aorist and the formula "answered and said" is the common sign of normal narration in John's Gospel, occurring 79 times. This pushes Thomas's confession into narration and past-story time. This is the default confession. This does not undervalue or even call the confession into question, but it surely indicates that it is not the story's climax, as is often claimed. The confession is what is expected. Rarely in the New Testament is Jesus called God (Attridge, 1989, p. 58). Bultmann insisted the phrase was cultic (1971, p. 538), but its closest parallel is to the title of the Emperor Domitian who ruled during the Gospel's time frame (81-96 A.D.). He required that he should be addressed as "our Lord and God" (*dominus et deus noster*, Suetonius, *Domitian*, 13; Lindars, 1972, p. 615, in support; Schnackenburg, 1982, 3:333, against; Brown, 1970, 2:1047, probably no, but not so sure.) John has used imperial titles before. At the end of the narrative of the Samaritan woman's conversion, Jesus is proclaimed as savior of the world (4.42), clearly an ironic usage. Here too a confession exposes the pretensions of the Roman emperor. Thomas's confession acknowledges what Jesus has already told Mary. Jesus is God's agent, the bridge between my God and your God, creating the new family of God. "Whoever has seen me has seen the Father" (14.8).

Jesus' response to Thomas's confession is in the present tense, the foreground, indicating that the narrator wants to draw it to an audience's attention. The question "Have you believed?" is slightly ironical, challenging Thomas to examine his belief. The beatitude is cast in two aorist participles, describing full actions. This is the risen Jesus' default position. The contrast is between seeing and believing. Truly blessed are those who believe without seeing, like the beloved disciple. In the end, the narrative comes back to its first example of faith. Lindars has observed, "Being absent when Jesus appeared to the disciples on Easter night, Thomas was virtually in the position of the Christian who has not seen the risen Jesus, and he should not have needed a further appearance in order to come to faith." (Lindars, 1972, p. 616).

Period 4.8 concludes the whole unit. The construction of its cola signals a shift in voice. The first two cola are long and in continuous style in sharp contrast to its final six cola, all of which are quite short and arranged in a tight ABCCBA pattern.

The rhetoricians warn against excessively short cola. For example, Aristotle warns "A short one often causes the hearer a bump; for when [his mind] is rushing toward what is to come and its measure, of which he has his own definition, if he is pulled up short by the speaker's pausing, he necessarily trips, as it were, at the abrupt close" (*Rhetoric*, 3.9.5, Kennedy, 1991, p. 241). While such short cola for a conclusion seem problematic, yet the final six cola are carefully constructed to serve as a conclusion to the argument of chapter 20. The first colon, ταῦτα δὲ γέγραπται "these things were written" contains a large number of alpha sounds which contrasts with the final colon which is elongated with a large number of long vowels. The use of the perfect, rather than the aorist, to describe the writing of the "book" indicates the book's continuing validity. The book is center stage, at the apron, drawing the audience's attention. Furthermore, writing in the ancient world is strongly connected with auditory activity. One writes so that others may hear. The second and fifth cola are built around πιστεύω (*pisteuo* "to believe"). The textual evidence concerning the tense of the verb in colon 2 is inconclusive (Metzger, 1971, p. 256). From the point of view of a sound analysis, I would argue that it is a present tense, matching the tense of colon 5. Furthermore, the present aspect indicates the center stage point of view, viewing coming to faith as a process, not a completed act (aorist). The purpose of writing/hearing is the bringing of one to faith. In between cola 2 and 5 are two commata, which are confessions of faith. Thus cola 2 and 5 form an *inclusio* "set of brackets" around the confession of faith, Jesus is the Messiah, Son of God.

This final period argues that faith now comes through hearing, not seeing. The audience of the book confronts in its sound, in hearing it, the conditions for believing.

In the future, I hope we can begin to envision fidelity in translation to be full fidelity to the whole composition, to sound and visualization, to the amphitheater quality of the biblical text and not just to the signified, the denuded message. With such an enriched understanding of translation, the technological possibilities opening up before us promise a new age in translation where we can hear, see, and experience, where we can hear the Word of God not as silence but as *logos* "speech."

8

Multimedia Communication of the Biblical Message

Eugene A. Nida

Culture and Communication

New media communication provides an increasingly effective method of making the message of the Bible more meaningful to people. For the Bible Societies, the potential for new media is unprecedented. Although the dangers of misusing such media are also very real, this should not discourage the Bible Societies from exploiting any and all means for making the Scriptures more accessible and relevant to particular types of audiences.

Using symbolic systems other than printed texts or spoken words for communicating biblical truths is not entirely new. From the earliest centuries, Christians have employed singing and chanting to make the message of the Scriptures more attractive and meaningful (see essay by J. Ritter Werner in this volume). The wording of the Gospel of John 1.1-18 points quite clearly to a poetic structure that was no doubt often sung or chanted. Compare also Mary's Song in the Gospel of Luke 1.46-55 and the prophecy of Zechariah in the Gospel of Luke 1.68-79, as well as the Psalms and many other poetic passages of the Old Testament.

But even in printed texts, differences of typeface, format, and book covers have also carried messages. When the Bible Societies published so-called "red-letter" New Testaments and when the printed Luther German text contained certain verses in bold type, many people strongly objected because this would imply that some words of the Bible were evidently more authoritative than others—a canon within the canon. The use of an unconventional cover for the Good News New Testament also offended many people who insisted that displaying names of major world newspapers on the cover was nothing less than sacrilege.

The Bible Societies did not publish anything less than a complete book of the Bible for many years. But after the Second World War, Gilbert Darlington, the treasurer of the American Bible Society, published, at his own expense, the Sermon on the Mount in several European languages. This opened the way for widespread distribution of selections from the Scriptures in hundreds of languages, something represented before that time only in lectionary traditions.

During the Middle Ages when relatively few people could read, the message of the Scriptures was often communicated through paintings and statues. The 14 stations of the cross were frequently painted on interior church walls, and colored glass windows portrayed the resurrected Christ, the Virgin Mary, Jesus and his disciples, and even God creating the world. In some churches the entire ceiling featured paintings of biblical events (see essay by Gregor Goethals in this volume).

In northeast Romania, the outside walls of churches were often covered with biblical scenes, especially the story of Adam and Eve and the two ladders, one labeled with sins and leading to hell and the other labeled with virtues and leading to heaven. One church wall even depicted Plato confirming belief in eternal life (an early widespread misinterpretation of the writings of Plato). This painting of the outside walls of churches may have resulted from the fact that these churches had such massively thick walls and such narrow windows that interior paintings would have been scarcely visible.

The architecture of churches can also serve as a medium for communication, for example, the so-called "Fish Church" in Stamford, Connecticut. This church was built in the shape of a fish in order to represent the early Christian symbol of a fish, for which the letters of the corresponding Greek word could stand for "Jesus Christ God's Son Savior." The placement of the pulpit at the center of the platform in some churches also became an important symbol for those who insisted that the proclamation of the prophetic word had priority over the Eucharist.

Drama and ritual often communicate the events recorded in Scripture. The manner in which ornately bound Bibles are paraded with clouds of incense in Orthodox churches is certainly a way of exalting the sacred character of the Word of God. The rituals of baptism, marriage, and internment are also media communications of Christian traditions, and the supernatural values associated with the Mass are so great in some countries that consecrated wine is often stolen and sold at a high price to local sorcerers.

Churches throughout the world have been employing media in their various programs for many years. For example, in one Presbyterian church in Cameroon, the hesitant but expectant dance of a young woman moving slowly up to the front of the church portrayed the angel's proclamation to the Virgin Mary. But suddenly another dancer came dashing into the church to announce with jubilant shouts of joy the birth of a coming Savior. And as the messenger danced the good news, the young woman began to subtly adjust her movements and rhythm to match those of the messenger, thus producing a powerful message through dance.

In many Sunday schools in Africa the teacher first tells a biblical story and then the children act it out, and in some churches people immediately dramatize a sermon, which is a far more effective device than having a preacher repeat his outline at the end of the sermon.

New media presentations cannot, however, escape the thought worlds of the source and receptor cultures, that is, the beliefs and values of the biblical world in contrast with those of the receptor cultures. Present-day Christian congregations in the Western world simply cannot understand the concept of collective responsibility, which so often forms a puzzling element in the biblical accounts, for example, the devastating plague suffered by the people of Israel because King David counted the fighting men of his kingdom.

A Thai Buddhist found the four Gospels equally confusing; in fact, he interpreted the four Gospels as the accounts of four reincarnations of Jesus. What surprised this Thai was that Jesus evidently reached Nirvana after only four reincarnations, while according to Buddhist tradition it took Gautama a thousand reincarnations. Most devout Buddhists find even the verse John 3.16 almost incomprehensible. The statement "God so loved the world" seems nonsensical, because they regard loving this world as the root cause of sin and evil. And the final statement about "having everlasting life" appears incredibly cruel, because this would mean that no believer would ever escape from the wheel of endless rebirths into the benign nothingness of Nirvana.

Culture and Context

All communications are associated with cultural settings consisting of multidimensional contexts that provide clues to what a statement must have meant in the source culture and what it is likely to mean in a receptor culture when translated into words and/or into new media. This concern for contexts is not merely a matter of radical differences between obviously different cultures, such as China and Great Britain, but these contextual distinctions are also crucial factors in diverse subcultures of a single language. The beliefs, ways of reasoning, and values of some subcultures in the United States differ radically from one another, as anthropologists and sociologists have often pointed out. African Americans, Hispanics, and Caucasians represent quite different ways of life. Accordingly, what is perfectly acceptable to one subculture is not necessarily meaningful or relevant to another. For example, a Gospel published in Black English was completely rejected by those in New York City who customarily use this form of language among friends. They regarded such a publication as paternalizing. Similarly, a Gospel illustrated by drawings in which the biblical characters were depicted as West Africans was strongly condemned by local people. Many of their leaders had been in the Middle East and were offended that the biblical characters were depicted as being Negroid.

Unrecognized cultural features may also radically alter the interpretation of a passage of Scripture. For example, in some countries the parable of "A Treasure in a Field" means that Jesus would be advocating illegal activity, because in such countries all discovered treasures belong to the government and must be turned in to the authorities.

Rather than discuss some of the more general aspects of nonprint media in historical and cultural contexts, it seems much better to concentrate on the important contribution that the American Bible Society has made to understanding and appreciating the benefits and the problems of new media communication through a series of three videos and accompanying CD-ROMs: *Out of the Tombs* (Mark 5.1-20), *A Father and Two Sons* (Luke 15.11-32), and *The Visit* (Luke 1.39-56). The selection of these specific stories proved very useful because they differ widely in content, length, and potentiality for different new media treatments. Accordingly, they have proved to be particularly important as a means of studying successes and failures in the use of new media.

These three videos are technically excellent. The effective use of color, light, sequencing, quality of voice, dramatic settings, focus, transitions, and highlighting of persons and events is photographically excellent. No wonder these programs have received such high commendation from people in the industry.

New media presentations of the biblical message can take several different forms: (1) a presumed historical reproduction of a major biblical account, for example, *The Ten Commandments* and *Jesus Christ Superstar* (this type of production is a multimillion dollar undertaking and tends to sensationalize and to add, as well as to delete, significant portions of a biblical text); (2) a parallel set of events in an entirely different, but modern, setting, for example, *Out of the Tombs* and *A Father and Two Sons* (employing a translation that carefully reflects the meaning of the Greek text but is also easily understood in an oral medium); (3) the celebration of an event by means of words, music, and dance, for example, *The Visit* and the rap edition of *Out of the Tombs*; (4) a present-day illustrative example of a biblical account, for example, an African-American traveling salesman giving aid to a white racist who has suffered from a holdup or a shootout, after which the biblical parable of the Good Samaritan could be portrayed or simply told; (5) the oral form of a biblical text in some attractive symbolic setting, for example, the African-American storyteller reciting the account of *Out of the Tombs* or the actor chanting a biblical text in different symbolic settings, for example, from the basement to the tower of a tall church; and (6) the spoken form of a biblical account with appropriate background music to provide an attractive emotive setting.

Fidelity and New Media Translation

But irrespective of the form of new media presentation, there are some basic elements that must be carefully considered, especially if fidelity to the biblical message is an issue: (1) selection of a biblical event or theme that lends itself to new media treatment, (2) the nature of the translation, (3) the voice of the narrator or chorus, (4) the roles of the narrator and/or chorus, (5) the actors, (6) the setting, (7) the order of events and transitions, (8) additions and deletions, (9) supplementary information required to make a text understandable, (10) background information in related CD-ROMs, (11) testing the results of viewing videos and using CD-ROM background information, and (12) scenarios.

1. Selection of a Biblical Event or Theme

New Testament parables would seem ideal subjects for new media treatment, but since the action in such parables is usually very limited, producers often make certain additions. Producers could resolve the problem of length, however, by introducing background information that would make the parable more meaningful.

New media translations might also consider the treatment of some Old Testament accounts, for example, highlights in the life of Samson but with the emphasis on the tragedy of his life and not on his Rambo exploits. The story of Naaman's leprosy might focus on intercultural understanding of religious differences. Producers could treat certain themes in the Bible, for example: riches, pride, family, and forgiveness, with obvious present-day examples of success and failure in these areas of life.

The choice of subject matter largely depends on the total length of the video and on the potential audience. Producers should, therefore, find some valid way to involve members of a potential audience in the process of text selection. They could obtain such information as part of the process of testing the results of existing videos, as discussed in section 11 below.

2. The Nature of the Translation

Any translation of a biblical text for new media must pass the test of "rapid oral comprehension," which means that the translation must represent in vocabulary and pronunciation the most widely acceptable forms in the usage of the intended audience. And it must also be sufficiently intelligible and accurate so as to prevent possible misunderstanding. This implies that translators must avoid such features as long left-hand extensions (e.g. long clauses or series of prepositional phrases before the verb), technical vocabulary, remote pronominal reference, and literary subtleties. Such translations must also possess a rhythmic flow in both sound and semantic content, because people comprehend an oral text largely by means of rhythmic units (see essay by B. Brandon Scott in this volume), and not by strings of isolated words.

Unfortunately, some persons believe that the quality of a translation for new media use depends primarily on strictly adhering to a list of words based on frequency of usage. But frequency alone does not provide an adequate criterion for intelligibility. For example, the English word *knee* is not a high-frequency word, but it makes no sense to talk about *the bend in the middle of the leg*. Instead of some arbitrary criterion of frequency, translators would do better to think in terms of "transitional probabilities," that is, the extent to which what precedes tends to anticipate what follows. The greater the transitional probabilities the more likely it is that what follows is understood by what precedes. For the English language, the Bible Societies are fortunate to have the Contemporary English Version, which has been specifically designed for oral/aural communication and can serve as a model for other languages.

3. The Voice of the Narrator or Chorus

The voice of anyone speaking in a new media production, whether narrator, chorus, or actor, should sound believable and sincere. These qualities are delightfully present in the beautiful diction of the African-American storyteller in a special rendering of *Out of the Tombs*. But many professional actors and narrators have an artificial quality in their voices, a kind of "professionalism" that raises doubts about what they say. People tend to treat with suspicion those who are paid to talk.

The voices in new media must, of course, involve clear enunciation, but at the same time they should not sound pedantic, artificial, or too professional, although truly professional speakers do not sound professional. In addition, the voice of a narrator, chorus, or actor should not be readily classifiable as to socioeconomic class or status unless this is a vital feature of the new media production, as in the case of the rap edition of *Out of the Tombs*. Nor should a voice imply some particular personal role. For example, the voice of the narrator in *A Father and Two Sons* sounds so gushy that in combination with the extravagant gestures, it suggests a hard rock entertainer.

Interestingly it is much easier to understand the words in these three new media productions when only one person speaks or sings the text than when several people speak or sing together. In order to make the message as intelligible as possible, the use of antiphonal sets, which are so common in various parts of the world, might help. For example, one person sings a short unit of a song and the group then responds with the same unit. This procedure not only makes the text more intelligible but also emphasizes what is being communicated.

4. The Roles of the Narrator and/or Chorus

The roles of the narrator and/or chorus (see section 9 concerning background information) must be carefully distinguished. The narration of the biblical text should probably be assigned to one person because, as already noted, people can more readily hear a single voice than the combined speech of several persons. But neither the narrator nor the chorus should have a role in the story line. This very thing produces a conflict of roles in

A Father and Two Sons. After the announcement of the title, the father and the two sons ride up on horses, but then the female narrator rides up on a fourth horse. This same narrator becomes one of the enticements in the reckless living of the younger son, and she finally appears as a guest at the banquet. This switching of roles confuses the viewer too much, especially in a very brief production.

The role of the narrator should only speak the text so as not to confuse the text with background information (see section 9). The chorus (or perhaps only a single person with a distinctly different voice or appearance) should provide background information about the location of this text in the Bible, accompanying passages that help explain its meaning (e.g., the two brief parables preceding the parable of *A Father and Two Sons*) and the "big idea" of the selected text. The chorus could also explain or call attention to various elements of the biblical text as the production unfolds.

Some persons may feel that all such supplementary information should be contained exclusively in the CD-ROM portion of the production, but people are not likely to search for more background information unless they have already found such data very helpful. No doubt some of the urgency for such background information should be a crucial element in the program for testing present or future video productions (see section 11).

5. *The Actors*

Videos in which the actors speak their own roles differ vastly from those in which a narrator speaks the entire story line. This latter approach is certainly simpler to produce and involves fewer misrepresentations, but there is considerable value in actors performing their roles by means of relevant utterances.

Even when a narrator produces a text in an actionless setting, for example, the African-American storyteller, the story might become more relevant if she had appeared speaking to a group of fascinated youth. In fact, it seems unfortunate that she only glances at the video audience at the very end of her narrative account. As now filmed, the storyteller seems to talk to herself.

The roles of actors are inevitably affected by their appearance, movement, and facial gestures. In the video *Out of the Tombs*, the person representing Jesus has a facial appearance that is glacial and a somewhat strange and unnatural gait. One of the persons associated with this production explained this rather zombie type of behavior as an attempt to suggest the divine nature of Jesus. But this suggests an unreal Jesus which reminds us too much of the Gnostic heresy that sought to separate the earthly Jesus from the heavenly Christ. In contrast with this deadpan Savior, the demoniac becomes the hero of the event.

The actors in the rap version of *Out of the Tombs* and in the chorus treatment of *The Visit* are excellent. They not only communicate well but give every evidence of enjoying what they do. This adds immensely to the dynamic quality and sincerity of the video.

6. The Setting

The setting of any new media production takes on great importance because it provides the context for the event. However, *Out of the Tombs* completely neglects the biblical setting of Jesus arriving with his disciples, and the healing focuses on sunshine and water rather than on the role and words of Jesus. The biblical account is by no means as sensational as the leaping attack of the demoniac: this episode not only runs contrary to the biblical account but also suggests a manic state, something quite different from most biblical accounts of demon possession.

The setting of *A Father and Two Sons* is also sensationalized by making the story into a "Western" with four persons riding up on expensive horses. Such a context seems inconsistent with the proposal of a son wanting to have his share of an estate. Would not a porch or the interior of a home seem more appropriate and believable?

The setting of the rap performance (*Out of the Tombs*) in what appears to be an empty part of a church might work more effectively if it were on a street corner in Harlem and staged in front of a delighted audience, with which the viewers of the video could identify. The setting for the chorus presentation of *The Visit*, however, seems particularly appropriate because the story of Mary's visit is a very personal matter. The attractive use of color in the garments and the scenery is especially fitting, and results in an excellent setting for the intimate account of Mary's Song.

7. The Order of Events and Transitions

Any shift in the order of events, for example, flashbacks, may confuse viewers unless the video carefully marks the transitions. When the two young boys enter near the end of *A Father and Two Sons*, many viewers tend to confuse the identity of the children. Although the photography representing the two boys, reflected in the highly painted vehicle, is technically excellent, one may ask if there is enough transitional buildup to make ready identification of them as the two grown sons when they were young.

In some instances the video spends so little time on a particular setting that many viewers simply do not grasp the significance of what it portrays. For example, a mirror and a female figure appear in front of the demoniac (*Out of the Tombs*), evidently as a means of explaining his manic action, but a number of viewers will not realize that this represents a typical psychiatric interpretation of such aberrant behavior, namely, narcissism and sex. This interpretation, however, does not accord with the beliefs about demons as reflected in the New Testament.

8. Additions and Deletions

This brevity of passages that seem appropriate for video treatment and the temptation to sensationalize the content places considerable pressure to add to or to delete elements in the biblical text. For example, in order to highlight the demoniac's inhabiting the tombs, the video omits the account of Jesus arriving in Gerasa with his disciples; instead the demoniac appears in the tombs and ready to pounce upon Jesus (clearly an addition). This addition tends to shift the focus of the passage from Jesus' relations with a Gentile community to merely a miraculous casting out of demons. We really need background information that will explain why Jesus later refused to let the healed man join him and his close followers.

Furthermore, in order to bring Jesus and the demoniac together, the character representing Jesus walks into the cemetery with a bouquet of red roses and places them on one of the tombs. Not only an addition, this action further suggests to some persons an event entirely alien to the biblical text, namely, that Jesus must be honoring a girlfriend who has died.

We must suspect all additions and deletions because they are not part of the biblical text and because they also introduce elements that can lead to serious misunderstanding. But this caution about additions and deletions should not be extended to the need for adjustments in wording so that the text can fit an accompanying new media code, for example, some of the expressions in the rap version or in the sung portion of Mary's Magnificat. And additions are certainly needed in introductions so that people can better comprehend the essential elements in a biblical account, as noted in section 9.

9. Supplementary Information Required to Make a Text Understandable

One of the serious problems with the short videos produced by the American Bible Society is that people unfamiliar with the Scriptures simply do not grasp what the stories of *Out of the Tombs* and *A Father and Two Sons* are all about. It is not enough to say that these presentations are based on the Bible with a reference to the book, chapter, and verses. People need to know that the land of the Gerasenes was a part of Palestine occupied by Gentiles who raised pigs and ate pork. The focus of this account is that the people who had collectively hired others to herd their pigs showed more concern with their economic losses than with the healing of a social outcast. Furthermore, the herders were greatly alarmed because the healing of the demoniac not only destroyed their livelihood but also exposed them to great financial loss. No wonder they rushed about to the various towns to spread the word about what had happened to the demon-possessed man.

The video of *A Father and Two Sons* makes much more sense if hearers know that according to Jewish custom the older son inherited twice as much as any other brother or sister. Moreover, the older brother's insistence that he never disobeyed his father in any way shows the extent of his self-righteousness. No wonder the younger brother wanted to leave home! But in order to understand this parable, we must take into consideration the previous two parables about the joy in heaven when people repent. The accompanying CD-ROM can highlight this information, but the appreciation of the meaning of the biblical account in the video requires some such background information.

Producers may have to add such background information to a narrator's introduction or to the comments of the chorus made at the beginning of or at crucial points during the video. The distinction between the narrator and the chorus then becomes similar to the different typefaces used in printed Bibles to distinguish the text from section headings, chapter summaries, and footnotes.

10. Background Information in Related CD-ROMs

The three CD-ROMs produced thus far appear basically factual and noncontroversial. That is to say, they do not take up some of the doctrinal problems implied in the text, for example, the family relationship between Jesus and John the Baptist in *The Visit*. The CD-ROM information provides essentially supplementary material, though not interactive material, as the format implies. For anyone who wishes to know more about a particular passage or about the sociocultural context of New Testament times, the information is extensive and well designed, except that a person can easily get lost trying to track down specific data.

In order to develop truly interactive material, producers must give users information as well as the opportunity to make some decisions on their own. For example, one of the programs makes the suggestion that a person might wish to translate a particular section of the biblical text, but most people do not know a foreign language well enough to translate from Greek or English into another language. However, the producers might introduce certain aspects of what is involved in translating by selecting a particular text in English and then asking people to consider altering the text to fit the vocabulary of younger children or of youth who find a particular Bible translation hard to understand. Such problem solving would nevertheless require considerable background information, and it is doubtful if many persons would really be interested in such a challenge.

People could, however, learn a great deal about translating using carefully guided inquiries about different English translations of the same text. The program could ask them helpful questions with alternative answers about the pros and cons of particular renderings. In this way, people could discover something about differences in manuscripts, alternative interpretations, diverse levels of language, and distinctions in sociolinguistic dialects. These real issues in Bible translating could make the CD-ROMs both interactive and interesting.

In order to respond to the concerns and interests of a wide constituency, the supplementary information in the CD-ROMs has to be largely factual, but this inevitably restricts the size of an intended audience.

Furthermore, most people do not read the Bible for information about ancient customs or historical events, but for help in solving personal problems. Such homiletic CD-ROMs would be endlessly elaborate because of the infinite variety of human experience. In addition, such supplementary information would go far beyond what has been the tradition of the Bible Societies, namely, to regard the application of the Scriptures to people's personal lives as the responsibility of the churches as the "communities of faith."

11. Testing the Results

In view of the high cost of new media productions and in order to improve the quality and effectiveness of future videos and CD-ROMs, it is essential to conduct adequate testing of viewers' responses. Such testing, however, must go beyond mere market distribution. In order to understand precisely what people get out of such programs, it is essential to elicit reactions from randomly selected viewers immediately after they watch the programs, a week later, and, if at all possible, a month later. People trained in how to obtain valid information should do the interviewing. They should not ask people, "Did you like the program?" but rather "What part of the program did you especially like? What part was most interesting? Do you think some people might have difficulty understanding the narrator's voice? What kind of people are likely to learn most from such a video? What age group would enjoy this video most? What kind of churches would welcome such videos?" As in all such interviewing, the more informal, the better, with the questions focused on the reactions of other people, including their difficulties in understanding. But if people volunteer information about their own problems of understanding, so much the better. Interviewers should never imply, however, that the interviewees are in any way incapable of understanding and appreciating the production.

This type of questioning may seem unnecessary in view of the positive reactions to this material by people in the industry, but such people often have little or no knowledge about the Bible or about the cultural symbolization of the source and receptor cultures, or about the subtle theological implications of the text. The results of interviews, however, are indispensable to those immediately responsible for future productions, to the leadership of the Bible Societies, to those asked to serve as consultants for future programs, and to those responsible for developing principles and procedures for guiding other societies in undertaking new media productions.

Some persons have suggested that new media productions created in one language and culture could be used in many other parts of the world, but this is not only unlikely but exceptionally risky. For a production to "grab an audience," it must be expertly fitted to the experiences and values of the people in question. Accordingly, the use of such a video in a quite different part of the world would introduce too many misleading features.

12. Scenarios

If consultants, Bible Society leadership, and translation committees are to provide real help in creating fully satisfactory video and CD-ROM programs, it is essential to develop scenarios at three stages. First, when they agree that a particular biblical text appears amenable to new media presentation, those persons responsible for production should create a tentative scenario of two or three pages outlining some of the high points and stating clearly the purpose and focus of the production. After approval of the preliminary scenario, they must prepare a detailed scenario including the settings, actions, types of actors, clothing, narrators and/or chorus, and accompanying music and dance so that all persons concerned may have adequate input (at this stage they should also provide some estimate of total cost). Finally, they should develop a shooting scenario so as to maximize efficiency in moving from one photo perspective to another and in using actors, narrators, and chorus. Such scenarios must also take into consideration the contents of the corresponding CD-ROM.

Conclusion: Principles and Procedures

In order to maximize the cooperative efforts of various societies in new media productions, the leadership of the Bible Societies should clearly state the principles, procedures, and purposes of new media programs, including the advantages in reaching out to new audiences and the problems due largely to significant differences in the interpretation of texts presented in quite different sociolinguistic contexts. They should state clearly that the use of new media is not designed to replace the printed text, but to lead people to the text.

Such a statement should take into consideration the wide range of visual materials that Bible Societies, churches, and commercial companies have produced. For example, the Bible Societies would find it useful to study carefully the new media productions of the Church of Latter Day Saints (Mormons), which has invested extensively in video productions of high quality.

Principles, procedures, and process must focus on the problems of diversities in cultural contexts because these lie at the core of all issues involving comprehension. Clarence Jordan's translations of major parts of the New Testament in the Cotton Patch Version are exegetically admirable, but due to the radical diversity in cultural context, the translations have not reached the constituency that Jordan sought to enlist in the cause of social and economic justice. Having Jesus born in Gainesville, Georgia, referring to Peter son of John as "Rock Johnson," and having Jesus condemned to death by the archbishop and elders in Atlanta involved so many radical differences in setting as to appear to some people as sacrilegious.

Parables do not involve such serious problems of context because they are not strictly historical, even though they are very true. But providing actual events with different contexts poses almost insurmountable problems for many Bible readers. That is precisely why the production *Out of the Tombs* seems much more difficult to relate to than *A Father and Two Sons*.

New media represents a gold mine of opportunity for effective communication of the biblical message, but without sensitive understanding of cultural differences, the theological import of the text, and the role of contexts, the payoff will be only fool's gold.

9

The Imaged Word: Aesthetics, Fidelity, and New Media Translations

Gregor T. Goethals

Introduction

Imagine that a powerful religious leader comparable to Jesus appeared in the late 20th century. Imagine also that this figure made such an impact that print and electronic media covered every "event," capturing conversation, gesture, dress, setting, and audience.

Now, fast forward into the 21st century, 100 years later, and reflect upon what the translation enterprise might be like. The quantity and complexity of media reports of the life and teaching of that figure would be staggering. Sorting through books, newspapers, film, TV and radio archives—not to mention faxes and camcorder tapes—we would be overwhelmed by questions of fidelity.

Among the questions that might overwhelm us are several that we will raise in this chapter: Does the presentation and meaning of the figure in the 21st century conform to the presentation and meaning of the figure in the 20th century? Under what conditions, with which media, and with what audience expectations in mind did we transfer the meaning of this figure from one century to another? What adequacy norms governed this transfer of meaning? All of these questions combine into a single one: Does the target text, with its words, images, pictorial style, and cultural values preserve the wholeness of the source text, with its words and (implied) images, sounds, and cultural values?

By contrast, reports about Jesus of Nazareth are relatively scarce, devoid of explicit media images and sound. Yet in both instances, those who did not directly encounter Jesus or our fictional, 20th-century savior would be equally dependent upon symbolic accounts for knowledge of who they were and what they taught. William Ivins has reminded us of our inevitable reliance upon interpretative accounts: "[A]t any given moment the accepted report of an event is of greater importance than the event, for what we think about and act upon is the symbolic report and not the concrete event itself"

(1968, p. 180). Thus faithfulness originates with attention to those texts that report events in Jesus' life.

New questions about fidelity arise as our society becomes increasingly driven by image technologies. Visual artists, especially those in film and television, are asking probing questions: Can we apply the concept of fidelity to modes of communication other than texts? Can word and image be integrated in a way that remains faithful to the original symbolic report? Are there criteria and adequacy norms for an authentic transference of meaning from text through image and sound?

Although a thorough exploration of these questions is far beyond the scope of this chapter, I would like to open up areas for further exploration and dialogue. During the last several years, the American Bible Society (ABS) has begun a series of new media translations using a combination of word and image in videos and CD-ROMS. However, before we look critically at these productions, we need to address, at least briefly, a contentious issue that continues to haunt religious communication: the use of images and their relationship to text.

This chapter begins by exploring where and how Christians first related texts to images. A short summary of scholarly studies in this area can draw attention to functional integrations of text and image that emerged early in Christian culture. At the same time, this will provide an opportunity to observe different formal relationships and the diversity of styles that appeared over time.

The second part of this chapter looks at changing relationships between images and text after the Protestant Reformation and the invention of printing. Traditional roles of images dramatically changed, especially in churches which adhered to the teachings of John Calvin and Ulrich Zwingli—radical reformers who completely eliminated pictorial representations in worship space. How, then, did this aniconic aesthetic affect the integration of text and image?

In exploring this question, we turn to the predominantly Protestant ethos of 19th-century American society. While some artists wished to portray biblical themes, they found no context or demand for these. At the same time, the printing and circulation of the Bible was growing rapidly, and it became common to include illustrations. In these biblical illustrations, we can identify the formulation of a "religious art"—a particular style that continues its influence even today.

The last section looks at contemporary attempts to re-vision image and text in translation and in the transference of religious meaning. During the 20th century, the vital interaction between text and images was rediscovered, not by religious groups but by secular advertising firms. Using sophisticated technologies and extraordinary combinations of image, word, sound, and motion, commercial institutions virtually resurrected the power of the icon and illuminated manuscripts.

Amid a secular renaissance of the imaged word, the ABS began to experiment with contemporary technologies and to explore new ways of combining word and image. Certain vital questions have gathered and propelled the collective work of translators, scholars, and artists: How was the wholeness of image and word achieved in traditional religious forms? What do new communication technologies offer to translation and to the integration of word and image today? How is a diversity of form and symbol developed in a multicultural environment? This essay attempts to pursue these questions.

Envisioning the Word

In the early history of the church, new social and cultural environments gave shape to varying forms and styles of a Christian art; the relationship between word and image developed along rich, diverse lines. Amid formal, stylistic differences, however, two contexts for visual representation emerged relatively early in Christian history and remained constant up until the time of the Reformation and the invention of printing. Image and word were creatively joined in liturgical spaces and in illuminated manuscripts. Church walls and parchment surfaces provided the contexts for integrating word and image. Concrete images, which were themselves enhanced by the light and space of architectural forms, enlivened the spoken words and action of ritual. In book illumination, the written text and image became an artistically unified whole. In either context, the function of the art forms is clear: to transfer and extend meaning from word into image. In the brief overview which follows, a few examples will describe how, in early Christian communities, images played a significant role in the communication of religious meaning.

The Early Church: Signs and Symbols

Archeological evidence confirms that visual representations were used by early Christians in ritual and ceremonial spaces. In his work, *Ante Pacem*, Graydon Snyder examines the "distinctively Christian archeological data" (1991, p. 2) that begins to appear about 180 A.D. Before that date, he hypothesizes, material remains cannot be clearly separated from a non-Christian culture. Although a rich literature existed well before the second century, it took over 100 years for distinctly Christian forms of visual expression to appear. Studying catacomb art before the Peace of Constantine (325 A.D.), Snyder focuses our attention on the images made by members of small Christian communities amid social change and conflict. In such precarious and unsettled living conditions, their symbols were shaped as much by the turbulence of their lives as by their religious text.

Snyder significantly contrasts the late second-century cryptic symbols found in the Roman catacombs with the narrative imagery that appeared later with the Peace of Constantine. Instead of pictorialized texts, one finds in the catacombs simple, linear signs, such as an anchor and fish. These images, Snyder contends, function like "a metaphor in linguistic expression....Signs are much more quickly produced means of communication. They represent that which cannot be expressed easily by words or even narrative" (p. 13).

Insofar as they reflect the multiple social conflicts or paradoxes in which the group exists, the selection and use of such signs is not mystical or secret: It grows out of the boundary experiences of the early Christian community. Snyder resists, for example, the explanation of the anchor as a coded literary reference to the redemption of the cross. The earliest Christians, he observes, stress deliverance and victory, rather than death and resurrection. "Understood in terms of social conflict, the anchor, fish and ships are all things that can endure in an alien environment. Therefore, the anchor implies security in a hostile, if not negative, culture" (p. 15). He also notes that the anchor symbol was found frequently in the third century but then basically disappears in the Constantinian era (288-337 A.D.).

Other cryptic symbols appeared in the catacombs which were more directly related to biblical texts and to a long history of scriptural references. At the Catacomb of Priscilla, in the Cubicle of the Velatio, simply-painted representations portray events in the life of the deceased woman, as well as an orant—a conventional symbol of a person at prayer, standing with arms extended upward. In the same small space, one also finds a depiction of the Three Hebrews in the Fiery Furnace, and, at the top of the ceiling, a figure of the Good Shepherd. Snyder acknowledges the importance of patristic literature for the appearance and interpretation of these biblical motifs. At the same time, these biblical symbols are significantly related to the cultural context of the early church. Snyder underscores their metaphoric suggestion of deliverance and victory for Christians in the midst of social conflict. There exists, he argues, a "dialectical tension between the symbol of the social matrix and the biblical scene of the revealed religion" (p. 45).

Early in the 20th century, archaeologists excavated the ancient site of Dura-Europos, uncovering extensive and rich imagery related to liturgical and biblical texts. Fragments of wall paintings located in a synagogue and a Christian building have opened up new areas of scholarship about Jewish and early Christian paintings; they have also provided new insight about the interdependence of visual representation and words in religious communication. Here, liturgical functions as well as social context comprise the matrix for visual imagery.

In a small room of the Christian building that served as a baptistry, a font is the central feature. Within an arched, semicircular niche of the baptistry is a sketchily drawn Good Shepherd figure; he is standing, carrying a large sheep on his shoulders as he watches over a small flock. In the lower left area is a crude, almost graffiti-like representation of the Fall: Adam and Eve, a tree and serpent. On the preserved sections of the baptistry walls are cryptically painted figures suggesting biblical motifs and stories. Like the catacomb paintings, they are evocative rather than narrative. Although the baptistry is small, there are several isolated sets of figures on the walls. One of these is a sketchy representation of Christ's healing of the paralytic, showing only the figure of Christ and the healed man as he takes up his bed and walks. Other vignettes depict Jesus walking on water; Jesus reaching out to a sinking Peter as the disciples watch from a boat; Jesus with a woman at the well; and the confrontation between David and Goliath.

In his report on the Christian building at Dura-Europos, historian Carl Kraeling concludes that this selective grouping of biblical vignettes symbolize the victory over sin and death achieved through the savior figure, Jesus Christ. The images on the walls reinforce and resonate with the experience of the individual whose entry into a new life is marked by the rite of baptism—through the waters of the font. With other scholars, Kraeling stresses that any attempt to understand these images must first take into account the general history and cultural context to which the decorations belong. This context should include, for example, the pictorial decorations of the Jewish synagogue at Dura-Europos, as well as those of the surrounding pagan temples. Second, he notes that any interpretation should be linked to the purpose which the baptistry served: solemnizing the baptismal rite. Third, any analysis of these images must take into account the literary sources available to the small Christian community in the mid-third century, sources which informed the baptismal practices and doctrines of a local congregation (1967, pp. 178-179).

The analyses of Snyder and Kraeling remind us of the enormously complex relationships that images have to biblical texts, to liturgical rites, and to the social matrix in which the church exists. To more completely understand the images, we would need to study the texts recited during particular rites, the oral or written Scriptures, the cultural context in which artistic styles mingled, and the sociopolitical circumstances of a local community. Moreover, as we rethink the relationships of image and text in today's electronic world, we need to remember that even the static images of the early Christians were experienced in a dynamic context of ritual words and actions. Enlivened by the movement and sounds of liturgy, visual images were integrated into a vital composite of religious meaning.

Visual Narratives for Liturgical Settings

The catacombs and the baptistry at Dura-Europos represent only a very modest appropriation by Christians of the rich formal language of classical art. After the Peace of Constantine and during the Constantinian era, visual arts and architecture began to play a much larger role in religious communication. As great public churches were built, liturgical spaces were adorned with paintings, sculptures, and mosaics executed by skilled artisans. As Snyder has emphasized, it was only then that a narrative Christian art appeared. Like the earliest art of the small communities, however, the selection of images continued to be dependent upon biblical text and liturgical practices. The Church of San Apollinare Nuovo in Ravenna, Italy, built between 494 and 526, offers an excellent example of how images reinforce ritual practice and biblical narration. Originally constructed during the reign of the Arian ruler, Theodoric, the decorations were later altered by Orthodox Christians. The complexity of the designs illustrate a dramatic change in symbolism and in the quality of workmanship that appeared under the patronage of Christian rulers.

Unlike the sketchy vignettes of the catacombs and Dura-Europos baptistry, the program of mosaic decoration in San Apollinare Nuovo is unusually elaborate, both in composition and symbolic detail. Three levels of shimmering mosaics cover the interior wall surfaces. On the left wall, at the lowest level, stand figures of female martyrs processing toward Mary, who is seated on a throne and holding the Christ Child. To the right, on the south wall, a parallel procession of male martyrs moves toward Christ. These processional figures are later replacements made by Orthodox Catholics during the reconstruction of the building. Earlier, the mosaics at this level had depicted King Theodoric and members of his court.

On a second level, occupying the space between the clerestory windows, one sees majestic, individual portrayals of patriarchs, prophets, and apostles. Above these are panels narrating sacred stories from the Gospels. Mosaics on the north side represent episodes from the teaching and ministry of Christ, such as the Raising of Lazarus, the Healing of the Paralytic, and the Freeing of the Man Possessed by Demons. Opposite, on the uppermost level of the south wall of the nave, a symbolic sequence moving from the altar toward the western entrance tells the story of Christ's passion, death, and resurrection.

The uppermost level of mosaics are not to be taken simply as a visual narration of biblical texts. While they do perform this function, they also bear liturgical and political meaning. In his studies of the churches at Ravenna, historian Otto von Simson has shown how these are at the same time representations of the liturgical dramas: "the Savior's life, death, and resurrection did not happen once in the dim past...but take place mystically within the faithful themselves as they are enacted in the liturgy" (1948, p. 79). The biblical subjects at San Apollinare Nuovo appear to be selected and arranged to reinforce the liturgical rites that occur in the sacramental time and space.

Von Simson also carefully analyzes the political and cultural influences on the symbolism of the mosaics in San Apollinare Nuovo. The lower level of mosaics indicates significant changes in the sociopolitical status of the church. Unlike earlier Christian communities, the churches of this later period are often imperial churches. The original prime space was filled with mosaic images of the Ostrogoth king and his retinue, processing symbolically toward the representations of Christ and the Virgin. Moreover, he suggests that the procession of the virgins and martyrs may reflect the pageants of the ancient world and homage paid to a ruler. In San Apollinare there is an interrelation of political and theological iconography in which a political legacy is transformed (von Simson, 1948, p. 119).

From the Constantinian period up until the time of the Reformation, liturgy provided an essential context for the interaction of word and image. Even as forms, technologies, and cultural conditions changed, worship spaces remained a constant context for the transference of meaning from text to image. For example, while the brilliantly colored windows of Chartres Cathedral differ in form and technique from the mosaics at San Apollinare Nuovo, they both are best understood in terms of liturgical rites, biblical texts, and changes in the nature of the church and its leadership. Great church interiors maintained the religious-image lexicon for the mass populace. The adornment of ritual spaces offered to worshipers a consistent encounter with a shared visual text. Here were depictions of sacred stories and persons from the Old and New Testament, alongside heroic figures from the lives of saints.

Illuminated Manuscripts

Historically, a liturgical setting provided the most direct engagement with biblical texts: listening to sacred Scriptures read aloud and hearing them interpreted in a homily. As manuscript illumination developed, opportunities arose to see text and illuminations when the Gospel was raised aloft in a worship service. Yet, the great manuscripts were primarily accessible to the clergy and to a ruling class who might commission texts and illuminations for private devotional use. Though limited in circulation, manuscript illumination became a rich, vital reservoir of diverse pictorial forms in European medieval culture. The illuminators frequently modified the models from which they worked, developing an amazing variety of styles. In addition, artists also transposed manuscript illuminations into other media, such as paintings and sculpture. A brief highlighting of particular combinations of word and image in illuminated texts can be useful today, especially as we explore interconnections between the verbal and visual in new electronic media.

Such highlighting will give us a sense of how illuminated manuscripts raise in their own way the issue of translational fidelity. Among other things we may ask about the function of illuminations in manuscript. How do these images interface with words? In contrast to the interaction of words and images in ritual, do we see a new concept of text evolving, one which includes both calligraphy and imagery? In addition, does the combined shaping of word and image add information or offer new perspectives on the meaning of the text?

In contrast to illustration in the ancient world, early Christian and medieval illuminations were intricately related to the text itself. Carl Nordenfalk (1995) points out that classical illustrations guided readers, since the columns of writing on long manuscript scrolls were unnumbered and lacked a system of references or indexes. As the papyrus roll was gradually replaced by the vellum codex, the leaves offered a new support for illuminations and gave artists particular spaces and boundaries within which to work. Nordenfalk dates the oldest miniatures in painted frame to the fourth century.

As early Christian illuminators began to depict biblical subjects, they turned to Greco-Roman models, adapting their visual vocabulary and syntax for the representation of stories from Scripture. Then, as missionaries went out from Rome, they carried with them manuscripts whose illuminations reflected the classical style. These became the models to copy, giving monasteries in remote parts of Europe the impetus to create new manuscripts. At the same time that the classical aesthetic influenced local styles, it was itself transformed by indigenous, non-classical visual language and syntax. Three manuscripts may indicate this dynamic and the diversity of styles in relating text and image.

The Rossano Gospels

The holdings of the Diocesan Museum in the Archepiscopal Palace at Rossano, Italy include parts of a Gospel book from the sixth century known as the Rossano Gospels (or Codex Rossanensis). While there are relatively few pictures in this important manuscript, they are large in relation to the overall size of the page which measures approximately 11 by 10 inches. Two representations of Pilate's Judgment take up a full page. Other illustrations, interspersed with a Greek text, take up about a third of the top area of the page. Several of the illustrations of the life of Jesus use continuous narration to tell the story, sequencing images that move the story forward in time. Beneath the broad band of text and illustration at the top of the page are four columns of texts, each capped by a small portrait bust of a prophet.

One continuous narration depicts the Last Supper, following the accounts found in Mark 14.12-25 and Matthew 26.17-29; to the right at the same level of the page is a representation of Christ washing Peter's feet, described in John 13.1-17. In representing the Last Supper, the artist has arranged the figures of Jesus and the 12 disciples around a semicircular table. The full figure of Jesus is seen in a reclining position on the far left, with one of the disciples in a comparable pose on the far right. Between these two figures, abbreviated portrayals of the disciples suggest similar reclining positions around the table. All are attentively looking at Jesus—except one, presumably Judas, who reaches over with his hand into the large vessel on the table. (Matthew 26.23: "One of you men who has eaten with me from this dish will betray me," Contemporary English Version [CEV].) In the depiction of Jesus washing the feet of Peter there is a similar spatial treatment. We see the complete figure of Jesus as he bends over and draws water with cupped hands to pour over Peter's feet. Peter is shown seated on a stool with his feet in a large basin; he leans over slightly so that his hands reach down and almost touch those of Jesus. The artist uses the technique of overlapping to position the remaining 12 disciples behind the two major figures.

While the two sections of the continuous narration have no elaborate spatial background, there are, nevertheless, residual elements of a classical aesthetic. Like the mosaic panels at San Apollinare Nuovo, the essential vocabulary of the visual narration is the human figure: Gesture, expression, and spatial grouping collectively form the basic carrier of meaning. Whenever the story demands a background, sufficient elements are included to conform to the texts. For example, at the top of one page is an illustration of Christ's entry into Jerusalem. Jesus rides astride a donkey while two disciples follow. In the background we see a tree; one youth is in the tree while another struggles up the trunk. Waiting to greet Jesus are groups of people with palm branches. Just beyond these figures is a cryptic symbol of a city gate. Projecting above the city wall, small architectural shapes indicate that Jesus is about to enter the city of Jerusalem.

Faintly resembling late Roman painting techniques, the illustrations in the Rossano Gospels reveal a limited use of shadowing to suggest plane and space. Yet the modeling of the faces is quite simple and the garments are executed primarily through line and areas of color. The overlapping of figures is a major device for grouping the disciples and reinforces the artist's attempt to situate the figures in space. At the same time, it is clear from the way the Last Supper table is tilted upward that the illusionist techniques of Roman art are no longer operative. Without elaborate backgrounds, and with only the simplest techniques to place figures in space, the scenes function as continuous panoramas which, closely integrated with the Greek text, move the story forward in time. Integrated this way, text and image communicate as a unified, inseparable whole.

With regard to the issue of fidelity, the Rossano Gospels present an interesting case study. Their illustrations draw subject matter directly from the biblical narrative, providing an essential unity between image and word. At the same time, the modeling of the figures represents sixth-century tastes, not first-century tastes, so that in the visual realm we see the search for what Nida (1984) terms functional rather than formal equivalence.

The Utrecht Psalter

Pages from the Utrecht Psalter witness to the tradition of narrative illustration seen in the Rossano Gospels, but the style in which the story is told is radically different. Dated about 832, but possibly based on models linked to a manuscript 400 years older, the manuscript originated at Hautviliers, France, near Rheims, and consists of texts and illustrations of the Book of Psalms (Hinks, 1962, p. 116). In the pages of the Utrecht Psalter we see a unique integration of visual image and text. Each page is organized into three columns of text. Black and white pen drawings, placed in the margins of the page, depict the dramas of the Psalms. (See Figures 1, 2.)

While the human figure is still the essential locus of meaning, its formal gestural language is expressionistic. If we look at Psalm 57, for example, we see in the drawing, and read in the text, the basic theme of praise

University Library, Utrecht, Ms. 32, fol. 32r. Reprinted with permission.
Figure 1: Illustration from Utrecht Psalter, Psalm 57

and trust in time of trouble. While the text begins with the words *Miserere mei*, the psalmist quickly moves to voice confidence in God's care. The exuberant drawing at the bottom of the page is existential, expressing the terror of the psalmist's situation, and, at the same time, the wonder of God's protection. Vigorous, rhythmic lines crisscross each other, creating several spatial zones. God and the heavenly host. Visually reign above. At the center is the psalmist who is "among lions." Below him are the enemies who have fallen into a pit dug by themselves, but intended for the psalmist. To the right and left are the "attackers," armed with bows and arrows and lances.

The Imaged Word 143

University Library, Utrecht, Ms. 32, fol. 32r. Reprinted with permission.

Figure 2: Detail from Figure 1, Psalm 57

The central figure, in the shadow of angelic wings, faces upward toward heaven in a gesture of praise: "May you, my God, be honored above the heavens; may your glory be seen everywhere on earth" (Psalm 57.11 CEV).

Although the imagery clearly has a narrative function, the figures are not positioned in a fixed theatrical space; nor are they staged on a particular plane. Instead, dynamic, black and white vignettes range freely in a visual poetic motion that parallels the rhythm of the text. As words and images move together, the lines themselves seem to sing: "I feel wide awake! I will wake up my harp and wake up the sun" (Psalm 57.8, CEV). In this illumination, words and drawing seem inseparable; indeed, the lines seem to perform the text rather than simply illustrate it.

Here, too, we find implications for the issue of translational fidelity. Like the images in the Rossano Gospels, those of the Utrecht Psalter reinforce the subject matter of the biblical text, thus preserving a unity between word and image. This unity is also mirrored in the dynamic, linear motion and rhythms of the visual style that parallel the poetic voice of the Psalm text. At the same time, the unusually expressive technique of this ninth-century black and white pen drawing revitalizes and gives fresh meaning to ancient words.

Book of Kells

In the illuminations of the Book of Kells we see another type of integration of word and image, one that is more abstract than either the Utrecht Psalter or the Rossano Gospels. Dating from the late eighth or early ninth century, the exact origin of the manuscript is still debated. Some scholars believe it was made in Iona, Argyll; others believe it originated in Kells in Ireland. Some believe that work on the manuscript was started in Iona and taken up again in Kells as the community fled from the assaults of the Vikings.

The Board of Trinity College Dublin, reprinted with permission.
Figure 3: Arrest of Christ, Book of Kells

The pages in the Book of Kells are comparatively large, measuring 13 by 9½ inches. Unlike manuscripts in which artists tried carefully to follow the classical models, the Book of Kells represents a stunning example of the insular tradition—an ornamental, rather than narrative art form. Thus, the use of the human figure was minimal and always highly abstracted. Primary attention was given to pattern and surface detail, characteristic of the ornamental art that adorned their weapons and garments. When artists in the scriptoria of the northern monasteries began to transpose to illuminated manuscripts the geometric shapes of jewelry and the dynamic, organic forms of nature, the figural art of the Mediterranean tradition was significantly transformed.

Two pages exemplify the unusual, ornamental integration of text and image present in the Book of Kells. One full-page illustration depicts the arrest of Christ. (See Figure 3, page 144.) Characteristic of the insular tradition, the dramatic action is framed by an ornamental border; however, here the border takes on an architectural quality. It is open at the bottom and two columns form the right and left boundaries of the frame. Unlike any kind of classical columnar order, the columns are a composite of geometric shapes, within which are interlocking spirals. Moreover, two arcs spearheaded by an abstracted animal head spring from the capital shapes. These meet at the center and the interlacing tongues of the animals wedge the two arcs into a semicircle. The text lies inside this architecturally prescribed half-circle, flanked by swirling curvilinear floral forms.

Within the fantastic archway and beneath the text is the visual drama of Jesus' arrest. Placed in the center of the composition, Jesus is hemmed in by a soldier to his right and left; each has grasped one of his uplifted arms. Larger than the other two figures, Jesus looks straight ahead, directly confronting the viewer. Turned toward Jesus, the soldiers' faces are seen in profile. Their clothing is represented primarily through pattern; robes are flattened and organized by lines that suggest the movement of the figures. Even though he is being seized by the soldiers, Jesus is portrayed as a figure of authority. Extraordinary visual elements—the frontal position of Christ, the piercing eyes, the intensity of color, the forcible linear design of his garments—all transform this central figure into a powerful icon.

More remarkable still is a visual pattern that signals the crucifixion that will soon follow (see Figure 4, page 146). If one carefully studies the directional lines of Jesus' form, it is possible to detect a condensed cross shape. There are blue areas of Jesus' clothing, set off by a contrasting red color of the cloak, establishing the essential linear cross patterns. His outstretched arms extend these further. Beginning then with Jesus' extended arms, one can follow the blue shapes downward and see an implied intersection slightly above the knees that are pulled inward. Then the diagonal linear forms move downward to complete an elongated X-shaped cross.

Like other illuminations in the Book of Kells, the border of the Crucifixion page functions almost like a mandala, defining sacred space. Its essential shape seems rectangular, but it leaps in and out to form subordinated geometric shapes. Two of these surprise detours are on the right; each forms a small rectangular area where we see the heads and shoulders of a small group of people. On the left there is another similar grouping of human faces. Closer examination reveals that the meandering, rectangular border is really a fantastic creature that frames the page. From its mouth come flaming curvilinear lines that weld together the beginning and end of the ornamental border. Springing from this creature is a large decorative capital letter, intricately designed with abstract interlacing and small fantastic figures. Here begins the text.

The Board of Trinity College Dublin, reprinted with permission.
Figure 4: Crucifixion Page, Book of Kells

In this illumination, however, the text is more than text. The artist has shaped letters into a visual object. On this page are several words, the last ones forming an "X"-cross which fills almost half of the lower part of the page. Text is visually transformed and *becomes* image: the cross. The visual and verbal are fused into one cohesive symbol of the brutal climax of the Incarnation. Yet, except for the three little groups tucked into the border, there are no visual references to human beings. Moreover, fantasy, even humor, continues to run wild in the playful ornamental border. At the same time, the abstraction, the imaged word of the cross, has become a stark and terrifying witness to the horror and despair of the crucifixion of Jesus.

The paucity of narrative human figures, and the use of geometric abstractions, fantastic organic forms, and ornamental frames indicate how far this manuscript has moved from the visual vocabulary and syntax of the classical aesthetic. Moreover, just within these three illuminated manuscripts—the Rossano Gospels, the Utrecht Psalter, and the Book of Kells—we have a striking diversity of style and creative impulse. In the Book of Kells, the figures are defined by flat patterns of color within stylized shapes; there is no attempt, as in the Rossano Gospels, to suggest spatial depth or particular scenes. Likewise, the size and treatment of the figures in the Book of Kells contrast with those of the Utrecht Psalter. In short, the manuscripts we have seen illustrate a surprising range of aesthetic orders used to combine word and image in the creation of religious meaning.

This new visual vocabulary and syntax of the Book of Kells raises again the issue of fidelity in a visual medium. How does this use of visual space convey meaning? How does its meaning relate to the meaning of the original text? Does the fusion between text and image in the cross (the lexical and the illustrative) capture some essential unifying moment in the narrative and transfer its meaning to a new medium or create a new meaning altogether?

Biblia Pauperum

During the 14th century, illuminators and wood block engravers began to adapt images seen on church walls and to transpose them to pages which were then made into a form of book. In his study of the history of reading, Alberto Manguel has called attention to the popularity of these large picture books. Accessible to the poor, the books juxtaposed scenes, using words only minimally. These few words appeared as captions on the page, or were sometimes given the treatment we have seen in modern cartoon strips (1996, p. 101). According to Manguel:

> Chained to a lectern, opened to an appropriate page, the Biblia Pauperum would display its double images to the faithful sequentially, day after day, month after month. Many would not be able to read the words in Gothic script surrounding the depicted personages; few would grasp the several meanings of each image in their historical, moral, and allegorical significance. But the majority of the people would recognize

most of the characters and scenes, and be able to "read" in those images a relationship between the stories of the Old Testament and the stories of the New, simply because of their juxtaposition on the page. (p. 103)

While some have argued that the Biblia Pauperum was primarily intended as a thematic guide to prompt the priest, Manguel counters that no document exists to confirm its purpose; these large picture books, he contends, probably had many different functions and readers. Most importantly, the books allowed Christians familiar with the stories to enter and participate in an iconographical universe of text and image.

From early Christian communities through the development of late medieval culture, the integration of image and text took place in liturgical spaces and in illuminated books. Over these several centuries, this integration gives witness to continual innovations in style and to shifting emphases in religious symbolism as well. These innovations reflected changes in the church's role in society; they were likewise generated by shifts in translation and liturgical practice. And, of course, innovations arose from the creative imagination of artists and architects as they shaped liturgical spaces and crafted illuminated books. From the brief selection of images presented, we catch only a fleeting glimpse of the spectrum of styles and formal relationships between image and text.

Following the Reformation and the development of the printed book, the contexts for combining visual representations and words were dramatically altered. In the 16th century, radical religious reformers emptied churches of paintings and sculptures. Later, sanctuaries in many predominantly Protestant countries were no longer adorned with visual images, and artists turned to other subjects and patrons. Painters interested in religious themes depicted biblical subjects on portable panels or turned to print making. Rembrandt, for example, continued to explore religious themes both in his paintings and etchings. As revolutionary printing technologies appeared, new opportunities for book illustration arose. By the 19th century, the illustrated Bible reintroduced religious imagery into a Protestant ethos. To reflect on these changes, we will look at some facets of 19th-century American culture.

Reforming Image and Text

The formidable Reformation leaders, Ulrich Zwingli and John Calvin, would have been pleased with the kind of architectural space developed by some of their followers who settled in America. While churches in Geneva and Zurich had to be whitewashed and stripped of images, in New England there was no legacy of medieval art and architecture to reform. Puritan settlers could start afresh to build churches according to principles of worship established by Zwingli and Calvin. Neither reformer, however, would have objected to religious painting and sculpture outside of the worship space.

Their rejection of art was specific to liturgical and devotional functions: Art was not to be used to assist or enhance worship. Calvin, for example, did acknowledge that the visual arts might be useful in narrating historical events, both religious and secular.

Even though the reform leaders would tolerate art outside of a liturgical context, many settlers of the New World brought with them additional objections and prejudices about the visual arts. Fleeing from oppressive authorities, many associated the visual arts with intolerant political and religious institutions and with the privileges of wealth. Thus, in the early years of American culture it was difficult for visual artists to find work, and those who desired to depict religious motifs felt the difficulty more acutely. Outside of a meager demand for portraiture and the decorative and serviceable arts, they found little demand for their profession in the predominantly Protestant sections of the country.

In Search of Religious Symbols

In the early 19th century, several American artists sought to find appropriate subject matter for the nation's religious and democratic principles. Two painters—Washington Allston (1749-1843) and Thomas Cole (1801-1848), for example—wished to use the Bible as a primary source for subject matter and symbols. Allston was approached about a commissioned painting for the rotunda of the United States's Capitol. In his correspondence, the artist made it clear that he did not want to do "battle-pieces." Nor, he said, could he think of an appropriate subject from American history that "belongs to high art." Indeed, for this painter the Bible was the appropriate source of subject matter for the Capitol project. "This is a Christian land," wrote Allston, "and the Scriptures belong to no country, but to man. The facts they record come home to all men, to the high and the low, the wise and simple....Should the Government allow me to select a subject from them [Scriptures], I need not say with what delight I should accept the commission" (Flagg, 1892/1969, p. 233). However, unable to come to an agreement on subject matter, Allston turned down a commission eagerly sought by his contemporaries. Allston, who was deeply influenced by Samuel Taylor Coleridge, turned increasingly to philosophy and to lectures on art.

Thomas Cole, Allston's younger contemporary, also wanted to create paintings that could evoke strong moral and religious feelings. In pursuit of these artistic goals, he frequently turned to biblical subjects. At the same time, the painter was deeply committed to the natural environment, taking long walks through the Adirondacks, filling his sketchbooks with drawings and notes of his observations. In 1825, Cole's work came to the attention of John Trumbull, William Dunlop, and Asher B. Durand, all respected artists who discerned in Cole's landscapes an exceptional talent. Cole's paintings were introduced to a wider public audience at an 1828 exhibition of the National Academy of Design. Along with his landscapes were two works he referred to as a "higher style of landscape." The subject of one was the biblical story of the Garden of Eden; the other was entitled The Expulsion from the Garden.

The Expulsion from the Garden of Eden (1827-1828) tells its story almost entirely through elements of landscape. When viewed from a distance, the painting appears to be a dramatic composition of light and dark. Rays of light break through an opening in the center of the composition to illuminate the garden. Crossing over into the world of toil and death, Adam and Eve confront dark forms whose rugged, torn contours are illuminated only by the brilliant glow from the portal. Instead of the magnificence of Eden, they walk into a grotesque landscape in which all of nature is embattled. Trees are ravished and uprooted by storms. Stags that leapt playfully in Eden are now being devoured by a beast; a vulture awaits the carnage. The cactus has replaced the lotus of Eden. The only illumination outside Paradise is generated by nature's violence—a volcano and lightening bolt in the far distance. Although the human plight is central to the biblical story, here Adam and Eve are relatively small figures in the composition. Natural forms have assumed the principal role in conveying the meaning of this visually-narrated scene from Genesis.

Cole had an unusual eye for the grandeur of the environment, and his landscapes found a wide, appreciative audience. In an "Essay on American Scenery" (1836), he wrote movingly about the special privilege of artists in this country who might view nature fresh from creation. Cole was widely celebrated for his landscapes that could evoke all the particular wonders of American nature. While the painter's biblical and mythological themes were appreciated by fellow artists and intellectuals, they were not generally popular. Cole frequently expressed disappointment about the public's preference for his "views" and the failure of his religious compositions to sell. During his career, he constantly sought patronage for his religious and allegorical paintings. (See Noble, 1853/1964, p. 159).

Cole, like Allston, was also a writer, and we learn a great deal about his concern for religious art through his journal, miscellaneous notes, and letters. After his death his letters and journals were compiled and edited by Legrand Noble and published in 1853. These writings, together with his paintings, show the hopes and frustrations of a painter who wanted to produce art that was distinctly religious. He was a traditionalist who believed that paintings fulfilled an important function in churches. Even though people were no longer dependent upon pictures for learning Christian Scripture, Cole was convinced that painting and sculpture could continue to perform a teaching role. Recalling the place of images in early Christianity, he suggested that 19th-century Protestants visit the catacombs to learn about the early consecration of art. He sharply criticized the church for rejecting painting and sculpture in places of worship, arguing that the principles that guided Christian art and architecture through the centuries could still be useful for this new country. He noted that while serviceable arts and utilitarian forms contributed to the well being of a society, they did not meet its spiritual needs. Spirituality was, in Cole's view, the responsibility of the fine arts. If American artists were not at work for the church, it was not, he contended, that they lacked the capacity for important religious art, but only that they lacked the opportunity (Cole, unpublished notes).

If painters like Allston and Cole were frustrated by the lack of demand for religious paintings and liturgical art, the sacramental functions of images to render visible an invisible faith were finding other channels. By the 19th century, the art and science of printing had developed significantly; illustration techniques included lithography as well as traditional engraving. These and later printing technologies would have considerable effects upon the expression of religious sentiments. The depiction of humanistic religious epics, the subject matter which Allston and Cole so earnestly wanted to paint, found a viable context in the production of large illustrated family Bibles.

Historian Colleen McDannell has examined in rich detail an inclusive spectrum of popular religious art forms—statuary, cards, vials of holy water, cemeteries, posters, illustrations, Bibles and a host of religious objects that frequently fall between the cracks in traditional histories of art. Sorting through an abundance of artifacts associated with popular Protestant and Catholic Christianity in America, she emphasizes the relationship between religious belief and its material manifestations. These connections have often been neglected in the study of American Protestantism:

> What is needed is a more nuanced understanding of the relationship between body and mind, word and image. As "multimedia events," religious practices are areas where speech, vision, gesture, touch, and sound combine. The assumption that Protestantism broke the Word/words away from visual or tactile perception is not correct. A radical division may have been intended but not entirely achieved. (1995, p. 14)

Of particular importance for our concern with religious text and image is McDannell's analysis of the Bible as a primary devotional object, embedded at the center of family religious life and rituals. "There can be no doubt," she writes, "that during the 19th century, Protestants, black and white, rich and poor, owned Bibles. The peak years (1810-1870) of both ABS Bible distribution and commercial Bible publishing paralleled the extraordinary growth of Protestant denominational institutions" (p. 72). Bibles printed without images, such as those published by the ABS, were satisfactory for ordinary reading and study. McDannell observes, however, that a large number of Bibles sold were used in additional ways. "No longer merely a religious tool, the Bible became a revered possession that activated sentiments and memory. Bibles assumed qualities that transformed them from acting as a saving text to functioning as a saving object" (p. 73).

By the end of the 19th century, however, the popularity of these large family Bibles had declined. The sense of the tomes as holy objects of family ritual diminished; they returned to "being a source of sacred scriptures" and "spiritual uplift" (p. 101).

Formulating Religious Art

Although the elaborately illustrated Bibles went out of fashion, the visual styles developed for their religious narratives and supplementary studies have continued into the 20th century. Even as 20th-century artists and revolutionary technologies (film, color photography and printing, television) began to change our imagistic world, the characterization of religious figures and depiction of biblical stories continued to follow the 19th-century aesthetic. This traditional academic style has arguably become a kind of artistic canon. Predominant for over a century, especially in the United States, it is now almost synonymous with "religious art." In fact, that aesthetic is so deeply entrenched that it is difficult for artists to offer alternative representations of religious subjects.

Though admittedly there has been some development and change, 19th-century Bible illustrations serve as prototypes for a dominant form of religious art. To understand better the aesthetic involved, we will examine the visual vocabulary and syntax of these illustrations. In addition, we will compare and contrast this style with biblical representations of earlier centuries. The purpose of this comparative study is both to place the current formulation of religious art into a broader perspective, as well as to formulate the question of fidelity in terms of 19th-century Bible translation and illustration.

The library of the ABS holds two "Sampler" Bibles. Large in size, measuring about 14 by 20 inches, these books present a collection of features from which selections could be made to form a composite Bible of one's choice. These were issued by Bell & Parsons in Columbia, South Carolina, with 10 copyrights secured from 1872-1885 and published by P. W. Ziegler & Company, Philadelphia and Boston, 1886. An inserted note advises: "The agent should make himself familiar with all the features, and mark all to which he wishes to refer. Be sure to have an appropriate word for every important thing" (American Bible Society, 1886, first notice). Inserted at intervals are pink printed notes specifying the various combinations of texts and illustrations that could make up as many as six variations of the "PICTORIAL FAMILY BIBLE." (See Figure 5.) All of the styles offer a basic choice of the "King James Old Version alone" or a combination of it and the "Revised Version of THE OLD and NEW TESTAMENTS in PARALLEL COLUMNS."

The basic selection, Style 1, offered the following: "over 90 valuable Scriptural tables or helps to study the Bible"; "Brown's Concordance"; "a history of all Religious Denominations"; "a marriage certificate and Family Record"; "20 full page engravings from the famous designs of Doré and other celebrated artists"; "TWO ILLUMINATED PLATES, a Temperance Pledge and a Presentation Plate"; and "THREE COLORED MAPS." Billed as a "Complete Cyclopoedia of Biblical Knowledge," additional features could be chosen to form more complex styles, such as full-page engravings of the "PARABLES OF OUR LORD"; "Scenes and Incidents in the Lives of the Patriarchs, Prophets, and Kings of the Bible"; "Illustrated Scenes and Events in

The Imaged Word 153

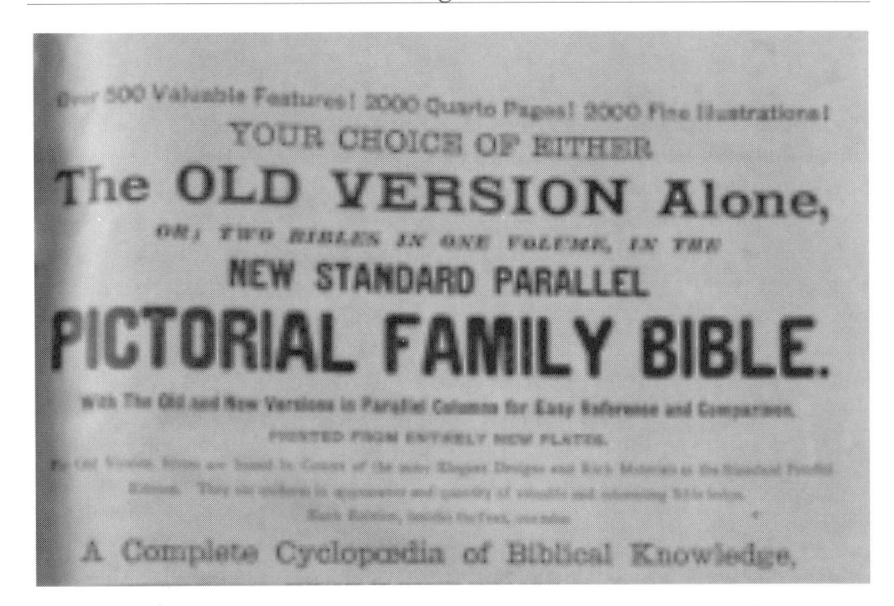

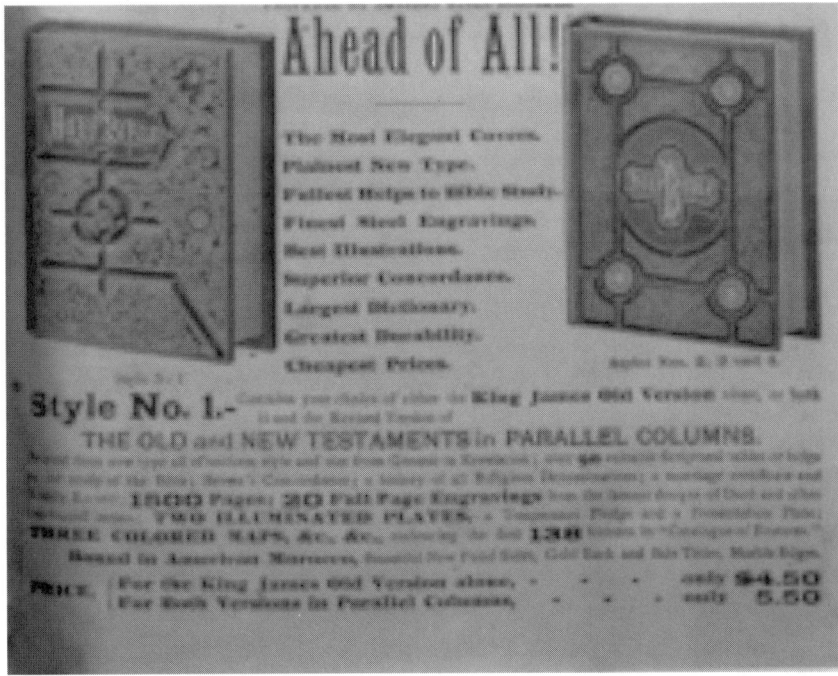

©American Bible Society, reprinted with permission.
Figure 5: Title page for ABS's Pictorial Family Bible.

the LIFE OF CHRIST"; and, "ILLUSTRATED SCENES AND EVENTS IN THE LIFE OF ST. PAUL" (Style number 3 notice).

The Picture Galleries

Both Sampler Bibles in the ABS library have a "Doré Gallery" from which illustrations may be selected. Gustave Doré (1832-1883), a French illustrator widely acclaimed for his draftsmanship, was particularly famous for his depiction of biblical stories. In addition to the ABS Sampler Bible (1865), he also illustrated, for example, Dante's *Inferno* (1861), Cervantes's *Don Quixote* (1863), and Milton's *Paradise Lost* (1886). Doré also painted and sculpted. In his large paintings, he generally worked with biblical and historical themes, paralleling the subjects he had explored as an illustrator. For the illustrated Bibles, Doré drew directly on wood blocks which were then engraved by artisans whose names appear on the right of the print. Thus the biblical illustrations retain a vital, direct connection with the artist's own vision.

While Doré was not trained in an art academy, his extraordinary mastery of figure drawing lent itself to the creation of pictorial dramas in which the human figure was the basic carrier of meaning. Although the artist may not have been familiar with the *Discourses on Art* of Sir Joshua Reynolds (1723-1792), Doré's treatment would have pleased the English academician. The features have been generalized to represent certain ideal human types. There are no eccentric particularities in the faces or figures. Biblical scenes are composed so that the viewer stands just inside the foreground of the picture, looking forward into the middle plane, and further into a distant background. The action was typically staged in an architectural or landscape setting, depending upon the biblical story. Doré's spatial compositions and use of idealized figures reflect a classical aesthetic that had been reinstated and refined by Renaissance artists. His skillful and dramatic images of biblical themes set the style of biblical illustration for decades to come.

Among the scenes in the Doré Picture Gallery of the 1896 Sampler Bible is The Judgment of Solomon (1 Kings 3.16-28). (See Figure 6.) The artist depicts the action in a courtly architectural setting. His left arm raised, Solomon is the commanding figure. Standing in a magisterial niche, between two fluted classical columns and framed against a richly decorated wall, Solomon is placed high above the other figures in the scene. Beneath the steps leading up to his platform are the other major players: the two women who are claiming the child, and one of Solomon's military officers, standing with his sword already drawn and holding the child aloft. He looks toward Solomon, awaiting the fatal command to sever the infant. The true mother has flung herself on the officer, clutching at his breast plate with one hand, while with the other she almost touches the sword in her struggle to reach the child. To the leftt of the composition is a second woman; she looks on passively, gazing down, focused on the one who has thrown herself against the soldier to protect the infant. Other figures, to the right and left in the middle ground of the engraving, occupy the space between Solomon and the major characters. Two lances on the right suggest the presence of other military figures.

The distribution of light in the illustration is effective in crystallizing the moment of crisis. Most brightly illuminated are the figures of the soldier and the real mother. The darkest figure in the composition—even darker than most of the figures in the middle area—is the false mother. The king,

Figure 6: Judgment of Solomon from ABS Sampler Bible.

while lighter than most other figures, still appears somewhat more shaded than the soldier and the pleading mother. The four major figures taken together form an ovoid shape, suggesting the emotional tension circulating amongst them.

In this composition, the artist has used human figures, particularly their definition and gestures, to capture the critical moments of the text which lead Solomon to his decision. The woman who, in the textual biblical account, screams and agrees to give up the child is depicted as she throws herself at the soldier and grasps upward. The false mother, who asks that the child be cut in half, is cast in darkness and stands withdrawn from the other major figures. Using the dramatic potential of human figures, the artist has substituted visual action as an equivalency for words.

Doré and others domesticated the 19th-century academic style for its use in prints and illustration. More importantly, Doré's widely acclaimed success in biblical subjects established a prototype for images of Jesus and biblical heroes. In an example from the 1885 Sampler Bible, Jesus Healing the Sick (Matthew 4.24), we see a portrait of Jesus that became standardized in religious publications, continuing late into the 20th century. (See Figure 7.) The composition reinforces the repeated emphasis of the text on Jesus' healing power. "He also healed every kind of disease and sickness" (Matthew 4.23, CEV), "and people with every kind of sickness or disease were brought to him" (Matthew 4.24b, CEV). The figure of Jesus is almost exactly in the center. Seen in profile, he reaches out to touch the sick. His right hand gently enfolds the forehead of a small boy, held in the arms of an older woman who has lowered the youth so that he may be touched. Jesus' left hand moves toward another man struggling to raise his body to meet the healing hand. To emphasize the dramatic presence of Jesus, the artist has organized the figures of the sick and diseased so that they circulate around him as they await healing. In the upper left of the illustration, another woman supports a slightly older youth; the eyes of both are focused on Jesus' hands. The figures on the left thus establish a sweeping curve which is met at the bottom of the picture by another group of older figures. A crutch accents the diagonal thrust of the one who lurches upward toward Jesus. Another man lying prone is supported so that he may look up at the healer. On the right, an upright figure supports himself with a crutch. His vertical position leads the eye upward again to two stalwart individuals. Their position and appearance suggest that they might be disciples. In the background, at the top left section of the design, two decorated columns with lintel place the crowded scene in an architectural setting.

The faces and figures of each person in the composition—including those of the diseased—are carefully abstracted and generalized. Most idealized are the features of Jesus and the two robust men standing behind him, presumably disciples. Both stand tall, pensive, and attentive; the bare arm of one is tight and muscular. The kneeling, robed figure of Jesus is the brightest area of the composition. Lean hands, elegantly tapered fingers, and

Figure 7: Jesus Healing the Sick, from the ABS Sampler Bible.

gentle gestures distinguish his persona from the others. The artist has carefully refined the facial features of Jesus. More idealized than any of the others in the composition, his profile is crisply drawn with clear, sharp lines. The contour lines seem to indicate, like many academic models, a synthesis of classical Greek features: the clean line of the forehead; deep set eyes; flawless, straight nose; cleanly chiseled mouth and chin. The hair of Jesus is wavy and flows neatly to his shoulders. Somewhat less robust than the men standing behind him, Jesus appears younger and intensely focused on the persons around him.

Doré's masterful figurative design became exemplary for other biblical illustrators. The various editions of Sampler Bibles offer examples of

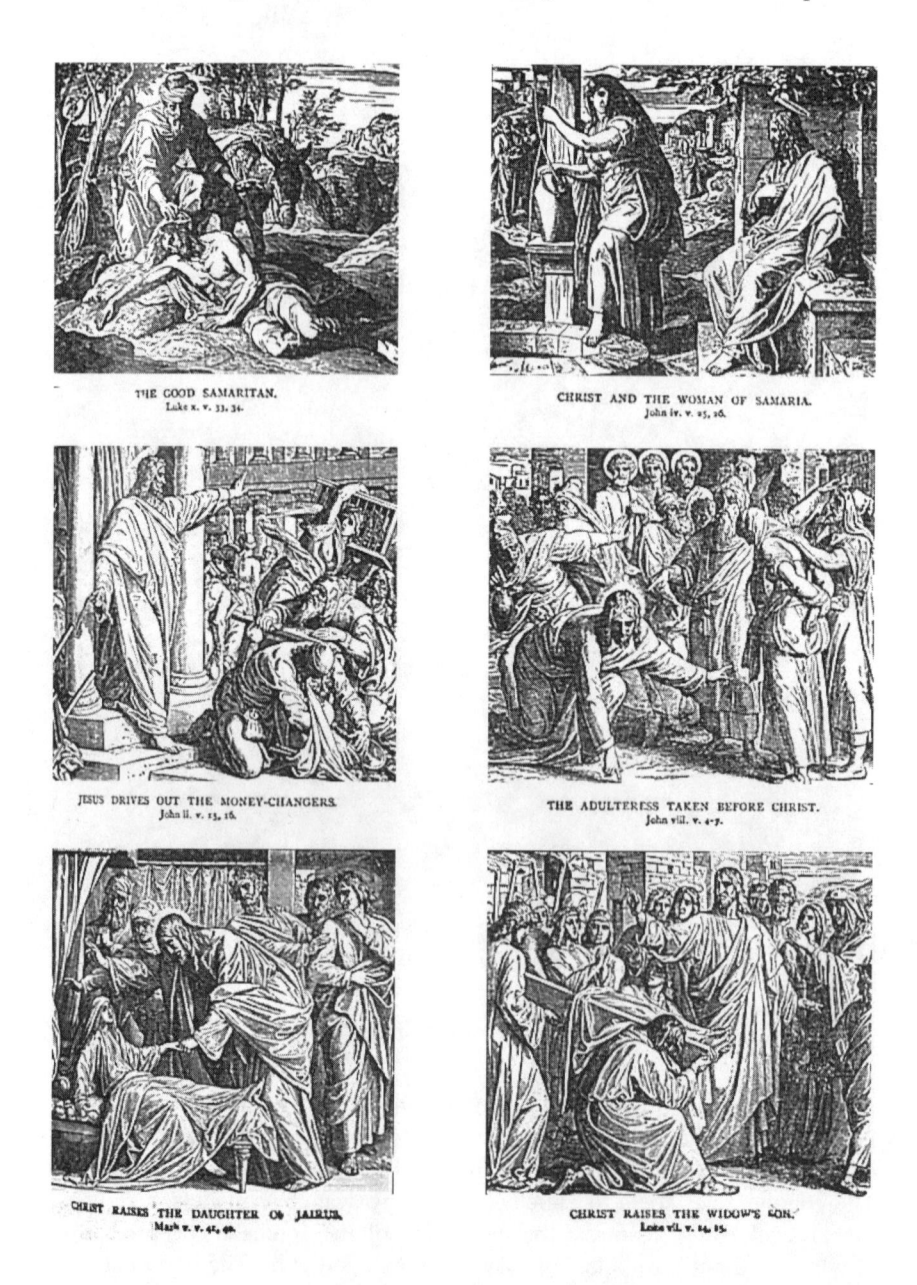

©American Bible Society, reprinted with permission.
Figure 8: A six-illustration page from the 1886 ABS Sampler Bible, p. 9.

other artists in "THE GALLERY OF SCRIPTURE ILLUSTRATIONS." Their depictions of biblical scenes bear a striking resemblance to those done by Doré. Some of these illustrations occupy a full page, but smaller ones were also available for inclusion in particular editions. One sampler page (Figure 8), for example, contains six small illustrations. Five depict events in Jesus' ministry: Christ and the Woman of Samaria (John 4.25-26); Jesus Drives Out the Money-Changers (John 2.15-16.); The Adulteress Taken Before Christ (John 8.4-7); Christ Raises the Daughter of Jarius (Mark 5.41-42); and Christ Raises the Widow's Son (Luke 7.14-15). The final one, the first in the grouping, illustrates the parable of the Good Samaritan (Luke 10.33-34).

Since the representations are considerably smaller, detailed linear work is restricted. Certain stylistic features, however, do echo the formula of academic art. In each frame, the figures narrate the dramatic moment of the story, and the settings are rendered in perspective, defining the space of the action. In one frame, a classical architectural setting places Jesus at the entry of the temple, while the four figures in the right foreground cringe as he drives them out. In the background of the illustration, smaller figures help define distance, and two levels of columns locate the temple and action in a public meeting place. In two other frames, The Good Samaritan and Christ and the Woman of Samaria, distant landscapes identify the location of the action. The central figures occupy the foreground so that the viewer focuses on the interaction of the two major figures of the story.

Like the larger illustrations, human action—gestures and expressions—narrate the stories. In the Christ Raises the Widow's Son, for example, about 14 distinct figures look on as the widow's son is raised. Yet, the monumental figure of Jesus dominates; nearby four disciples, now easily identified by their halos, stand supportively behind him. Equally crowded with figures is the scene in which the adulteress is taken before Christ, who is depicted on the left side of the composition as he writes on the ground. On the right stands the woman and her accusers. One can surmise, however, that Jesus has already stood up and said, "If any of you have never sinned, then go ahead and throw the first stone at her!" Here he bends over for the second time to write with his finger on the ground. Behind the figure of Jesus, the woman's accusers have begun to leave one by one (anticipating the moment in the narrative when Jesus and the woman are there alone.) Although not mentioned in the text, the haloed disciples appear in the background.

In all of these small illustrations, the features of Jesus are generalized and idealized; his monumental figure is both serene and authoritative. The idealization is equally characteristic in the depiction of apostles, though the use of the halos sharply distinguishes them in the crowd. Indeed, most of the participants in these pictorial dramas are represented in stylized robes and are well-proportioned according to academic standards. Only in the faces of the money-changers and the accusers of the woman do we pick up shifty eyes and grimacing mouths that suggest mean or greedy spirits.

Realism, even caricature, emerges in the treatment of some characters in stories. The figures of Jesus and his disciples, however, are consistently idealized.

The idealization of facial features is particularly evident in another section of the Sampler Bible entitled "Lives, Transactions, Sufferings and Martyrdom of the Holy Apostles and Evangelists of Our Savior Jesus Christ" by Rev. W. F. B. Jackson. Small vignette portraits, executed in great detail, are inserted within the text. A careful look reveals the artists' attachment to the humanist models of academic art. A pensive portrait of Peter appears on the opening page of the article. Looking outward, the face is turned enough to display the clear sharp lines of forehead, brows, and a straight, shapely nose; a neatly tapered beard suggests his strong jaw and chin. Peter's graying hair is somewhat wavy and short; and the contour of his hairline adds to the portrayal of a mature man. Similar stylistic conventions are used in the portrait of Paul. Given a bushy beard and somewhat darker, thicker hair, Paul, turning now in the opposite direction, is positioned so that we see similar clear features of strong brow, nose, chin and fixed gaze.

While the illustrations of biblical passages vary in scale, there is little variation in style. A heroic humanism, developed as a canon of style and taste in 19th-century art academies, found its way into religious publishing and became the established syntax for "religious art." Thus, in a variety of formats—from full-page designs to small portraits—biblical stories are visually narrated through representations of idealized forms. Human figures—their gestures and facial expressions—and spatial perspective are composed into a visual narrative, capturing a key moment in a particular passage.

Other types of visual representations in the Sampler Bible functioned essentially as study helps for readers. These illustrative aids were typically executed in small line drawings and grouped together on a full page. Definitional drawings, they depict in a simple linear technique the details of ordinary life in ancient times. They illustrate customs and rites, and feature ornaments, tools, coins, and other familiar objects of everyday life in the ancient world. Frequently the line drawings are based on representations of art objects in Near Eastern and Egyptian cultures. In putting together a family Bible, one could also choose from the Sampler small illustrations of the flora and fauna and animals of biblical times. Some of these educational features, however, were large full-page color lithographs. One, for example, shows a priest fully attired with the breastplate and vestments worn within the temple. The colored illustration is entitled: "Furniture of the Tabernacle." The function is to provide visual information as directly as possible. Note, for example, the liturgical vessels lined up horizontally at the bottom of the composition. While there is some use of perspective to place people and objects in space, the primary goal is to identify or define discrete objects, not to dramatize the biblical texts. Definitional illustrations take objects out of their literary context. Unlike the narrative illustrations of Doré and others, these images perform an educational role enabling the reader to understand better the historical and cultural contexts of the Bible.

Text and image coexist on separate levels—in a nonintegrated form of communication. The biblical illustrations in the Sampler Bible exemplify how text and image developed a relationship of coexistence, almost as two modes of translation. Unlike the integrations of word and image seen in some medieval illuminations, the later printed Bibles allow word and image to occupy separate domains. As autonomous forms, words and images were given their own independent spaces, brought together, and bound as a book. The unifying principle of the printed book, which frequently encourages and accommodates a bifurcation of the visual and verbal, remains to this day a convenient form for translators who want to work with images and texts. Thus, with modern printing techniques, illustrated Bibles became lavishly adorned with full-color plates of biblical scenes and events.

Doré's visual treatment of biblical scenes raises interesting questions about fidelity and the criteria for measuring fidelity. Over time, the academic models he perfected have become an official canon of so-called religious art. Indeed, Doré's style, repeatedly copied, is now viewed by many as a symbol of fidelity, an authoritative genre for the transfer of religious meanings. The gestural and figural relationships he worked out have over decades ossified into a visual vocabulary and syntax for biblical illustrations. Is it possible that such canonization of a particular style for "religious art" has become an obstacle to fidelity?

Influence of Doré

Even though the popularity of encyclopedic family Bibles waned, the pictorial aesthetic formulated in them would endure into the 20th century. The large family Bibles were not the only public context for Doré's illustrations. In 1879, for example, The Fine Art Publishing Company in New York brought out *The Doré Bible Gallery*. The book contained 100 pictures and an accompanying explanatory page for each illustration. Such works not only contributed to Doré's popularity, but more importantly, they established a style of "religious art," particularly in the United States. As more sophisticated and cheaper processes of color printing developed in the present century, publishers focused on updating and refining 19th-century models whenever the need for "religious art" arose. This domesticated academic aesthetic thus became the basic and distinguishing style for visualizing religious texts. As late as 1993-1996, for example, the Russian Bible Society brought out a complete edition of Doré's biblical illustrations.

One can reasonably speculate that these dramatic biblical scenes and epic panoramas were an invaluable stimulus to movie makers. Just imagine, for example, how suggestive the Doré illustrations would have been to Hollywood producers like Cecil B. De Mille! Doré's great figural compositions might readily serve as a set of story boards for the Hollywood directors of a religious extravaganza. Doré's "The Tower of Babel" (Genesis 11.1-9), for example, contains many visual elements that would easily transpose to film. Organized spatially into zones that move from foreground to background, the groupings of figures narrate the biblical story. In the distance is a monumental conical structure, encircled by ramps leading to the top. At its base are minuscule figures which provide scale and enable us to grasp the immense size of the tower. Its spectacular height is emphasized by drifting clouds, some of which obscure the uppermost parts of the soaring structure. Though very small, the clusters of figures at the base of the tower suggest the hordes of people needed to build this monument. The scene is rich in details of stone, tools, and implements. Carts laden with huge blocks are drawn by men and oxen; wooden, crane-like forms are at the building site. Near the middle ground are larger figures working and talking together. Closer yet is a group of about eight persons in various cultural attire. Some are fully robed and wear turbans. The dramatic moment of the story is signaled by a single figure. Standing above the others on a large block of stone, he violently thrusts his head backward, stretching his arms and entire torso heavenward. A seated figure next to him bends down to hide his face and cover his head with his hands. Others close by seem astonished and alarmed. Is this the moment when the Lord went down to "confuse them by making them speak different languages"? The moment when pride is converted to humiliation? This and other Doré designs seem to anticipate the technology of sound and movement, a technology that would liberate the theatrical illustration and give the images new life in film.

Whether in epic movies, in illustrated Bibles, or in clip-art, the 19th-century formula for religious art has continued to flourish. Yet, even during the last years of Doré's career as an illustrator, monumental changes were occurring in art theory and practice. The academic formulae for visual representation were being questioned. Some artists forcefully challenged both the academy's aesthetic and its educative program. Impressionist artists, and later, post-impressionist painters eventually abandoned its canon of style and subject matter. By the end of the 19th century, few modern American or European artists were choosing biblical themes. The deep commitment of Cole and Allston to religious subjects was a thing of the past.

To be sure, an aging Albert P. Ryder did continue to do small, heavily painted panels of biblical motifs; but late 19th-century artists with religious sensibilities had begun to explore other kinds of symbols in communicating religious meanings. In the United States, George Inness, like the European painter Vincent van Gogh, sought to express in his landscape painting the presence of transcendent being in nature. In Europe, George Rouault, passionately interested in religious imagery, radically altered his painting style during the first decade of the 20th century. He moved from an academic style to a harsher, more expressionist rendering of biblical subjects. In addition, Rouault used non-biblical subjects to express biblical themes of suffering and redemption. Later in this century, Jewish artists like Mark Chagall and Ben Shahn developed their own approaches to religious text and image.

These artists, however, proved to be rare iconoclasts to the "canonized" 19th-century aesthetic of religious art.

In light of the dogged endurance of this enshrined academic style, we now want to ask: Has this visual formula become the exclusive way of defining and identifying "religious art"? Are there no other viable ways of envisioning and integrating biblical texts and images?

Re-Visioning Word and Image

One concern of this essay has been to draw attention to the rich syntheses of image and word which arose over time in Christian liturgical spaces and books. References to early church art and illuminated manuscripts were given to show the unique aesthetic forms growing out of particular experiences of faith and culture. Turning, then, to 19th-century America, we saw how illustrated Bibles set the tone and style for religious art in a Protestant ethos. In this final section, the emphasis will again be upon diversity and openness—in style, symbolism, and technology. Using contemporary examples, we will consider alternative ways of combining word and image in religious texts.

Danish Children's Bible

In 1995, the Danish Bible Society published an illustrated children's Bible, *Bibelen: Udvalgte fortaellinger.* The designs vary in size; smaller ones are six inches wide and range from two to three inches in height. A majority of illustrations are larger ones—full pages, without margins, 9 inches high and over 7½ inches wide. The illustrator, Esben Hanefelt Kristensen, creates a biblical world that astonishes us with its wonder and beauty. Not simply for children, adults also can rediscover the inspiration engendered by the ancient narratives.

Two examples indicate the artist's radical departure from stereotypical "religious styles." In his illustration of the Sermon on the Mount, Kristensen gives new life to this well-known New Testament scene. (See Figure 9, page 163.) Jesus sits on a crowning knoll of a small mount. His attentive followers are seated nearby. Gesturing with outstretched arms, Jesus is identified as teacher. His garment is white, while those seated just below him have light blue clothing. These small figures are located within an encompassing landscape. Atop the mount and along its slopes are rhythmic trees; lower down are lilies and flowers of the field. Birds in the air fly with the clouds, while a lone, colorful bird below glides among flowers. Small, stark, black figures, silhouetted against the brilliant colors of the landscape make their way up the mount. Their dark contours reveal a poignant diversity of human beings. Ascending the mount to reach the teacher are the old and bent, the lame, the blind, and mother and child. Below this group, and echoing its

164   *Gregor T. Goethals*

©Danish Bible Society, reprinted with permission.
Figure 9: Sermon on the Mount from Danish Children's Bible.

starkness, one can see black leaves and flowers scattered among more colorful ones.

In this composition, the artist has used pattern and color in a remarkable way. The figures at the top, for example, show very little shadowing, and thus become part of a richly detailed whole. Claiming the viewer's immediate attention, the dark human figures in the lower part of the painting lead the eyes upward to the small figure of the teacher. Along the way the landscape is saturated with a multitude of colors and shapes, woven together into a great tapestry of creation. The repetition and orchestration of simple forms and

©Danish Bible Society, reprinted with permission.
Figure 10: Last Supper from Danish Children's Bible.

colors resonate with the aesthetic of 20th-century artists such as Matisse. At the same time, the playfulness of these forms reminds us of the whimsy and imagination of Paul Klee. In his transformation of 20th-century styles, Kristensen has given new vitality to biblical illustration. Indeed, this Danish artist has done more than "illustrate;" he has created visual and functional equivalents which transfer the meaning of the text through images.

In another full-page illustration, that of The Last Supper, the figures are large and function as dominant design elements. (See Figure 10.) Jesus is the central figure, placed in the middle of the illustration. The table occupies the lower third of the composition and seated around it are the disciples. Since the figures are larger, we get a wealth of detail; nevertheless, the representation of faces and clothing is highly stylized. The features of Jesus and the disciples are Semitic, but greatly simplified. Pattern and color remain major pictorial devices. The figure of Jesus, for example, is framed by a window formed of composite rectangular shapes. Outlining the basic shape of the window are small blue and white squares. Within this rectangle is a smaller, solid blue one which defines the opening through which we see the deep blue light of night. This becomes the dark background against which the light of Jesus' face is seen. Above his head are small stars and the white, glowing shape of the moon, outlined in black. The wall which is pierced by the window is made up of colored, decorative stones, forming a luminous mosaic. The uplifted arms of Jesus—along with the use of light and color—strongly suggest the Pantocrator figure of Eastern Christian art. Almost unconsciously, one recalls the great mosaic of Christ at Cefalu: "I am the light of the world. Whoever follows me will never walk in darkness" (John 8.12, New Revised Standard Version). More prosaic types of religious illustrations usually focus so explicitly and unimaginatively on particular scriptural passages that they limit the depth of a viewer's response. By contrast, Kristensen's Last Supper is evocative and visually links this particular account to other representations, symbols, and texts.

Before his illustrations for the Danish Bible, the artist's work was not well known in Denmark. Since the publication of this illustrated Bible, Kristensen has been widely recognized and acclaimed as one of the country's leading artists. Such recognition is not shared by anonymous illustrators in Hong Kong whose biblical comic books we will examine next. Producing translations for the United Bible Societies (UBS), these anonymous artists are given templates for the visual forms and guidelines for the text within balloons. While the comic books they produce may not appeal to all, this format depends upon a creative integration of word and image.

UBS Scripture Comics

We shall look briefly at one example of the UBS Comics, "Man with a Mission: The Story of Paul," a 34 page, four-color publication measuring approximately 7 by 10 inches. The book's cover presents the dramatic conversion of Paul. (See Figure 11.) A muscular horse, startled by rays of descending light, suddenly rears, nearly throwing the rider who shields his eyes from the blinding light. Another horseman in the background witnesses the spectacle. This cover design does reveal residual elements of the 19th-century academic visual vocabulary and syntax. True, the aesthetic has been simplified, but in this popular genre, it also has been considerably rejuvenated. Like illustrations in 19th-century Bibles, representations of human figures, set in particular spatial contexts, narrate stories through facial expressions, gestures, and action. Except for the robes and beards, the biblical

Figure 11: Conversion of Paul in a Scripture comic.

heroes resemble other comic book heroes; St. Paul, Prince Valiant, and Superman are similarly cast in an idealized style.

Looking at Figure 12 (page 168) will enable us to identify a number of pictorial devices used in these biblical comics. The stories are generally

©United Bible Societies, reprinted with permission.

Figure 12: Page from Scripture comic about life of Paul the Apostle.

presented in sequences of frames. While these frames are typically rectangular, the page layout here has been diversified with lines that zig and zag, defining scenes with oblique angles. Images within these frames are shown in different perspectives: close-up faces, small and large groups of figures, and panoramic vistas. Reflecting the assimilation of a photographic aesthetic, the figures are cropped as though seen through the lens of a camera. Other pages use maps or combinations of maps and figures to illustrate the travels of the apostle. Occasionally, additional information for the viewer/reader is presented in small panels which can supplement the dialogue and help propel the action forward. In the top left corner, for example, is a small rectangle with the text: "After a rest in Tarsus, Paul and Silas crossed the mountain to Derbe."

The defining element of the comic book style is the use of balloons. The balloons, choreographed with the framed images, carry the dialogue of the story; sometimes they indicate the thoughts and feelings of characters. Sounds extraneous to the conversation of the speakers—loud, unexpected noises, for example—are typically presented in very large outlined words that burst into the space of the frame. Using various combinations of balloons and images, these comic books translate in a mode of continuous narrative.

In an unexpected way, the cartoon style has reintroduced the concept of religious text—word and image—as a unified whole. The popular art of comic books draws our attention to new possibilities of aesthetic forms that integrate text and image. Most biblical comic books currently recycle traditional religious art styles. Yet, one can speculate about combining other types of art with biblical passages in a comic-book format which defines "text" as an integrated spatial unity of image and word.

Of course, comics are not the only contemporary genre in which pictorial representations and words form an indivisible whole. This artistic unity is evident in advertising art as well. Producers of commercials long ago rediscovered this communicative power. In TV, as well as in print advertising, word and image merge, simultaneously engaging our attention on both a verbal and visual level. In addition, when word and image are conceived as an indivisible whole, they form a single pattern—a gestalt, or highly integrated structure, whose meaning cannot be derived simply from its individual elements. This way of viewing text and word did not, however, arise suddenly in the 20th century; recall that the Book of Kells gives evidence of a similar formal unity.

ABS New Media Translation Program

In an effort to explore such combinations of text and image, the ABS began, in 1990, research and experimentation in new media translations. (See essay by Hagedorn in this volume; Goethals, 1997; Werner, 1997; and Pettus, 1997.) Working collaboratively, a team of scholars and artists initiated a series of prototypes combining moving images and sound. In our brief review of early forms of Christian communication, we saw how word and image became composite, synthesized forms in ritual and illuminated manuscripts. A primary goal for this ABS research and experimentation was to achieve similar faithful translations through new media, translations that would reflect an aesthetic in which image and word were a symbolic whole—an inclusive text, encompassing moving images, sounds of the human voice, and music.

Conclusion

The discussion of experiments in combining images and texts is not an attempt to foster another stylistic dogma. Rather, it simply presents some alternative ways of incorporating visual representations in biblical translations. These were chosen in part because they were designed for a broad audience. For some, this may signal a shift of focus to "popular" religious art. Throughout this essay, however, there has been a deliberate attempt to avoid the polarization of a "popular" and "high" religious art. Whenever such a simple stylistic evaluation occurs, it is all too easy to defend one or the other on the grounds of education, class, or taste. In addition, the lines between high and popular culture drawn by critics in the past have become irrelevant in the artistic milieu of the last 25 years. The social and cultural conditions which brought into play terms such as "avant garde," "reactionary," "authentic," "traditional," "fine art," and "low-brow art" no longer exist.

Today a more productive discussion might be directed to critical issues in religious symbolism, such as (1) the sacramental role of the visual arts, (2) the possibility of diversified, multicultural styles, and (3) fidelity to biblical messages. Participants in conversations could include translators, religious book publishers, manufacturers of religious artifacts, church leaders, theologians, and artists.

The first issue has been addressed for decades by anthropologists, art historians, and liturgists. Even a casual glance at an introductory art history syllabus will indicate the inextricable relationship between the visual arts and the making of religious meaning. In addition, many theologians, medieval and modern, have reminded us time and again of the human drive to render visible an invisible faith. Yet, it has been hard, as Colleen McDannell has reminded us, for some to recognize and appreciate the sacramental impulse manifest in both Protestant and Catholic popular arts. Through careful documentation and analyses, she argues eloquently against an aesthetic dualism growing out of gender and class.

Even as the sacramental role of the visual arts is being vitally reconsidered, conversations about a diversity of styles are limited, often derailed by debates about marketability—what will sell. As marketing strategies arise, the "taste" of the audience becomes the focus of attention. In the Epilogue of her book, for example, McDannell tells her readers: "We need to take seriously Roland Marchand's quip regarding the need for advertisers to know their audience: 'It isn't the taste of the angler that determines the kind of bait to be used, but the taste of the fish'" (1995, p. 274). She elaborates:

> We already know the "taste of the angler" regarding appropriate art and religion; it is now time to understand the "taste of the fish." Bright

colors, realism, duplication, and sentimentality in Christian art may hold no spiritual appeal for those schooled to appreciate subtle shades, abstraction, singularity, and emotional distance. Those who define art (like religion) as something that challenges and provokes the spirit may find it difficult to understand those Christians who find comfort and reassurance in the familiar. If we define having a personal relationship with an image or object as superstitious anthropocentrism, then we will never understand how these things function in the religious lives of Christians. James Martin writes that "Art is about beauty and religion is about holiness." But, we must ask, who defines the beauty of art and the holiness of religion? (p. 274)

Perhaps the greatest challenge to marketers and art directors—and to the angler/bait/fish concept itself—is the reality that we fish are not all alike, neither in our material predilections, nor in our spirituality. A cookie cutter approach to communication simply cannot do justice to the mystery of religious experience. Indeed, there is an arrogance in the assumption that each and all will be inspired by one single aesthetic—whether that of comic books or abstraction, Mozart or Lawrence Welk. In a growing consciousness of audience diversity, some religious and secular institutions have increasingly utilized focus groups in making decisions about imagery. Yet, the testing is essentially dependent on what is currently presented to them. If, in religious publishing, for example, focus groups receive only the old homogenized images—bearded men, open Bibles, halos, praying hands, and candles—what is to be learned? Except perhaps that they "approve" of what has been marketed as "religious art" for decades. If there are no attempts to experiment with diverse styles, the information gathered is rather useless. If we are to learn something from market testing and focus groups, presentations will need to display and offer a variety of visual forms and styles. Why not develop testing processes that include an openness to symbol, style, and technology?

We began this essay with a question about the role of the visual arts in translation. Our inquiry led us to examine historical and contemporary examples of ways in which word and image were united in order to transfer religious meaning. We have seen that for an artistic vision to be faithful, it must transfer meaning from source to target in a unifying way; that is, it must preserve the interaction between word, sound, and image that makes up the meaning of the texts we translate. Over time, artists within different traditions have created for themselves, and those they represent, unique syntheses of image and word. In this respect, faithfulness in translation also assumes that there are many visions.

Medieval Christendom testifies to such an "open" faithfulness. Art and theology reveal a diversity of image use and text in the transference of religious meanings. Umberto Eco has noted some of the seemingly contradictory dimensions of medieval aesthetics which we today find difficult to reconcile. "Their aesthetics," he writes, "like all their thinking, expressed an optimum synthesis. They saw the world with the eyes of God" (1986, p. 118). Today, experimental translations, which present a total way of knowing (word, music, image), may refresh and renew our concept of faithfulness to text, drawing us, perhaps, deeper into the wonder and mystery of a Creator God.

10

Midrash: A Model for Fidelity in New Media Translation

J. Ritter Werner

The video translations produced by the American Bible Society (ABS) combine three media: text, music, and image. Of the three, music is pivotal. When a video is played, the musical performance sounds the text and informs the images. This is accomplished by setting the words musically, reflecting the text's lexical, syntactical, and rhetorical nuances, and by performing the new composition in such a way that the images can flow in a natural, parallel rhythm. This is a formidable task, since all three media have individual technical and aesthetic requirements to communicate artistically thoughts and feelings to contemporary audiences.

This task is further compounded because biblical communities require that video translations be faithful to the Word as they have received it. This is difficult to do, since the current norms for fidelity are print based, and are not in themselves *una voce*. The performative or imaginative aspects of a biblical text are, for the most part, either ignored or left to personal artistic interpretation.

In an important exception to this general state of affairs, Fry argues convincingly that print-based norms for faithfulness need to be expanded to cover situations in which a biblical text is experienced from "...a range of elements including (but not restricted to) words" (1987, p. 42). He then proceeds to raise issues concerning the dangers inherent in text selection, the options for restructuring texts in non-print media, and the effects of media on the biblical message. At the end of the article Fry cautions:

> In every nonprint presentation, there will not be "equivalence" of the same order as we expect to find when we produce a new text which is in the same medium as the source text. So we probably should not use the term "accuracy" or attempt to define faithfulness in the same terms as for print medium productions. (p. 58)

Shortly after the appearance of Fry's article in the *United Bible Societies Bulletin*, the ABS established a Multimedia Translations Program within its Translations Department, which produced three major new media translations and several minor ones. Each project began with a source-target analysis of the Greek text and established equivalent word-sound-image domains for the linguistic, paralinguistic, and extralinguistic characteristics of the original. This exercise followed guidelines for functional equivalence in biblical translating as established by de Waard & Nida (1986).

Although Nida's work was important in each production, the information gained was skeletal, except for the linguistic parameter. The paralinguistic features of the source text, which marked musical changes of voice, timbre, dynamics, melodic inflection, rhythm, tempo, and form, could only be inferred. The extralinguistic features, which among other things concerned the physical nature of the text and its recital, were even more nebulous. The connections therefore between the source text and the target were tenuous at best. Fry's caution proved true in practice. Equivalence for paralinguistic and extralinguistic parameters were not of the same order as for the linguistic.

This reality did not stop research, but re-directed it to vast secondary musical and artistic sources based on the biblical texts. Early examples were found in liturgical books, ancient sacred spaces, and the patristic writers. Later examples were found in music manuscripts, works of art, and contemporary scholarship. This research enabled the ABS new media team to determine lines of continuity or discontinuity within the tradition that connected the Greek text and the new media productions. It also established a benchmark for making decisions about larger rhetorical issues for text, music, and image.

The introduction of secondary sources, while beneficial to the new media process, raises the question of fidelity. Is Fry correct in his intuition that accuracy in such a process is skewed, and that new media translations cannot demonstrate fidelity in a meaningful way? Or, must the definition of "translation" and "fidelity" take into account the realities of new media translation? If Fry and others are correct, new media presentations will forever be a secondary art-form governed by aesthetic or personal taste. If not, the relationship of the biblical tradition to the history of its transmission needs to be defined and understood, and new norms, theories, and approaches for fidelity established for new media translations.

Tradition and Transmission

Biblical tradition comes alive in its transmission. The goal for this activity is to unite humanity, individually or corporately, to God. The process is straightforward: to teach, preach, witness, or pray the Word of God. The effect, however, is profound. To move human hearts and minds toward God, the transmitters of the biblical tradition need to transfigure the text by one or more media. History bears witness to this reality. Virtually every medium has at one time or another communicated the Word of God. In the arts of movement we see this in music, poetry, narrative prose, and dance. In the arts of repose it takes the form of architecture, sculpture, painting, printing, and the manufacture and illumination of manuscripts and printing (Mocquereau, 1989, p. 37). Not only have these various media been used individually, but they have also been combined at times to produce, what Richard Wagner called, a *Gesamtkunstwerk* "wholistic work of art" that combines text, music, visual, and gestural elements. The ancient liturgies of the east and west exemplify this well, as do the great Baroque Oratorios and Passions in 18th century Lutheran Germany.

Every age, medium, and genre has successfully transformed biblical texts that have united humanity to God. There are exceptions however. Sometimes success or failure is due to the chosen medium. Sometimes it is due to the talent, abilities, or inclinations of a particular musician or artist. Other times it is due to the spirit of an age, which may accept or reject a work of art based on its ability to reflect a particular worldview. This transmission history needs to be understood by new media translators because their work forms part of the same history. This is no easy task, however, given the sheer amount of material that has been produced over the last two to three millennia. We need a methodology to sort through, limit, and evaluate the artistic creations of the past, and at the same time, to help new media translators create fresh works of art. The method that I propose is midrash.

Midrash

A simple contemporary definition of midrash is, "A dialogue with a biblical text" (Cohen, 1992). In the Hebrew Bible, its triconsonantal root—*d-r-š*—often connotes a seeking for God not only in public worship and private prayer, but especially in Scripture (Bloch, 1978, p. 30). In the Rabbinic reformation of Judaism, after the destruction of the temple, midrash became a process of study, explanation, reinterpretation, and adaptation of the past biblical tradition for the ongoing spiritual life of the community (Fishbane, 1985, p. 1). Eventually this word also referred to the literature produced by the midrashic process.

Traces of its origins are found *within* the Hebrew Bible (Fishbane, 1985, p. 3) as for example, in Ezekiel chapters 40 through 48. These chapters describe the restoration of the temple and the liturgical life of the Jewish nation after the Babylonian Captivity. G. Ricciotti commented:

> It seems undeniable that Ezekiel worked...on the fabric of preceding legislation, especially that of Deuteronomy: this would explain the parallelism of the laws; but at the same time the sacred writer was not content with a mere transcription: it was his intention to change the ancient law which he adapted to the future nation. (quoted in Bloch, 1978, p. 35)

Midrashic elements are also part of the Greek Bible. In Matthew's account of the Sermon on the Mount (Matthew 5-7) the evangelist has Jesus reinterpreting Judaic Law and practice. In Matthew 19, within a dialogue with a rich young man, Jesus glosses the Decalogue and then calls the man to greater perfection. In Matthew 22, in a dialogue with an expert in the Law, Jesus distills from the whole Law and Prophets the two great commandments. In each example Matthew has Jesus engaging in midrash by reinterpreting and adapting the received biblical tradition for the benefit of his contemporaries. These and other examples of midrash in Matthew's Gospel forge an inner-biblical link between the two Testaments, which give this authoritative Gospel great substance, depth, and power. The same is true for other books in the Greek Bible.

Midrashic activity did not cease with the close of the two canons, but was institutionalized for Jews in the synagogues and houses of study, and for Christians in the churches and catechetical schools. The focus of these sacred places was *logos* worship, that is, "...the promulgation, reproduction, and veneration of the sacred *word*" (Werner, 1984, p. 151). In these environments, midrash was *the* tool to create biblically-based homilies, hymns, prayers, devotional instruction, and commentaries. Such Jewish literary monuments as the *Mishnah* and the *Babylonian Talmud*, and such Christian writings as the *Didache* and *Hexapla* are the fruits of these *logocratic* environments. So too are such liturgical documents as the seventh century A.D. "Old Gelasian" Sacramentary and the ninth century A.D. Masoretic Text of the Hebrew Bible, the latter combining the original consonantal text, vowel letters and points, and cantillation marks into a single document.

Since systematic use of midrash in these institutions is reflected in their respective literatures, modern scholars can enumerate and delineate its characteristics. In her concise and stimulating monograph, *Midrash*, Bloch outlines the essential and fundamental traits of this venerable method in the rabbinic tradition:

(1) Its point of departure is Scripture.
(2) Its purpose is homiletical.
(3) It is a study attentive to the text.
(4) It adapts the past tradition to the present.
(5) It produces works either for edification or for practice
—*Haggadah* or *Halakah*. (based on Bloch, 1978, pp. 31-33)

These five traits have important implications. Since it begins with Scripture, midrash is an activity of a biblical community, not an end in itself. This leads to the second point: the primacy of homiletical purpose means that certain members of a community use midrash to serve everyone, not a sub-group of scholars, artists, or *literati*. A "homilist" must read and study the biblical tradition carefully and slowly using all rhetorical tools available to ask and ponder the implicit and explicit questions contained in the text (Cohen, 1992). After this careful reading and questioning comes the heart of midrashic activity: to create a work of piety or practice that *explains, reinterprets*, and/or *adapts* the original biblical tradition for a contemporary biblical community. At this creative point Bloch states that the Scriptural tradition is "actualized," and that this actualization:

corresponds to the way in which Israel—and later the Church—has always understood Scripture as the word of God. It always involves a living Word addressed personally to the people of God and to each of its members, a Word which makes clear the divine wishes and demands and calls for a response, never theoretical, and a commitment: the fidelity of a people and each of its members to the demands which the Word makes manifest. Revealed at a specific point in history, this Word is nevertheless addressed to men of all times. Thus it ought to remain *open indefinitely to all new understandings of the message, all legitimate adaptations and all new situations*....So long as there is a people of God who regard the Bible as the living Word of God, there will be midrash; only the name might change. Nothing is more characteristic in this regard than the use of the OT in the NT: it always involves midrashic actualization. The newness resides in the *actualization itself*, in the present situation to which the ancient texts are applied and adapted. (Bloch, 1978, p. 33; emphasis added)

Midrash and New Media Translation

The similarities between Bloch's outline of rabbinic midrash and the new media translation are striking. The same process governs source-target research. The departure for every translation is Scripture in the original language. The intended audiences are people in the pew, in Sunday School, and hopefully those curious about Jesus Christ. Each text receives great attention. In new media translation each text is read slowly and carefully, using linguistic, paralinguistic, and extralinguistic tools to ask and ponder implicit and explicit questions. Finally, translators adapt each text by creating new media works of art that actualize the ancient tradition in contemporary words, sounds, and images for the edification or practice for a living, biblical community.

The similarities continue among the historical examples. As previously stated, many musical and artistic creations continue the biblical tradition by teaching, preaching, witnessing, or praying a particular text authentically, while others do not. Upon examination the more successful follow the midrashic process to a higher degree than the less successful. We can use Bloch's outline normatively, therefore, to sort through, limit, and evaluate secondary sources. The best examples function as midrash, and are worthy of emulation.

These descriptive and normative uses of midrash can also be extended to cover the larger issues of accuracy and fidelity raised by Fry. If new media translators carefully model their process on the descriptive and normative components of midrash at every step of their work, then they will attain accuracy. If a particular creation actualizes the Word of God, so that a biblical community responds with a deeper commitment to God, then fidelity will meaningfully describe, "...the presentation as a whole, and how this accords with the overall message, perspective, and purpose of the biblical author," or the general biblical tradition (Fry, 1987, p. 42).

At this point I have taken Fry's comments and pointed them in a different direction. In his perspective, accuracy and fidelity are word-, sentence-, and paragraph-bound in a source-target continuum. To go beyond these lexical parameters, even within the principles of functional equivalence, precludes their meaningful use. In my perspective, accuracy describes the care taken in new media research and translation, and fidelity describes the continuity of response from the source text to a biblical community via a new media performance.

I shall demonstrate the validity of this perspective by doing a new media translation of the Lord's Prayer, and documenting my source-target and midrashic research. For purposes of understanding and appreciation, however, I would like to place this work within its historical context.

Historical Context

New media translation is rare in western biblical history. The musical and scribal disciplines usually maintain a respectful distance, even though musicians, especially cantors and composers who use sacred texts, are fellow custodians and transmitters of the biblical tradition with ancient and modern scribes who engage in translation. The normal situation is for each discipline to study the contents of the received tradition within the parameters of their respective media, and to preserve and communicate its meaning for succeeding generations (Fishbane, 1985, p. 23). There have been, however, a few important situations when the musical and the scribal disciplines overlapped.

The first was at the beginning of the Christian Era, when the biblical tradition was spreading from its eastern Mediterranean birthplace to all points of the compass. To teach, preach, witness, and pray in these new lands, the biblical tradition was simultaneously translated into many vernacular languages and the ancient cantorial practice musically adjusted to fit the natural rise and fall of the voice in the respective languages (Avenary, 1963, p. 3). The resultant corpus of biblical texts and accompanying musical figures or tropes featured rhetorical meaning beautifully amplified by simple but powerful melodic patterns (de Waard & Nida, 1986, p. 78). This *ars nova* was revolutionary in the ancient world:

> [It] supplanted the splendor of virtuoso techniques [of late Hellenistic music], and the colorful plethora of instruments and performers; and even the subtle accompanied song, *citharody*....The combined forces of Jewish and Christian [cantorial practice] put an end to the instrumental trend in music, and advanced the prevalence of the word and its message. (Avenary, 1963, p. 3, italics added)

Another example of the musical and scribal interaction was just before the turn of the first millennium. At that time the Masoretes re-formed the

Hebrew Bible. Their composite text included the addition of accent signs to mark the mid- and end-points of sentences, plus accent signs to establish the inner relationship of the words within these larger units (Waltke & O'Conner, 1990, p. 22). The end result was a text that provided musical inflection for every word in the Hebrew Bible. The accenting of larger units continued the thousand year old tradition that also prevailed in Christian cantorial practice (Revell, 1971, p. 214). The accenting of words within each unit, however, was new. Since this accentuation system fixed the relationship of the words in the text to the syntactical and sense units, the accents controlled the text, not vice versa (Revell, 1979, p. 142). The result was an elaborate recital practice that added dignity, solemnity, beauty, and clarity to the public cantillation of the Hebrew Bible, and at the same time, that provided a tool for assuring accuracy and fidelity (Waltke & O'Conner, 1990, p. 28).

A final example occurred during the German Reformation. According to a report by Johann Walter, a leading musician in the Wittenberg Chapel, Martin Luther composed cantillation tones to sing the Epistle and the Gospel in the *German Mass* of 1526 (Leupold, 1965, p. 55). For the Epistle, Luther adapted the eighth Gregorian Psalm Tone, making it more melodious, and extending its range for the termination (p. 58). For the singing of the Gospel, he adapted the Latin Passion tones from Holy Week, retaining three separate sets of melodic figures or tropes, the first for narrative, the second for Jesus' words, and the third for other voices (p. 59). Luther also recomposed individual tropes, making them more stepwise and syllabic to better fit the genius of the German language. As he commented in *Against the Heavenly Prophets:*

> To translate the Latin text and retain the Latin tone or notes has my sanction, though it doesn't sound polished or well done. Both the text and notes, accent, melody, and manner of rendering ought to grow out of the true mother tongue and its inflection, otherwise all of it becomes an imitation in the manner of the apes. (quoted in Leupold, p. 54)

While Luther's melodic adaptations for the chanting of the German Bible were effective and musically sensitive, they had minimal impact: most churches did not use them, including his own in Wittenberg. He wrote to Justus Menius, "The last melody for the Epistle and Gospel pleases me better, although our people here do not use it; but I wish you and others would make use of it" (quoted in Leupold, p. 59). From a musical perspective, Luther's development of German hymnody and congregational singing had a much greater impact on the worship life of German congregations. The German tropes, however, did provide the basis for the singing of the Passion narratives in German during Holy Week. This tradition provided the liturgical setting for J. S. Bach's two great Passions.

All of these examples occurred at exceptional moments in western history. The establishing of logocentric cantillation came when the ancient world used music almost exclusively for pleasure and not for serious communication (Avenary, 1963, p. 3). The Masoretes developed their accentuation system as the ancient, oral cantillation tradition was dying, or being distorted. Luther adapted Gregorian melodies for the chanting of the German Bible at a time when polyphony had eclipsed simpler monophonic music. We are presently entering another exceptional moment in history as more people, "...prefer their communication and information to supply sound and images, and not simply silent words in print" (Burke, 1993, p. 102). For this exceptional moment the musical and scribal disciplines must once again overlap to provide new media performances of biblical texts that are accurate, faithful, and beautiful.

Source Analysis of Matthew 6. 9-13 (Lord's Prayer)

Greek

9b Πάτερ ἡμῶν ὁ ἐν τοῖς οὐρανοῖς,
ἁγιασθήτω τὸ ὄνομά σου,
10 ἐλθέτω ἡ βασιλεία σου,
γενηθήτω τὸ θέλημά σου,
ὡς ἐν οὐρανῷ καὶ ἐπὶ γῆς.
11 τὸν ἄρτον ἡμῶν τὸν ἐπιούσιον δὸς ἡμῖν σήμερον
12 καὶ ἄφες ἡμῖν τὰ ὀφειλήματα ἡμῶν,
ὡς καὶ ἡμεῖς ἀφήκαμεν τοῖς ὀφειλέταις ἡμῶν
13 καὶ μὴ εἰσενέγκῃς ἡμᾶς εἰς πειρασμόν,
ἀλλὰ ῥῦσαι ἡμᾶς ἀπὸ τοῦ πονηροῦ.

Transliteration

9b: Pater hemon ho en tois ouranois
hagiastheto to onoma sou
10: eltheto he basileia sou
genetheto to thelema sou
hos en ourano kai epi ges
11: ton arton hemon ton epiousion dos hemin semeron
12: kai aphes hemin ta opheilemata hemon
os kai hemeis aphekamen tois opheiletais hemon
13: kai me eisenegkes hemas eis peirasmon
alla rusai hemas apo tou ponerou

Linguistic Analysis

Matthew's form of the Lord's Prayer is the center of both the the cultic instruction of Matthew 6.1-18, and the entire Sermon on the Mount, Matthew 5 through 7. Betz (1995) calls it, "a literary masterpiece," which echoes Luther's comment that it is *unendliche Rhetorica* "infinite Rhetoric" (p. 375). Tertullian (200 A.D.) called it *breviarium totius evangelii* "an epitome of the entire Gospel" (Evans, 1953, pp. 4-5).

Its structure is straightforward, and we follow the analysis of Betz (1995, ch. 5), de Waard & Nida (1986, pp. 78-85) and Smyth (1984, pp. 671-683). It opens with an invocation, verse 9b, followed by two sets of three petitions: verses 9c-10, and verses 11-13. The first three petitions, which state God's obligations to humans, are the most succinct with parallelism, common grammar, syntax, word order, the same number of syllables, and parallelism of sound at the end of each petition. The parallelism is broken with verse 10c: *hos en ourano kai epi ges,* which probably modifies, and therefore, binds the first three petitions together.

The second set of petitions, which states basic human needs, is introduced in verse 11 with a wonderfully rhythmic colon, *ton arton hemon ton epiousion dos hemin semeron.* The use of alveolar (t,d) and velar (n) consonants signals the ear that a new section is beginning (Crystal, 1980, p. 372), while the re-introduction of the pronoun *hemon* also binds this verse to the invocation. The fifth petition in verse 12, which asks for forgiveness, continues the rhetorical density. The parallel lines are in opposition, and again *hemon,* which is repeated at the end of both lines, binds the two lines to each other and to the invocation. The two lines of the sixth and last petition, which asks for protection, are antithetical. "[It] forms the climax of all petitions, and the last word, 'evil,' names the issue that has been in the picture from the beginning" (Betz, 1995, p. 405). Also, the continued use of derivative forms of the *hemeis* in this verse, and in the entire second section *hemon, hemin, hemeis, hemas*, juxtaposes the three uses of *sou* in the first set of petitions.

Paralinguistic Analysis: General Observations

A paralinguistic analysis of a biblical text notes those elements that occur naturally in the recital of a passage of Scripture, and/or any graphic signs in a source text that help a person know how to vocalize a particular passage (Nida, 1984, p. 2). Therefore, this musical analysis primarily concerns vocal sound (timbre and dynamics), full and partial cadences, and melodic inflection. For the purposes of source analysis vocal sound is unknowable, and while some major and minor pauses can be inferred in a source text, early manuscripts contain no graphic signs to mark cadences. Melodic inflection is graphically noted in the ancient manuscripts with extra-lexical marks invented by Aristophanes of Byzantium (c. 257-180 B.C.). The three accents are the acute, the grave, and the circumflex.

Of the three the acute accent (*oxytone*) is the master tone (*ho kyrios tonos*); its higher pitch has primacy (Stanford, 1967, p. 151). In modern music terminology, a syllable that is sung on a higher pitch possesses a tonic accent. The grave accent (*brytone*) is the default tone; its low pitch is assigned to all unmarked syllables, or to syllables that lose their acute accent in context. In all cantillation traditions this "default tone" is called the reciting tone or tenor. The circumflex, variously called *ditonos, oxybarys, symplektos,* or *peristomenos* (Allen, 1987, p. 122), is the most melodic; it combines the acute and grave accents over ultimate or penultimate long vowels and diphthongs (Smyth, 1984, p. 37). Its also retards the tempo during performance, since the high and low pitches are vocalized in rhythmic succession (Buck, 1955, p. 163). In later cantillation traditions this kind of melodic activity often occurs at cadence points.

Since the pitch in this system is not fixed, the distance between the grave and acute accents is not known. Dionysius of Halicarnassus (first century B.C.) states that, "the melody of speech is measured by a single interval, approximately that termed a 'fifth,' and does not rise to the high pitch by more than three tones and a semitone, nor fall to the low by more than this amount" (Allen, 1987, p. 120). We do not know whether the grave and acute pitches outline Dionysius' fifth or not. Aristotle, for example, mentions a tone between the acute and grave accents: the *mese* (*Ars rhetorica*, p. 3.1.4). By implication the interval between the various accents could be smaller if it was calculated from a central point. The interval of the fifth would be the ambitus of the scale, not the distance between the grave and acute accents. This is very important for the circumflex which glides from the grave accent up to the acute accent and then back. A wide interval, like a fifth, would almost turn this melodic figure into a yodel, which does not fit ancient comments on this expressive accent, or the melodic figures that are recorded in the Greek ekphonetic system which is based on the ancient accent system (Stanford, 1967, p. 165).

Paralinguistic analysis, therefore, is very limited. Timbre and dynamics are unknowable, full and partial cadence points can be inferred, and the three accent marks give places of possible melodic activity. Given these limited parameters, is a paralinguistic analysis worthwhile? If we follow Dionysius of Halicarnassus, who thought that melody needed to be subordinate to the requirements of music, the answer in no. If we follow the lead of the musical writer Aristoxenus, who thought that the natural melody of speech is reflected in word-accents, the answer is yes (Allen, 1987, p. 118). Allen states that some examples of ancient Greek music seem to follow Dionysius, with, "...little correlation between the linguistic accents and the music..." (p. 118). However, he also points out that some musical inscriptions from Delphi from the late second century B.C. seem to follow Aristoxenus, so that

> there is a tendency to agreement between the music and what we believe to have been the melodic patterns of speech....So far as the high pitch is concerned, a syllable which would bear the acute accent is nearly always marked in the musical inscriptions to be sung on a higher note than any other syllable in the word. (p. 120)

Stephanus, a late Christian grammarian, also seems to follow Aristoxenus. In commenting on Aristotle's *Rhetoric*, he advises "those reading the Holy Gospels to learn the high, low and...*[surmatike]* (long-drawn out) kinds of intonation" (Stanford, 1967, p. 154).

Paralinguistic Analysis of Matthew 6.9-13

Taken as a whole, the musical parameters of this passage reinforce the linguistic characteristics through the interaction of the three melodic accents with the flow of each colon and/or its division. This is particularly true with the multiple uses of the circumflex that define the invocation (9b), the close of the first section (10c), and the end of the entire prayer (13b).

> 9b: *Páter hemôn ho en toîs ouranoîs*
> 10c: *hos en ouranô kai epi gês*
> 13b: *allà rûsai hemâs apò toû poneroû*

Musically these circumflexes slow down the tempo, over three vowels to set off the invocation (9b), over two vowels to prepare for a breath at the mid-point (10c), and over four vowels to signal the final cadence (13c).

With the beginning, middle, and end well defined by the multiple use of the circumflex, the structure of the internal verses is defined by the acute accent. This is especially true for the first set of petitions, verses 9c-10b.

> 9c: *hagiasthéto to onomá sou*
> 10: *elthéto he basileía sou*
> 10b: *genethéto to thélemá sou*

In all three cola there is the same melodic beginning and end, with a gradual rise to the first acute accent, and a falling from the last acute accent per line to the grave accent on the closed sound created by the final diphthong *ou*. This makes audible the parallelism, common grammar, syntax, and word order.

Both the acute and circumflex accents are used in the second set on petitions, verses 11-13b, to highlight the individuality of each petition.

> 11: *Tòn árton hemôn ton epioúsion dos hemîn sémeron*

Remembering that this fourth petition echoes the invocation with the use of *hemon*, the *ton* with a grave accent forms an iambic, melodic pick-up to the melodic pattern acute-grave-grave-circumflex over the words *arton hemon*, which is the same melodic pattern for *pater hemon*. Also, the three acute accents emphasize the most important words of the verse, *arton, epiousion,* and *semeron.*

> 12: *kai áphes hemîn ta opheilémata hemôn*
> 12b: *hos kai hemeîs aphékamen toîs opheilétais hemôn*

This antithetical parallel verse opens with the same melodic inflection as verse 11, grave-acute-grave-grave-circumflex, which helps to tie the two petitions together. Also, the four circumflexes over the first-person plural pronouns help to emphasize that, "...forgiveness of sins involves interrelated acts—God's forgiveness is somehow bound up with the forgiveness of obligations others owe to us" (Betz, 1995, p. 401).

13: *kaì mè eisenégkes hemâs eis peirasmón*

The sixth and last petition begins with four grave accents, which make the acute accent over the ultimate of *peirasmon* stand out as the only line to end on a tonic accent. This, in turn, clearly marks the midpoint of the antithetical *isocolon,* and musically signals that the final cadence is about to be sung. This same musical technique will be seen in later, notated examples.

    This analysis takes at face value Aristoxenus and Stephanus who say that melodic inflection is related to the accent marks in a text. However, Allen cautions,

> we know virtually nothing about "melodic syntax," i.e., the way in which such patterns interacted with one another and with clause—and sentence—intonations in continuous speech. To judge from what we find in living tonal and melodically accented languages, their interactions may be extensive and complex. Given the melodic patterns of the word-isolates in such languages, it is of course possible to derive the melodic sentence-pattern from them—but the latter is not usually a simple summation of the former. (1987, pp. 128-129)

The preceding observations, therefore, are not made to uncover the *Urmelodie* of the Lord's Prayer, but to find places in the text that receive musical emphasis, and other places that do not. As Nida tells us, "Meaning exists only because there is contrast" (1984, p. 15). According to this analysis of the source text, the paralinguistic and linguistic contrasts run parallel to each other. While this might be a small point in isolation, it will prove very helpful in analyzing notated examples.

Extralinguistic Analysis

In the Sermon on the Mount extralinguistic analysis is primarily concerned with body language and its meaning. The only explicit gesture in the text is at the beginning of chapter five, "When Jesus saw the crowds, he went up the mountain; and after he sat down, his disciples came to him. Then he began to speak..." (Matthew 5.1-2a; New Revised Standard Version). By sitting, Jesus assumes the posture of a teacher. By gathering around, the disciples and crowd become his students. The attitude of these students is given at the beginning of chapter six: "Beware of practicing your piety before others in order to be seen by them..." (Matthew 6.1) Applied to prayer, this means that the students will "...go into their rooms and shut their doors and pray to their Father who is in secret" (Matthew 6.6). They are also not to "heap up empty phrases" (Matthew 6.7), but pray simply and succinctly with the Lord's words. (Matthew 6.9b-13). There is a hint in verse 11—"Our daily bread, give us today"—that the prayer is to be humbly prayed once a day. Since Jesus was Jewish, he probably assumed that his students would stand during prayer, and like Hannah, speak under their breath, while moving their lips with no audible sound (Betz, 1995, p. 362; Millgram, 1971, p. 352).

Summary

In an *Excursus* on the Lord's Prayer, Betz observes that it stands in the middle of the Sermon of the Mount and that this prominent location is no accident. "[It] creates the image of a praying Jesus in the center with his disciples surrounding him" (1995, p. 373). This devotional comment was made by a biblical scholar who possesses formidable linguistic tools for analysis. Remember that he named this section of Matthew's Gospel a "literary masterpiece." I think that it has been successfully demonstrated through the analysis of the paralinguistic and extralinguistic parameters that accompany the text that the Lord's Prayer is more than a literary masterpiece. The interconnection and correlation of these three elements are of the highest degree, to the point that the Lord's Prayer is also a great work of performative art (LaRue, 1970, p. 16). From this point of view it is very understandable why this pericope has been lifted out of its original context and used liturgically in the administration of the sacraments and in the public and private prayer of Christians in all ages, both east and west. It is also understandable why musicians throughout history have attempted to preserve musical features of this text, long after other parts of the Gospels fell silent. There is an almost unbroken tradition of musical settings of the Lord's Prayer, at least in the west, from the formation of the canon to the present. It is from this tradition that the following musical examples will be presented and compared to this source analysis.

Three Examples of the Lord's Prayer

It is in this section that midrash as a method can help to sort through, limit, and evaluate the musical settings of the Lord's Prayer. Remembering Bloch's first, second, and fifth traits of midrash, I have chosen settings of Matthew's text that have been used for the edification of people in the pew. I will then apply the third and fourth traits of midrash to analyze the linguistic, paralinguistic, and extralinguistic characteristics of each setting to determine how well these three parameters correlate and bring the tradition forward.

All of the examples are simple monophonic settings from the fourth to the 16th centuries. Since the Greek Orthodox tradition speaks the Lord's Prayer in its liturgies, these examples are from the western branch of Christianity: two Latin versions from the ancient and medieval periods, and one from the English Reformation during the Renaissance period. All are logocentric melodies, meaning that the text forms the creative focus of the music. Finally, all demonstrate how a change in any one parameter profoundly affects every aspect of a particular setting.

The Mozarabic Pater Noster

Pater Noster   **Mozarabic tone**

℣. Pa-ter noster: qui es in cae-lis. ℟. A-men. ℣. Sanctificetur no-

men tu-um. ℟. A-men. ℣. Adveniat re-gnum tu-um. ℟. A-men.

℣. Fiat voluntas tu-a: sicut in caelo et in ter-ra. ℟. A-men. ℣. Panem

nostrum quo-ti-di-a-num: da no-bis ho-di-e. ℟. A-men. ℣. Et

dimitte nobis de-bi-ta nostra: sicut et nos dimittimus debito-ri-bus

nos-tris. ℟. A-men. ℣. Et ne nos in ducas: in-ten-ta-ti- o-nem.

℟. Sed li-be-ra nos a malo

Figure 1: Score of Mozarabic Pater Noster.

This sung version of the Lord's Prayer appears in a French Cistercian manuscript from the late 12th century (Caldwell, 1978, p. 31). However, Peter Wagner, the early 20th century chant scholar, dated this psalmodic melody to fourth-century Spain, and his evaluation is still accepted by modern scholars (Angles, 1954, p. 82). From a linguistic point of view, the text is a formal equivalence translation of the Greek into "vulgar" Latin. This common form of the language was used throughout the Roman Empire by early Christian writers, including Tertullian, and for the so-called *Italia* translation of the Bible (Buck, 1955, p. 27). The Latin follows the Greek syntax and word order except for three instances. The first is in verse 9b. Since Latin has no definite article, the Greek phrase, *ho en tois ouranois*, has been translated into a relative clause, *qui es in caelis*. The second is in verse 13a. There, the translator, taking advantage of a wonderful alliterative opportunity in the Latin, changes the Greek word order, *kai me eisenegkes hemas*, into *et ne nos inducas*.

The third instance is structural. The original prayer has been recast into a litany. If standard liturgical practice was followed to perform this setting, the invocation and the first five petitions (verses 9b-12) were sung by a deacon and each answered by a congregational "Amen" (Jungmann, 1959, p. 222). The final petition was evenly divided between the deacon and the congregation. Since the litanic form can be considered an extralinguistic parameter of this setting, an important question for new media translation arises. Was this recasting of the original prayer into a litany a midrashic attempt to adapt the tradition to a fourth-century liturgical need? I would say yes, especially if we look at the paralinguistic parameter.

This Mozarabic setting of the Lord's Prayer, following the Hebrew Psalms, divides lines of the text into parallel parts with static medial and a final cadence formulae (Caldwell, 1978, p. 34). These formulae are also used in the oldest musical version of the Christian psalmatic Hymn the *Gloria in Excelsis Deo*. The first few verses, as found in the *Liber Usualis* (1961) on page 57 can be seen in Figure 2.

Sing the first few lines of this *Gloria*, especially the *et in terra pax hominibus bonae voluntatis*. Notice how the original formulae clearly divide the verse. Now, sing the Mozarabic *Pater Noster*, printed at the beginning

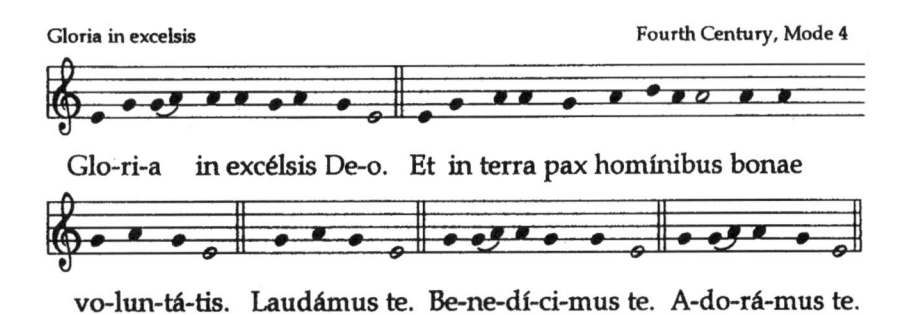

Figure 2: Score of *Gloria* in *Liber Usualis*.

of this section. Notice how the same formulae divide the text into parts, but that the *Amen* response *interrupts* the formulae. From this I would conclude that the *Amen* was consciously added to the psalmatic formulae to transform the melody and the prayer into a litany.

This conclusion is strengthened when we consider how the early church viewed the Lord's Prayer rhetorically. Tertullian comments in *De Oratione*, "Jesus Christ our Lord, has marked out for the new disciples of the new covenant a new plan of prayer" (*novam orationis formam determinavit*) (Evans, 1953, pp. 2-3). According to Gordon J. Bahr, this comment indicates that the Lord's Prayer was considered an "outline" of *how* to pray, not a verbatim formula (1965, p. 154). In other words, early Christians treated the Lord's Prayer like Jewish people treated the Eighteen Benedictions, or *Amidah* according to Sephardic practice (Hertz, 1985, p. 130), that is, as a traditional pattern of prayer used when approaching the Divine Presence (Millgram, 1971, p. 103). Parenthetically, this might help to explain the different versions of the Lord's Prayer in Matthew and Luke, the changes in the petition's order in Tertullian, and the addition of the doxology in sources like the *Didache* (Lake, 1977, p. 321). For our purposes, this view of the Lord's Prayer helps to explain why this prayer was re-cast into a litany. The creator wanted to provide a congregation the opportunity to give their assent with a resounding "Amen" to a public declamation of each petition. To this end, the text was divided into rhetorical *topoi*, and a standard psalmatic formulae was adapted to sing the restructured text.

The Medieval Pater Noster

The fourth century is also the period when evidence starts to accumulate for the inclusion of the Lord's Prayer in the Eucharist. The practice originated in the Greek-speaking East, and then "migrated" to the Latin-speaking West in the Gallican liturgy. In both traditions the congregation performed the entire text (Staeblein, 1962, p. 944). Pope Gregory the Great is credited for introducing the prayer into the Roman Rite, placing it immediately after the canon *super oblationem*, that is, sung over the consecrated bread and wine on the altar (Jungmann, 1959, p. 463). The congregational participation, however, was limited to singing the last phrase, *sed libera nos a mallo*, while the rest of the text was sung by the celebrant, *a solo sacerdote* (Staeblein, 1962, p. 944). For this reason the medieval manuscripts of the *Pater Noster* are found in liturgical books, such as sacramentaries and missals (Steiner, 1980, p. 229). The earliest notated sources come from southern Italy in the 11th century, but the internal melodic construction reflects a much older tradition, as early as the fifth to the seventh century (Jungmann, 1959, p. 468).

While the *Pater Noster* text used in the Roman Rite (see Figure 3) is the same as the Mozarabic (a formal equivalence translation of Matthew), its recitation within the Eucharist is part of a new extralinguistic context. This is reflected in the instruction or rubric given to the celebrant while

Midrash: A Model for Fidelity 189

Pater Noster   Medieval chant

℣. Praecéptis sa-lu-tá-ri-bus mó-ni-ti, et di-ví-na in-sti-tu-ti-ó-ne

formá-ti, audemus dí – ce-re: Pa-ter noster: qui es in cae-lis.

Sanc-ti-fi-cé-tur no-men tu- um. Advéniat re-gnum tu-um. Fiat

volúntas tu-a: sicut in cae-lo et in ter-ra. Panem nostrum quo

-ti-di-á-num: da no-bis hó-di-e. Et dimítte nobis dé-bi-ta nostra:

sicut et nos dimíttimus debitóribus nostris. Et ne nos in dúcas:

in-ten-ta-ti- ó- nem. ℟. Sed lí-be-ra nos a ma- lo.

Figure 3: Score of a medieval *Pater Noster*.

chanting the prayer, "Extend the hands, and stand with eyes fixed on the Sacrament" (*Extendit manus, et stans oculis ad Sacramentum intentis*) (*Missale Romanum,* 1956, p. xliv). The specific focusing on the blessed elements before their reception either develops or changes the original meaning of Jesus' words, depending on your theological point of view. As we have seen in the linguistic analysis, the second set of petitions is for specific human needs, and the fourth petition—"Our daily bread, give us today"—refers to, "...all that is necessary for nourishment. Rhetorically the term *bread* is a synecdoche, i.e. understanding one thing with another" (Betz, 1995, p. 399; Smyth, 1984, p. 684). In the context of the Roman Rite, *bread* refers to the Eucharist. Rhetorically the word *bread* is still a synecdoche, but it now stands for the sacramental body of Christ. This interpretation of the Lord's Prayer did not begin in the Middle Ages; as early as the second century Tertullian writes:

> we prefer the spiritual understanding of GIVE US TODAY, OUR DAILY BREAD. For Christ is our bread, because Christ is life and bread is life: *I am*, he says, *the bread of life:* and a little earlier, *The bread is the word of the living God which hath come down from heaven:* and again because his body is authoritatively ranked as bread—*This is my body.* And so by asking for daily bread we request continuance in Christ and inseparableness from his body. (Evans, 1953, p. 11)

With this type of theological reflection it is understandable why, two centuries later, Jerome translated the Greek word *epiousion* with *supersubstantialem* in the Latin Vulgate! It is also understandable that the paralinguistic and linguistic parameters were also profoundly changed in the middle ages to accommodate the new emphasis.

The medieval *Pater Noster* is based on recitation formulae used for the singing of prayers and lessons throughout the Mass. The primary characteristic of these formulae is that they are simple, static melodic figures, applied to texts in a prescribed way. A good musical description is given by Willi Apel: "Liturgical recitatives are fixed melodies consisting essentially of a monotone recitation with opening and closing formulae, each designed to serve for a great number of texts" (1958, p. 246). (To get a sense of the static nature of this cantillation tradition, sing the Mozarabic *Pater Noster* without the *Amen* response. See Figure 1 on page 186.) The medieval musicians loosened these fixed melodic figures, and applied them to the text in a more plastic manner, that is, they relaxed the rules. Instead of one reciting tone, there are two, which implies the concept of modulation. The use of two reciting tones was not new to the medieval *Pater Noster*. There are many examples in the Judeo-Christian chant tradition of psalm singing. The common term for a "modulating" psalm tone is *tonus peregrinus*, "wandering tone." The difference between the *tonus peregrinus* and the medieval *Pater Noster* is that the change of tenor in the *tonus peregrinus* occurs every half verse, while the change of tenor in the *Pater* only occurs for the last verse of the text. (Werner, 1984, vol. 2, p. 66.) Instead of having the medial and final cadence points in the same order for each verse, they are varied. The result is a melody that is still logocentric, and rooted in the cantillation tradition, but at the same time, moves closer to free composition, "...having a distinctive and individual melodic line...composed for one special text" (Apel, 1958, p. 246).

The development of distinctive and individual melodic formulae and cadences also changed the linguistic form of the text. The formal aspects of the Greek text can be outlined in the following way:

X – Invocation v. 9b
A – Petition v. 9c
B – Petition v. 10a

        C – Petition   v. 10b

        Y – Medial Cadence   v. 10c

        D – Petition   v. 11
        E – Petition   v. 12ab
        F – Petition   v.13a X   (X = a Final Cadence)

With the new melody the text is sung like a psalm:
        A – Invocation (v. 9b) B – Petition (v. 9c)
        A – Petition (v. 10a) A – Petition (v. 10b) B–Medial Cadence (v. 10c)
        A – Petition (v. 11) A – Petition (v. 12a)   B – (v. 12b)
        C – Petition (v. 13a) C – (v.13)   X – Final Cadence

In this outline, using solmizational syllables, "A" represents a formula with a reciting tone on *ti*, and a cadence on *sol*; "B" also represents a formula with a reciting tone on *ti*, but a cadence on *la*; and "C" represents a formula with a reciting tone on *la*, and a final cadence on *sol*. However, since the number of syllables and accents change in each verse, the repetitions of the three formulae are varied and distinct, except for the "B" singing of verses 9c and 10c.

As noted before, the syntax and the word order of the Greek source text and the Latin translation is basically the same, but the new setting has reformed the text into longer psalm-like antecedent/consequent-like phrases. This can be outlined as follows:

        Antecedent (9b)   Consequent (9c)
        Antecedent (10a)   Antecedent (10b)   Consequent (10c)
        Antecedent (11)   Antecedent (12a)   Consequent (12b)
        Antecedent (13a)   Consequent (13b)

This last outline almost looks "modern." The amazing thing is that it is *not modern*, but a creative development of a static cantillation tradition into a solo melody of unique beauty to demonstrate in sound the theology of the real presence. It is extraordinary how the linguistic, paralinguistic, and extralinguistic parameters interacted to produce this new work of art, which has been *the* model for new settings of the Lord's Prayer when the text is translated into other languages. The final example of this section is one of them.

The Our Father by John Marbeck

Before the Reformation there were at least five orders of worship in England for the Latin Mass and Offices. The most famous was the *Sarum Rite* at Salisbury (Clarke, 1959, p. 135). This situation continued during the reign of Henry VIII, who was liturgically conservative. However, Henry's

Anglican Our Father   John Marbeck, 1550

Priest: Let us pray. As our Savior Christ hath commanded and taught us, we are bold to say. Our Father which art in heaven, Hallowed be thy Name, Thy kingdom come. Thy will be done in earth, as it is in heaven. Give us this day our daily bread. And forgive us our trepasses, as we forgive them that trespass against us: And lead us not in-to temp-ta-ti-on. *People:* But de-li-ver us from evil. A-men.

Figure 4: Our Father setting by John Marbeck.

son Edward VI was a precocious student of the Reformation. At his coronation Archbishop Cramner called him a "second Josiah," and predicted that he would see that God is "truly worshiped." Under the young king, Cramner and other reformers were free to promote changes in the liturgy (p. 151). In January 1549, a bill approving an English prayer book passed both Houses of Parliament. The king gave his assent in March, and the first *Book of Common Prayer* came into exclusive use in the Anglican Church on Whitsunday of that year (p. 155). It was Archbishop Cramner himself who supervised the translation and rearrangement of the various services for the worship of the realm. The only problem with the book was its lack of music for singing the musical texts in the services. This omission was remedied one year later with the publication of *The Book of Common Prayer Noted* by John Marbeck, a musician of the King at St. George's Chapel, Windsor Castle (Marbeck, 1980, p. 13). One of the *noted* texts was the Lord's Prayer.

The most important use of the Lord's Prayer continued to be in the Eucharistic service, which was still called the Mass. Its recitation remained the same as its Latin predecessor, a solo text for the priest between the words of institution and reception of the elements. The linguistic and extralinguistic parameters, however, changed drastically. The entire service, including the Lord's Prayer, was in English. All retained Latin and Greek texts were translated, but texts based on older Roman theology were either dropped completely or re-written to reflect Reformation theology. In the new rite, receiving the consecrated elements was a "spiritual communion," not a reception of the actual body and blood of Christ. As Cramner said, "It is in the godly using of them (the elements) that they be unto the receivers Christ's body and blood" (quoted by Clarke, 1959, p. 353). It was in this new linguistic and extralinguistic atmosphere that John Marbeck composed his setting of the Lord's Prayer.

The Lord's Prayer in the 1549 *Book of Common Prayer* reads as follows:

> Our Father which art in heaven, hallowed be thy name. Thy kingdom come. Thy will be done on earth, as it is in heaven. Give us this day our daily bread. And forgive us our trespasses, as we forgive them that trespass against us. And lead us not in to temptation. But deliver us from evil. Amen.

Except for the words *trespasses* and *trespass*, and different punctuation, this translation was retained in the King James Version of 1611. This high level of correspondence probably reflects the attitude of Reformation translators about the nature of language, beginning with Tyndale. As George H. McKnight states:

> While Tyndale's translation has not possessed the authority over standard English possessed by Luther's translation over literary German, its phraseology and its turns of expression have been woven into the texture of English and for centuries have pervaded the language of English-speaking people not only in all parts of the world but in all stations of life, serving the needs of simple speech and of formal eloquence. To the zeal of William Tyndale in bringing a knowledge of the Bible within the reach of the "boy that draweth the plowe" is to be attributed the simplicity of biblical language and the purity of its vocabulary. (1956, p. 113)

The spirit of Tyndale's approach to language was emulated by the translators of the *Book of Common Prayer* who used simple vocabulary in eloquent ways. This can be seen in their translations of the old Latin Collects that were retained in the finely conceived *Prayer for Humble Access*, which paraphrased the Liturgy of St. Basil and the words of the Syro-Phoenician Woman in Mark 7.28 (Clarke, 1959, p. 339), and, finally, in the translation that they used for the Lord's Prayer.

Simplicity is the hallmark of the entire text. Most of the words used are one syllable, a handful are two and three, only one word, *temp-ta-ti-on* is four syllables long. When the words are built into phrases and sentences the sum total of syllables per line is less than the Greek or the Latin versions. The full text, therefore is "shorter" than its ancient counterparts. Except for two places, there are no "recessive" accents at the cadences; stress accents fall on the last syllable of most phrases. The English introduction to the prayer is half the length of the Roman Rite, and the long Latin extension, called the *embolism,* is completely dropped. This linguistic simplicity continues in the paralinguistic parameter.

The criteria for liturgical music used by Marbeck were established by Cramner. In a letter to Henry VIII he clearly states, "...that plain chant suitable for the English language should 'not be full of notes, but as near as may be, for every syllable a note'" (Marbeck, 1980, p. 27). In this call for syllabic vernacular chant Cramner was echoing Martin Luther's thinking. Marbeck followed Cramner's dictates to a tee. Starting with the *Book of Common Prayer* text, he carefully simplified the old medieval Latin melody to fit the English.

Marbeck had to simplify the tradition due to the differences between Latin and English, especially at cadence points. Historically the Latin accent could not stand farther back than the third syllable from the end (Buck, 1955, p.165). This "three-syllable law" regularized cadence point in Latin chant. They were either 1-2; 1-2-3; or a combination of the two, such as: 1-2-3, 1-2, 1-2. To use poetic terms the cadences were either *trochaic* (strong-weak) or *dactylic* (strong-weak-weak). A good example of this can be seen in the first phrase of the medieval chant with the rhythm of the melody notated above:

Páter nóster, qui és in caé-lis: sánctifi-cé-tur nó-men tú-um.

The text that Marbeck set did not have these "classical" cadences, since by the 16th century English had dropped most of its verbal inflection. What remained were simple cadences, such as 2-1, or 1-1; in poetic terms: *iambic* (weak-strong) or *spondee* (strong-strong). Therefore, Marbeck eliminates the four, five-and eight-note groups at cadence points, and replaces them with two rhythmic cadences of short-long (*iambic*) and long-long (*spondee*). Interestingly, he changes the pitch at these cadence points to have melodic variety, since the rhythmic parameter was so simple. In only two places does Marbeck come close to the medieval Latin melody: on the words *daily bread,* which, with long and short note values, is a chant-like 1-2-3-1-2 rhythm; and on the words *to temptation,* which again, with the long and short notes, musically retards the tempo with a 2, 1-2-3, 1-2-3, 1-2-3-4, thus telling the congregation to respond with the last line of the prayer, *But deliver us from evil, Amen.*

When Marbeck's *Book of Common Prayer Noted* was discovered in the 19th century, High Church Anglicans thought that they had discovered *the* musical link between Roman Catholic and Anglo Catholic worship. In a way they were correct. John Marbeck's work, however, is more than a footnote to the Tractarian Movement of the last century. He was a true son of the Reformation, a champion of a sung vernacular liturgy based on the insights of Luther and Cramner (Marbeck, 1980, p. 1). To this end he responded to the linguistic and extralinguistic changes of his day, and modified the paralinguistic parameter of the tradition. The result was an *Anglican chant* style, rooted in the past, but adapted for a new time, place, and language. From a new media perspective he is a hero, linking the cantillation traditions of Greek, Latin, and English. Without his pioneering work, 20th century new media translators would not be connected to the ancient past.

Conclusion

If this chapter were a full book, it would analyze other historical examples at this point. The powerful metrical translation of Luther, for example, would be discussed, since it is a wonderful example of the midrashic art, and links the Lord's Prayer to the western hymn tradition. The polyphonic settings of Willard, Palestrina, and Schutz, and the larger, Romantic settings of composers like Verdi, Liszt, and Tschaikowsky would be discussed as important choral adaptations of the tradition. Also, contemporary settings would be introduced to demonstrate how musicians are continuing to add to the midrashic tradition. Such analyses, however, are not necessary since this section demonstrates how to evaluate the linguistic, paralinguistic, and extralinguistic parameters of various settings of the Lord's Prayer with the tools of midrash, and shows how well they correlate in each example and bring the midrashic tradition forward. That purpose has been fulfilled with the analysis of the three chant settings.

From the perspective of contemporary new media translation it can be observed that all three settings of the Lord's Prayer are accurate and faithful translations of the source text in ways that silent linguistic translation is not. They are accurate and faithful, however, not by fixating on one parameter, but by responding openly to the linguistic, paralinguistic, and extralinguistic realities presented to them. Each in their day "actualized" the Scriptural tradition for a contemporary biblical community, so that their communities could, in turn, respond in faith, hope, and love to God and to neighbor. The three settings also demonstrate how powerful the Word of God becomes when the musical and scribal disciplines combine forces to make new translations. In this our ancestors have given us an example. For the future, it will only be through the cooperation of many disciplines that faithful, beautiful, and powerful new media translations will be produced.

A New Setting of the Lord's Prayer

Our Fath-er in the heavens: your Name be hallowed, your king-

dom come, your will be done, as in heaven, so on the earth.

Our dai-ly bread, give us to-day; and forgive us our debts, as

we for-give our deb-tors; and lead us not into temptation, but

de- liv-er us from e- vil. A - men.

Copyright © 1997, J. Ritter Werner

Figure 5: Our Father setting by J. Ritter Werner.

To be true to the midrashic process, I have to produce a new translation and musical setting for the Lord's Prayer. Given the popularity of the text among composers and editors of denominational hymnals from around the world, such an effort might appear unnecessary. However, since we are entering an era of new media translation, settings that combine the scribal and musical disciplines are necessary. Deeper lines of continuity need to be re-established between *all* of the parameters of the source text and contemporary performance. Also, contemporary, liturgical music practice needs to be rescued from the current creative aesthetic which elevates subjective inspiration over objective, logocentric settings that give primacy to the thoughts, feelings, and rhetorical structure of a text.

For the translation I have emulated the *Book of Common Prayer* by using a simple vocabulary. I have also retained the original rhetorical structure by employing a more Germanic word order in places. To this formal translation I have composed a new melody which imitates the characteristics of the ancient circumflex and the acute accents. In modern parlance this means that I have composed two-note motifs over important structural places in the text, and placed tonic pitches over important word accents. The result is a new text and tune that is organically connected to the source text, and at the same time communicates to an English-speaking congregation. Since my melody is inspired by the original melodic gestures, the last phrase does not "cadence" in a modern sense, therefore, following modern liturgical practice, I have added an *Amen* to bring the melody and this paper to a point of rest.

Finally, if you would like to hear the music examples sung by the author, please visit the website of the ABS Research Center for Scripture and Media at http://www.researchcenter.org. Click on "Studio" and go to "Audio Scriptures."

Section III

Seeking Fidelity:

Theoretical Perspectives

Seeking Fidelity: Theoretical Perspectives

Besides reflecting on the experience of new media translators, we also find resources to address the question of fidelity in translation in a number of theoretical perspectives. Two of the essays in this section draw on work in communication study and two on work in semiotics. In all instances the authors point out directions for further exploration. How might we pose the question of fidelity if we draw on traditions outside of translation study? Who else might have explored the issues of equivalence, faithfulness, and assessment in communicating across languages or genres?

Joy Sisley of King Alfred's College (U.K.) notes that biblical texts have long been presented in the popular forms of film and television. In most of these cases, the translator's assessment of fidelity never arises, though Baugh (1997) does raise that issue in his critique of Jesus and Christ figures in film. Sisley approaches fidelity, not as a critic, but as one who examines the contexts of production values, audience, and genre. Each of these influences the notion of scriptural authority. For her the question of fidelity takes on broader forms within the discursive practice of translation; she bases her discussion "on a definition of translation as rewriting, which recognizes the complexity of textual encoding and decoding with socially and culturally determined contexts." In this sense, fidelity becomes tied to the normative values of the evaluating group: the Bible Society or Church. Producers, critics, and audience members may apply different normative values–based on genre, for example.

The models of the communication process used in the early years of that discipline tended toward the static representation of input and output. As such, they fit the translator's notion of source text and target text rather well. Santa Clara University's Paul Soukup points out that these models privilege the text over the audience. He widens the overall inquiry by noting four models of the communication process (transportation, semiotic, ritual, and conversation), each of which suggests different criteria for fidelity, since each model calls attention to a different aspect of the overall process. He cautions that no one model suffices to explain communication or to guide research; for too long people have reduced concepts like fidelity and faithfulness to simple questions of equivalence based on a model of electronic circuits rather than on the human interaction that lies at the base of all communication.

Robert Hodgson, Jr., the manager of the American Bible Society Research Center for Scripture and Media suggests linking the question of fidelity to the philosophical work of Charles Sanders Peirce in semiotics. A semiotic analysis takes into account that the biblical text actually consists of multiple sign systems (linguistic, paralinguistic, extralinguistic) and that these combine into ever more complex sign systems. A faithful translation must manage the sign system and recapture it in a new language or in new media. Introducing the world of Peirce, Hodgson suggests a number of guidelines for translators and then guides the reader through several case studies, which illustrate his principles.

The final essay in this section provides a more comprehensive look at Peirce's semiotics, applying them to translation in a systematic way. Ubaldo Stecconi, on the faculty of the Ateneo de Manila University, begins by reminding us of the semiotic nature of translation in general–translations are never final; in fact, no work exists as an original until someone has translated it. By so doing, one begins a chain of interrelated signs. A translation, in the Peircean sense, becomes a set of relations among the "original," the interpretant, the translator's interpretant, and the reader. This redefines the whole question of fidelity from one of equivalence to one of inference, in Peirce's sense of "abduction."

Each of these essays, then, offers a new theoretical perspective on fidelity. Without claiming to resolve the issue, the authors invite further reflection on the process of translation and bring the project of this volume to a conclusion and a beginning. The volume began with an examination of the experience of translation in new media. That experience has led to a new sensitivity to qualities of the original texts. By taking new theoretical perspectives, we resolve, perhaps, one issue, but return to the process of translation.

Because the subject of translation is the Bible, this volume highlights the practical side of theology. Any theological discourse–following the Bible's lead–must take root in people's lives. The communication of the Bible leads theology to communication. A deeper understanding of that communication leads in turn to better translation.

11

Power and Interpretive Authority in Multimedia Translation

Joy Sisley

Introduction

New media technologies of the late 20th century have had a profound effect on western culture and society. The explosion of new communication forms has challenged societies whose cultural identity is founded, among other things, upon literary texts. The displacement of writing and literature by film and television alters the manner in which we communicate with each other and gives rise to new types of literacy. Indeed, some predicate the change from a literate to a post-literate society upon the introduction of new technologies, the development of new aesthetic forms and genres or signifying systems, and the creation of other social and institutional agencies that control their distribution.

The emergent and increasingly popular form of Bible stories translated into video or television is symptomatic of this trend. It *is* significant when video becomes the privileged format in which people encounter the Bible. Video translation challenges the very notion that the written form is a sacred text and as such provokes a paradigm shift in forms of biblical interpretation. Lynne Long (1995) describes a parallel paradigm shift with the introduction of printing as a change in the text/reader relationship, accompanied by a shift in the function of the text. She states that, on the one hand, an increase in text ownership through printing encouraged a more personal reader response, while, on the other, the growth in the area of individual response allowed the corresponding weakening of recognized authoritative institutions to maintain power over interpretations of those texts. Similarly, multimedia translation challenges the religious identity of Christian communities whose faith and authority is founded upon the written Word.

This chapter will focus on the ways in which biblical texts are rewritten through borrowing from popular forms of contemporary film and television. It will demonstrate how production contexts, audience address, and program form have an impact on the reception of multimedia translations and challenge conventional notions of scriptural authority. By illustrating the relationship between genre, authorship, and reception, I intend to pose broader questions about translation from one medium to another and the related issues of equivalence or fidelity.

I shall refer to the process of transforming Bible stories from print to screen as "translation" in preference to "adaptation," the term generally used within film theory. My use of the term "translation" is provocative. Firstly, a translations studies approach encourages a broader range of inquiry than is generally pursued in contrastive studies of literary and film texts. Secondly, treating adaptation as translation recognizes a displacement of literature and writing by film and television and potentially challenges the ways in which we talk about translation. The question, "Is this translation?" prompts an investigation of a constellation of issues about textual authority, interpretation, representation, and fidelity. My approach is based on a definition of translation as rewriting which recognizes the complexity of textual encoding and decoding within socially and culturally determined contexts (Lefevere, 1992).

I propose to treat translation as a set of discursive practices (Cattrysse, 1992) which necessarily involves questions about translation as a process of communication within a particular historical moment. By doing so, I will draw attention to the relationships between producer, text, and audience within socially and culturally defined contexts and will distance myself from the greater part of adaptation theory which is more limited in scope.

The focus on Scripture translation into video is exemplary because of the privileged status given to the Bible as a sacred text. Explicitly, the written text, the Word of God, both defines the community of believers and validates the authenticity of their religious experience. From a Christian point of view, the Bible is both the inspired Word of God, and God presented in material form as the written Word. Given the extraordinary authority of the written text, it should not surprise us that the history of Bible translation reveals a preoccupation with faithful interpretations. For believers, the text really ought to mean only that which its divine author intended. Therefore, as Detweiler states in his discussion of a sacred text, "[believers] will feel more constrained in their interpretation of the sacred text because it has, after all, a divine authority that commands reverence and restricts a free play of response" (1985, p. 214). In multimedia translation a requirement to remain close to the written text reflects that constraint.

While the notion of faithful translation as an objective fact has been abandoned in translation studies, within the context of translating religious texts it still makes sense to talk about fidelity because it leads us to investigate the nature of the translator's claims to faithful translation and the strategies used to authenticate that claim. Fidelity, then, is a discursive practice which concerns not only relationships between translators, texts, and readers (or translators, productions, and viewers) but also competing authorities within those relationships. The question of faithfulness is also a question of power—the power of different interpreters to legitimate their authority. Multimedia translation of the Bible highlights many of these issues because not only does it require new and diverse interpretive skills on the part of the translator, but also it includes a different set of professional production and distribution institutions than those involved in print publication. The following discussion will draw examples primarily, but not exclusively, from Bible Society work in order to draw attention to the ways in which particular translation strategies and production contexts circumscribe the relationship between viewers and video translation.

Approaches to Multimedia Translation

Bible Societies have adopted two approaches to the theory and practice of multimedia translation. One stems from a linguistic model of translation. The translation strategies adopted within this paradigm give priority to seeking equivalence between the two signifying systems of spoken or written language and film or video while attempting to bridge the gap between the different worlds of the audience for whom the text was written and contemporary audiences for the translations. In summary:

> The measure of **fidelity** (faithfulness of the translation compared with the original language texts) will be located primarily in the intended response sought by the original authors as encoded in the original language texts. Thus the images in a multimedia translation will be faithful to the images invited by the text in the minds and hearts of the original receivers. (Thomas, 1994b, p. 46)

This model treats translation as a process of *replacement* in which the translator acts as mediator between source and target texts. The translator strives to transfer an invariant core of meaning from source to target text. Faithfulness to the original text appears as an objective possibility, which can be evaluated, if only by its own criteria of fidelity. In this case the visual sign stands for the written in a relation of equivalence or one-to-one correspondence. It is "a *gesture* produced with the *intention of communicating*" (Eco, 1984, p. 16).

For example, in *Out of the Tombs* (American Bible Society, 1992), a music video translation of the story of the demon-possessed Gadarene man in Mark 5, the demoniac is represented as an adolescent delinquent tormented by the pressures and alienation of modern metropolitan existence, a portrayal that invites the intended audience to identify with the spiritual torment of the written story's protagonist. Similarly, the translation avoids a literal or mimetic visual representation of the demons and the pigs in favor of a symbolic destruction of the evil spirits portrayed by a cloaked figure who dissolves in a sea of flames. The image of the demons consumed by fire provides a metaphor that calls up a complexity of associated Christian images of hell and damnation, thus presumably establishing a one-to-one correspondence to the images conjured up in the mind of the reader rather than between the verbal sign "pig" and the corresponding visual sign. The translation curtails the possibility that such a creative treatment of the story might invite a variety of interpretations by anchoring the images to the spoken text, thereby reasserting the authority of the written Word as the source of biblical truth. However, to sustain the notion of fidelity to the source text, the translation must treat the written Word as transcendental and irreducible to any further signifying chain. The fact that the words on the page function as signifiers to the oral signified—a relationship itself arbitrary and dependent on convention—however, points to the ultimate impossibility of using this definition of equivalence as a guarantee of "faithfulness." This example illustrates the difficulties of using a translation strategy that attempts to create semiotic equivalents between word and image or the images invoked by the words.

The second paradigm treats translation as an act of intervention in the process of communication in which the video text *displaces* the centrality of the written text as the source of biblical truth and in which fidelity ceases to be a stable objective. This approach concerns the scriptural authority of a translation. In his address to the United Bible Societies Video Consultation in New York in February 1994, Basil Rebera argues that any discussion of faithfulness should recognize that "Christians and people of other faiths alike recognize only a written text as the Christian Scriptural source of revelation and authority" (Rebera, 1994, p. 3). Any attempt to express the Scriptures in another medium, therefore, cannot be described as translation in the terms understood by the Bible Societies. In the same presentation, Rebera links the issue of faithfulness to the original Word with a problem of authenticity. A translation cannot be faithful simultaneously to the written and audiovisual media because the two media function in different ways to communicate meaning. He discusses the problem of fidelity in fairly narrow terms by pointing to a distinction between the specific nature of images and the generic nature of language. A fat "animal" must always be represented by a pig, or a cow, or a sheep, or whatever, because a visual image cannot show an "animal." In this case he treats the photographic image as iconic in the Peircean sense in that it resembles its object more or less directly. He applies the same criteria of equivalence as the linguistic model by assuming that the meaning of the image is *intentional* in that it stands for the object it represents in a one-to-one relationship. However, his argument draws attention to a broader issue of the problematic difference between a person's image and the image of a person (Eco, 1984). For the scriptural authority of an audiovisual interpretation to be sustained, the viewer must accept a different type of representational relationship in which the image of a cow *stands for* an idea of the linguistic sign "animal." The sign is inferential rather than equivalent in so far as the image is used generically. Rebera's discussion of *Out of the Tombs* relies on this second dimension of signification. For example, when the young delinquent reappears at the end of the video dressed in a clean pair of slacks and a v-neck pullover, the audience is expected to interpret the image as a demonstration that the power of God can transcend evil. The signifying value of the image here is inferential because the reformed character's appearance constitutes proof of his redemption. The image of the young man, therefore, stands for a more general concept of redemption rather than Mr. X who lives on Y street in Z town. The difficulty arises in the generic use of the image when a gender or class reading takes it to mean that only white, middle-class, suburban males have the exclusive right to be liberated.

Both linguistic and textual approaches apply a set of normative values which assume that meaning inheres in the written text. This is consistent with the ideology of mission that underpins the Bible Societies translation program. It is predicated upon an approach to translation that privileges the author over the receptor and masks the processes of reading and interpretation. In either case a focus on the issue of faithfulness conceals more profound questions about the authorial power that underpins Bible Societies translation strategies. The important question is not whether *the* meaning of the text been preserved, but what is the function of the translation in its particular cultural and historical context? How and where does the locus of authorial power shift in these new translations? What is the effect of genre choice on the viewer's reception of the video? What if any new interpretations are suggested by such rewritings and in what ways does the translator seek to constrain the range of interpretive choices within a multimedia translation?

Translation and Interpretive Communities

Questions such as those above depend on the view that translation is a form of textual manipulation specific to a particular set of historical, institutional, and cultural contexts. Venuti (1995) argues that the discourses of fluency and transparency in English language translation are historically determined categories. For example, translation founded on a theory of dynamic equivalence reflects the 20th-century Anglo-American valorization of canons of accuracy or fidelity which is intended to preserve an illusion that the translated text is in fact the "original." The Bible Societies' linguistic model of multimedia translation assumes that one can achieve such transparency between source and target texts. On the other hand, the textual model perceives translation as a displacement of the "original" which threatens the authority of the source text. While Venuti aims to promote a theory and practice of translation that celebrates linguistic and cultural differences between source and target texts, his method of treating translation strategies as historically and institutionally contingent provides a useful approach to discussing faithfulness in multimedia translation. These arguments shift the terms of analysis from a comparison of source and target texts to the discourses of authorial power that support Bible translation strategies. The issue at the heart of translating the Bible from script to screen is one of faith and faithfulness. By this I mean, briefly, the perceived power of a multimedia translation to authenticate the Christian vision of the Bible as authoritative. The question becomes, faithful for whom? Made faithful by whom? According to what definitions of textuality? In this context, the notion of authority includes questions about the authorial power of the translator, the producer, and the institutions that validate the translations. Detweiler points out that "a sacred text emerges through particular authoritative figures in a community of believers who work to lend a given text divine endorsement and thus render it sacred" (1995, p. 215). Claims to divine authority may be part of the rhetoric of the text as suggested by Clines who demonstrates how by ascribing authorship of the Ten Commandments to God within the composition of the text itself, the real authors' intention of creating a set of moral and legal precepts written in the interests of the "*elites* and *power-holders* in Israelite society" is masked (1995, p. 32). Commentators who read the text uncritically buy into the ideology of the text which conceals the interested parties in the text's construction. Alternatively, the authority of the text may be constructed extra-textually. Jasper links the question of authority to the creation of a biblical canon which he defines as sanctioned traditions of reading sacred texts. Individual texts are read only within the boundaries of canonical orthodoxy whose "sacred truth" is thereby defended. The canon operates as "an instrument of principled, systematic exclusion" (Jasper, 1995, p. 23). Both writers take their cue from Fish who argues that the text's authority is established by interpretive communities who are themselves interested parties who seek to establish a stability of meaning:

> An interpretive community is not objective because as a bundle of interests, or particular purposes and goals, its perspective is interested rather than neutral; but by the very same reasoning, the meanings and texts produced by an interpretive community are not subjective because they do not proceed from an individual but from a public and conventional point of view. (Fish, 1980, p. 14)

The same kinds of processes appear to operate within multimedia translations in the ways that potential conflicts of interpretation are constrained or concealed.

One of the key points is how and why an audience perceives a multimedia production as a translation. The audience rarely links the perception to any objective notion of fidelity to the source text. Instead the perception relies primarily on three factors. The first is the degree to which visual representations conform to popular images of biblical stories that have been created and widely circulated through the cinema, Christmas card production, Bible story illustration, and other forms of illustration used in teaching and evangelism (see Goethals in this volume). In this sense, historical reconstructions of the period, which rely on western traditions of representation, are likely to be accepted by European and North American audiences as faithful representations of the written Word because attention has been paid to the authenticity of the translation's setting and *mise en-scène*. The degree to which these images are accepted in other parts of the world reflects the success of Christian evangelism in exporting them because this type of representation has a particular cultural currency among European and North American audiences.

The second factor that sustains the perceived authenticity of a video translation relies on the degree to which the video translation sustains interpretive conventions and canons of biblical criticism. The third factor appears in the discourses of authenticity within the video text itself, that is, in the ways in which the narrative and point of view of a video are structured to convince the viewer of its faithfulness to printed Scripture.

The series *Gospel*, produced by The Drama House for the British Broadcasting Corporation's Channel 2 (BBC2) in 1992 and distributed in the United States by Vision Video, incorporates many of these canons of authenticity. The series consists of a compilation of the Gospel accounts of events leading up to the birth of Christ presented as a verbatim performance. Several layers of interpretive authority are mobilized within the series. The seriousness of the producers' intentions are signaled by their use of the King James Version, a translation that is traditionally recognized by the Church of England as the authoritative translation. In this way, the twin powers of Church and State are invoked to authenticate the series. English viewers would recognize the series as authoritative because BBC2 broadcast it.

The British Broadcasting Corporation is a public broadcasting institution incorporated by Act of Parliament and funded by a fee levied on all television owners in Great Britain. The company has a strong identity as a producer of high quality arts programming which further endorses the importance of the series. The minimal staging and lighting of the performance, while allowing the actors to move around and interact with each other, draws attention to the importance of the written text. The acting style and intonation are based on received ways of performing Shakespeare plays. This makes an important intertextual connection with that other peculiarly British theatrical institution and reinforces the Bible as both sacred and classic text.

The authority of a video translation can also be validated extra-textually in a number of different ways. The most common is the practice of acknowledging biblical scholars who were consulted on the preparation of scripts and storyboards.

Lost But Found

The story of the Prodigal Son produced by the Malawi Bible Society (MBS) in 1992 clearly illustrates the power of interpretive tradition to authenticate a video translation. *Lost But Found* is an exemplar of the use of this parable in Christian teaching as an archetypal redemption narrative.

This version tells the story of a young man who has recently completed an M.A. in agricultural management, but shows no interest in taking up the role envisaged for him on his father's farm. He spends his time daydreaming about expensive cars, beautiful women, and a life full of excitement. He is a disappointment to his father and a source of annoyance to his diligent elder brother. Eventually, he persuades his father to give him the share of the property he expects to inherit and heads for the city where he squanders all his money on clothes, women, and drink. The cash is soon spent and the destitute young man is forced to beg from his former friends and rummage for food in rubbish bins. Several months later, the young man comes to his senses, literally wakes up on a rubbish heap on the outskirts of the city, and decides to return home and throw himself on the mercy of his father. As he approaches the house, his father runs out to meet him. The father throws a party to celebrate his son's return and everybody lives happily ever after, including the elder brother who is persuaded to enter into the celebrations.

The video transposes the parable of the Prodigal Son into a postcolonial African context. It incorporates Scripture passages as well as quoting directly from an English translation of the passage in the Gospel of Luke. The story functions as an analogy intended to convey the relevance of the parable to modern readers. The video narrative portrays a world parallel to the world of the Gospel story. It is set on the property of a wealthy farmer; the city is substituted but nevertheless signifies the foreignness of the cultural values, expectations, and social behavior that the Prodigal Son would have encountered living in a foreign country. The father, who believes his son to be dead, is overjoyed to see him again and forgives his earlier behavior. However, character, plot, and location merely account for the denotative levels of meaning within the text. The interpretive traditions on which the video draws are revealed through the narrative discourses contained in the expressive plane of the story.

There are two key narratives within *Lost But Found* that sustain its authenticity as scriptural and signify its relevance to the implied audience. I will begin with an analysis of the Scripture narrative. It is significant to note that the family portrayed in the video represents a particular set of Christian moral values. The characters are portrayed as a nuclear family of four who have adopted the habits and status of European colonists and missionaries. The conservative habits of the family contrast with the younger son's profligacy and serve to reinforce the message that Christian diligence and faith in God are somehow linked to success. In one scene, the father reads to the assembled family a passage from the Book of Jeremiah which states that a person who acquires his riches deceitfully will soon be parted from them and is nothing but a fool. The elder son, who criticizes his brother for being a good-for-nothing lazy bones, nods his head in agreement while the younger son refuses to listen and defiantly reads his magazine. The moral of the scene is clear and anticipates the fate of the younger son.

These representations reinforce the narrative closures in the video in order to communicate a message of redemption consistent with a particular interpretive tradition of the parable. For example, the video opens with a flash forward in which the son's homecoming is recounted in a sequence of parallel edits between a closeup shot of the son's dirty bare feet and the father's expensive leather shoes and ends with the son casting himself at his father's feet and giving a rehearsed speech asking for forgiveness. This pre-title sequence sets the pattern for the way the rest of the video is to be interpreted, inserting a narrative closure at the beginning that is mirrored by a similar closure at the end of the video. Not only does the elder brother enter into the celebrations of his brother's homecoming, but the video also concludes with the younger son singing *Amazing Grace*. Here is a sinner who has learned his lesson and returned to the bosom of his family. It is worth quoting extensively here from Gabriel Josipovici who describes the scriptural origins of this interpretive tradition and its development in St. Augustine's *Confessions*. Josipovici argues that in *Romans* chapters 7 and 8 Paul of Tarsus reconstructs the narrative of the Prodigal Son to authenticate his own conversion:

> We can now see clearly why Saul of Tarsus dramatized for his listeners what had happened to him and how he became Paul the Apostle. And we can also see that in this he was, after all, only doing what...all readers do: he was completing or continuing a series, and the series he chose to continue was that which concerned the Prodigal Son. Gone, however, is the elder brother, gone is the father's admonition to that brother, gone therefore is the familial tension which...made the parable an echo of the story of Joseph and his brothers. Instead what is developed is the story of the sinner who repents and is welcomed back....To compensate for the loss of the elder brother...there are new complexities. But these are all internal. What St. Paul is interested in is the state of mind of the Son before his return. (1988, pp. 244-245)

This aspect of the younger son's character and motivation is developed quite extensively in the video—in the build up to his departure, his arrival in the city, and his decision to return home. Viewers share his inner thoughts through a series of monologues and dream sequences in which he fantasizes about a better life, voices his joy at his arrival in the city, expresses his bewilderment at his destitution, and finally determines to humbly beg his father's pardon. When, at the celebration for his homecoming he bursts into song, the viewer is invited to identify with the character's spiritual journey of sin and repentance. This contemporary reading of the parable reinforces what Josipovici has termed "the Puritan conversion narrative" (1988, p. 248). From this perspective, therefore, it is possible to perceive the video as a faithful interpretation of that tradition in which the notion of fidelity becomes one of the discourses within the video used to authenticate and sustain the canonical authority of the written text.

If *Lost But Found* signifies its authenticity as Scripture through a reliance on a particular interpretive tradition, how does it signify its relevance to its implied audience? It achieves this through the contextual framing of the parable. The story is framed within a typical African narrative about the contradictions of post-colonial modernity by focusing on the perennial problems of urban migration and the consequent economic and cultural alienation. Within this framework the story functions as an analogy which relies on a rhetoric of metonymy. The son represents a generation of educated African elite who have become disassociated from their family roots by seeking independence and self determination in the city. The familial conflict in the video represents a competition between the two value systems of urban and rural life as well as between different generations. The younger son's selfishness and failure to live up to family expectations becomes symptomatic of these conflicts. The story of his journey into destitution draws attention to the worst aspects of modernization in developing countries and exposes the enormous gap between rich and poor. Eventually, he learns that what his father provided has more to offer than the distractions of metropolitan life.

I have attempted to demonstrate how the parable of the Prodigal Son has been rewritten to reinforce the contextual relevance of the story for urban African men and how it is also consistent with the dominant evangelical interpretation. In *Lost But Found* the parable's other discourses about the self-destructiveness of envy and the self-righteousness of the Pharisees are foreclosed by the redemption narrative. In conclusion, this highlights the fact that the meaning of the text is not a stable entity but is a product of interpretation in which "...interpretation is the source of texts, facts, authors, intentions" rather than being defined by them (Fish, 1980, p. 16).

Genre Analysis

My second example explores the ways in which the rhetoric of fidelity is embedded in the choice of genre. It also features a discussion of how we can use genre analysis to reveal interpretive contradictions introduced by the use of popular television genres. The processes are very complex and the analytical model proposed here is still tentative. Nevertheless, I believe it offers an important approach to uncovering the discourses of authorial power that underpin video translation. One must distinguish between the use of genre as an analytical concept in literary or biblical criticism, where it has a largely descriptive function, and film or cultural theory where critics use genre to analyze the ways in which the dominant ideology of the producing institution (cinema or television) is perpetuated and power relations between producers and consumers are sustained.

Cultural Studies sees genre as the product of three groups of forces: the production practices of a particular industry, the narrative conventions of the text itself, and the audience's expectancies and competencies. The production practices include commissioning, production, and marketing, and consist of a whole set of relationships between funders, creative teams, editorial teams, publicity agents, critics, and consumers. A Cultural Studies approach to genre looks at the ways in which these practices and relationships contribute to the meaning of a particular text. It emphasizes a notion of the cultural and historical specificity of these practices. Stephen Neale (1995) argues that it is critically essential to understand genres within an economic context, conditioned by specific economic imperatives, and institutional and industrial contexts. His argument demonstrates how the development of a genre is inextricably linked to the producing institution's primary motivation of economic survival that is predicated upon box office returns in the cinema, or income from advertising in television.

The narrative conventions of the text provide the grounds for how the story will develop, as well as for how the audience makes sense of the unfolding narrative and predicts its outcome. The plausibility of a narrative's construction is central to how genre works. For example, in a musical, the audience expects the actors to burst into song. When this happens, the audience sees it as normal within the bounds of the narrative conventions of musicals and therefore credible. However, if the same were to happen in a horror movie, it would not conform to viewers' expectations of the genre and therefore seem implausible.

Lastly, the narrative must be culturally credible. This does not mean "real" or "true" in any direct sense. Narrative truth is a discourse determined by what viewers believe to be true. Certain genres rely on establishing a transparent relationship between the real world and the world represented in the narrative. The narrative is constructed in such a way as to conceal discontinuities between one cut and the next and to disguise the gap between fiction and reality. The maintenance of narrative realism relies on the creation of a coherent and convincing fictional world supported by realist conventions such as the requirement that it should obey the laws of cause and effect, should conform to expectations about a character's psychology, or should present a coherent spatial and temporal world. Forms of realism operate as a complex network of representational convention and audience expectation dominated by a regime of narrative coherence and unity. In video translation, the generic conventions and translation strategy used will affect the way in which the discourses of fidelity to the real world of the book are structured.

Genres are empirical and historical categories constructed by authors, audiences, and critics in order to serve communicative and aesthetic purposes. The purpose of my next set of case studies is to observe how radically different interpretations can occur when a translation combines generic codes constructed within different institutional contexts.

Generic Choices and Fidelity

There appear to be three primary approaches to ensuring fidelity to the source text in use: faithfulness to the story's context, faithfulness to the letter of the text, and faithfulness to the spirit of the Bible. The approaches are reflected in the existence of several different generic categories that define the text/viewer relationship and reveal the theological or cultural identity of the translation. Briefly, these are history, analogy, adventure story, oral history, myth, and allegory. Each of these categories can be identified by a particular set of narrative and representational characteristics. The predominant genre is the history video in which the stated intention of the producer is often "to bring the stories to life" (publicity for Nest Entertainment Inc.'s *The Animated Stories*, a series of Bible stories on video). This genre draws on realist conventions of narrative representation that reveal a desire to replicate the historical (and geographical) context of the story or to maintain an acceptable degree of faithfulness to the historical and geographical context of the source text. Two requirements of narrative realism in the genre are that a harmonious and unified world should be represented and, therefore, that the narrative conventions themselves should remain invisible. The discourses of fidelity within this genre are characterized by a certain transparency which obscures the gap between the fictional world of the video and the real world of the biblical story, which is itself constructed.

The second generic category which I have labeled "analogy" finds a parallel social or religious problem suggested by the spirit of the written story and proceeds to apply an interpretation of the source to the contemporary context. An example of translation by analogy has already been discussed above. It establishes narrative truth by appealing to what viewers believe to be true in relation to their own experience. As with the historical genre, analogies are dominated by the narrative and aesthetic conventions of realism. The codes of fidelity are characterized by an emphasis on the relevance of the biblical story to the contemporary audience. In this case, however, the transparency of the relationship between the real world of the viewer and the fictional world of the analogy is achieved. Viewers, recognizing the analogy, willingly suspend their disbelief and make the connection between the two worlds.

Adventure stories form a popular genre for children's videos. In these stories the hero, who has God on his side, eventually triumphs over the villain and saves the world. The theology of good and evil is highly simplified and reduced to a set of binary oppositions. The "Christians" are the good guys and everybody else is a bad guy. The Christian ideology of good and evil is routinely imposed on interpretations of Old Testament stories as well as New Testament texts. A predominance of film animation (often cell animation), which in visual style and narrative construction make inter-textual references to the ideological world of Disney, characterizes this genre. The genre relies heavily on an ideology of realism manifest in the representational style used and the narrative coherence of the story.

The fourth genre, oral history, gives priority to the letter of the text and consists simply of a recitation by one or more actors. The sincerity of the actor's performance, the choice of translation, and, frequently, the choice of actor, underwrites the fidelity of this recitation. For example Biblenet Inc. advertizes *The Bible on CD-ROM*, an interactive program featuring Charlton Heston (who played Moses in Cecil B. De Mille's *Ten Commandments,* 1956, and won an Academy Award for his acting in *Ben Hur,* directed by William Wyler, 1959) as the storyteller.

A fifth generic category uses the narrative and representational conventions of myths and folk tales to retell Bible stories. A typical example of this genre would be the animated series *Testament* produced by the Welsh Channel Four and first transmitted on British television in 1996. The folkloric or mythical treatment of the series is conveyed through the visual style of the animators as well as the ways in which the stories are rewritten to provide a historical context for the biblical story. Finally, and more rarely, a text receives an allegorical treatment. Kristoff Kieślowski's *Dekalog* (1988) a ten-part television series of one hour plays, based on the Ten Commandments, is a rare, but outstanding example.

With the exception of the last two, these categories are created by, and within, a particular set of predominately Christian institutional production contexts, that is, by publishers and producers whose primary business is to promote Christian literature and other Christian materials. These translations borrow representational styles that conform to another set of generic rules and conventions particular to products created for mass consumption: music video, animation, epic cinema, contemporary drama, and so on. For example *Lost But Found* (MBS) is an analogy that uses contemporary drama. *A Father and Two Sons* (ABS) is also an analogy rendered as country music video. It is important to bear in mind the different motivations of the institutional bases for these translations. The combination of different generic traditions may likely produce interpretive contradictions and effects that exceed the discourses of the written scriptural text.

A Father and Two Sons

My next case study demonstrates how the choice of country music video affects our reading of the ABS's rendering of the parable of the Prodigal Son. Mark Fenster (1989) identifies a number of key characteristics that define the genre and distinguish it from other forms of music video. The central narrative frame of country music video is the filmed or taped performance intercut with visual segments that illustrate the plot of the lyrics. The performance is seen as a crucial aspect of the music's communicative and emotional powers. The visual representations complement and enhance the music that traditionally focuses on the family, family rituals, or the community, and that places value on "the country" as opposed to the city.

Country music video adopts a visual iconography of simplicity and ordinariness that draws on the narrative conventions and imagery of the Hollywood Western seen by many as archetypal of a classic American realism that mythically reconstructs American national and cultural identity.

We can see how the ABS has successfully manipulated this genre to reframe the story of the Prodigal Son. The narrative and visual realism employed in the video serve to underwrite both narrative and cultural plausibility of the video. It is believable because it conforms to the audience's expectations of the genre. In many ways the choice of genre well suits an interpretation of the Prodigal Son because the discourses of country music video and the redemption narrative in the Lucan parable converge. In this sense we can describe the video as a faithful translation both to its chosen genre and to its interpretation of Scripture. Significantly it allows both narrative discourses of redemption and envy to emerge by resisting narrative closure in the plot.

However, rather than achieving a functionally equivalent translation in which the images are "faithful to the images invited by the text in the minds and hearts of the original receivers" (Thomas, 1994b, p. 46), I would argue that the connotative levels of the text, produced by a combination of genres and representational choices made by the producers, invite interpretations that cannot necessarily be read into the authorial intentions of the parable. This is achieved in a variety of ways. American family values and family or community rituals are strongly reinforced within the video. The scene in which the father pleads with the elder son is represented by a series of flashbacks of the two brothers playing with their father. The images flicker as if the son were replaying them in a home movie. The final sequence contrasts this happy family scenario with the anger of the elder brother. The image freezes in a reflection in the windshield of his truck and then fades. In the party scene, images of a multi-ethnic group of people underwrites a mythology of community that is specific to American culture and the way it is inflected in the country music genre as well as in commercials for Coca Cola. Glimpses of a fiddle player and the ranch house in the background suggest a particular kind of party that contrasts with the party scene earlier in the video, which is dominated by strobe lighting and flashing police lights.

The connotative levels of narrative representation provoke contradictions that are presumably not part of the producer's authorial intentions. These arise from the particularities of genre choice. Whereas the plot of the video story remains open, imagery borrowed from other genres may introduce unintentional narrative closures. American viewers, who recognize the aesthetic conventions borrowed from the genres of the Hollywood Western or country music video, use their experience of these genres to make sense of the *Father and Two Sons* and in doing so unconsciously transfer the narrative closures of the Western and country music video into the interpretation. Similarly on the denotative plane of the ABS video the singer serves as the narrator, but the connotations of this image come from the motivations of country music video which are to promote the artist. Thus audience identification shifts from the singer as narrator to the singer as American blues star. This identification is reinforced by the packaging of the video tape which promotes the singer and her CD *Angel of Mercy,* which includes a recording of *A Father and Two Sons.*

Conclusion

In spite of the best efforts of the translator, multimedia translation generates interpretations that are constitutive of the cultural context, histories of reading, and the generic expectations of the translation's narrative form. Translation, therefore, encourages "unfaithful" interpretations and generates a new text/reader relationship. It displaces the central authority of the written word and gives rise to new sets of interpretive authorities that deny the privileged status of the written word. The process of multimedia translation creates a phenomenological problem for the faithful reader. If the Holy Book of the Bible loses its sacred and authoritative centrality, on what basis do Christian communities construct their religious identity? How do the faithful authenticate and validate their faith? And if the presence of God loses its connection with the material form of the Book, how do the faithful "know" God?

This is not the place to discuss the philosophy of multimedia translation. But it does suggest that the scope of the translator's task extends beyond faithful interpretation to a recognition of the processes of re-writing that involve audiences, producers, and productions in culturally and historically defined contexts and to an awareness of the communicative effects of nonprint media.

12

Communication Models, Translation, and Fidelity

Paul A. Soukup, SJ

The fact that people regularly translate from one language to another or—as the American Bible Society (ABS) New Media Translations Project has done—from one medium to another, may seem to make it easier to evaluate those translations. At some point, people can, and do, claim that one translation "works" while another does not, that one translation has greater aesthetic qualities than another, or that one translation is more faithful than another. The fact that people make such judgments, though, does not necessarily make it easier to explain theoretically how they make them.

Among other things, communication study examines both the process of communicating and the product. What might it contribute to an understanding of fidelity in translation? Various perspectives on communication, reflected in models of communication, can illuminate the process and, indirectly, the attendant question of fidelity. Without attempting any comprehensive treatment, I shall present four such perspectives: communication as transportation, communication as a semiotic system, communication as ritual, and communication as conversation. After a brief introduction to each, I shall examine the consequences of each for fidelity in translation. Finally, I shall offer some more general comments drawn from this treatment.

Early communication theory, following a kind of transportation model, fosters a view of fidelity that favors a sense of equivalence—something that can be measured. Later communication theory follows a more ritualistic view and asks what communicators do with communication; in this view, fidelity becomes more functional. Yet another approach sees communication as a manifestation of semiotic systems; in this view, fidelity manifests surface changes in a deeper structure (see essays by Hodgson and Stecconi in this volume). Finally, an interactive approach places communication as a conversational system; here fidelity takes on a different value—more a characteristic of the audience than of the text.

Communication as Transportation

In an influential review article, James Carey (1975/1989) proposed a distinction between communication as transportation and communication as ritual. By the former he characterized what had dominated North American communication studies through the mid-1970s: a sense that communication primarily involved the transfer or transportation of a message from one person or source to another through some medium or agent.

That kind of traditional communication study diagrams the communication process as a linear process involving a sender (or source), a message, a receiver (or target), a channel (or medium), a context, and various sources of noise. (See Figure 1.) Originally designed by Claude Shannon (Shannon & Weaver, 1949) as a tool for measuring the electronic transmission capacity of telephone circuits where one could compare an input signal to an output signal, the model, despite its mechanistic presuppositions, has found application in roughly identifying stages of communication. This model possesses a certain power since it diagrams various general aspects of communication and thus holds a certain universal applicability—describing communication in situations ranging from face-to-face interaction through written texts to electronic transmission. Eugene Nida and William Reyburn (1981) have successfully applied this model to translation.

The elements of the model identify key "places" in communication. The source or sender originates a message. Note that this implies that the source somehow determines or controls the message, thus becoming the "original" or yardstick against which to measure any copy or transported message. The receiver, or end location of the message, makes its version of the message available for measurement. If the message differs, then some distortion has occurred—due to "noise" in the channel through which the message passed or due to a change in context that affects the resulting process of understanding. This model works well to highlight what occurs in the transfer of a message from one place, or language, to another. It points out the places in which a message might undergo change due to the system of transportation—exactly what an engineer needs to discover. The model

Figure 1: Transportation model of communication.

applies to texts somewhat mechanically, but it does give a degree of insight into the communication process.

With this model, we could describe a translation in one of two ways. First of all, we could regard the translation as an intermediate process. A message source creates a message and transmits it through a medium (the translator) who in turn sends it on to the receiver. The process of translation may inject noise into the translation, though it should adjust the message to the context of the receiver. That very adjustment, though, makes the messages different in language and in presuppositions, as Nida points out in several places. Second, we could regard the translator as the creator of a new message, which reaches a receiver through some channel or other. In this instance, a double process of communication occurs: from the message source to the translator; from the translator to a receiver. In each case, one theoretically could measure the message at each end of the process and compare the two. The preponderance of authority or power remains at the point of origin—in the original, which acts as the yardstick for measurement.

From the sender-receiver transport perspective, fidelity becomes the demonstrated equivalence of the message transmitted from source to receiver. In the simplest (and original) application, one would measure the electronic signal at each end of the model and compare the two. Fidelity results when the received (or transmitted/translated) signal diverges little from the original. In more complicated settings—language translation, for example—one would have to determine an appropriate measure (Thomas, 1994a). Nida and Reyburn illustrate this move by showing how a word-for-word translation does not necessarily result in a faithful translation since it ignores idiomatic usage, cultural conventions, and so forth. They propose instead the concept of functional equivalence, preferring that the translation communicate the same function from one language or culture to another. For example, the biblical phrase, "to beat one's breast," may not communicate sorrow or repentance in all cultures; in some, a different action may serve that function. The faithful translation must change the linguistic phrase to convey the same meaning.

In this kind of linguistic translation, a bilingual speaker, one who understands both the culture of the original or source language and the culture of the target language, best judges the fidelity of the translated work to the original. The sense of measurement implicit in the Shannon model applies almost directly since such a speaker could quantify the degree of deviation of the target from source. Though difficult in practice, that kind of measurement remains fairly simple from the theoretical perspective of the model. (When applied to electronic circuits—the intent of the model—such measurement also remains fairly simple in practice.)

Multimedia translation poses a similar, but a more complex, situation. A message moves not necessarily from one culture to another but from one means of expression to another, usually within the same culture. The means of expression, though, do not parallel each other the way that languages do.

What should a measurement of fidelity measure in this case? This situation touches biblical work in two ways. On the one hand, the process is not completely new for the biblical message, since it has historically undergone a major media transition from oral performance to written text. However, that transition characterizes not only the Bible, but a wide range of texts, and so the conventions of writing have evolved to encompass the rhetorical and oral cues of the spoken word—often slavishly. When people heard words read back to them, they could acknowledge the functional equivalence of the "translation" to writing. One could argue that writing became less a translation than an encoding or a means of storage. (See the essay by Scott in this volume for some examples of this.)

On the other hand, multimedia translation *is* new for the Bible (or any other texts) since it involves both restoring the written text to a performative form and supplying interpretive elements from the rhetorical or oral cues. And so, from the perspective of the transportation model, multimedia translation faces at least five challenges, which I will list in increasing order of difficulty. Throughout this, I am presuming that the translation of a text—the biblical text—has been put into a multimedia form. (See Sisley's essay in this volume as well as Rebera, 1994 for more on these things.)

First, how should one determine the functional equivalence of paralinguistic features? Texts do record rhythm, rhyme, pacing, but an oral performance must go beyond these and include tone of voice, gesture, inflection, and so forth. Visual interpretation adds still other paralinguistic features, ranging from movement to interaction distances.

Second, multimedia translation, of necessity, must include extratextual material. How can any measure apply to this? The receiver ends up with more data than the biblical source presents—for example, the multimedia translation has to specify appearance of actors (body type, clothing), geographical setting, set decoration, and so on. Perhaps one should measure this as noise or as input from a second source (the translator), but the end product certainly differs from the original. As such, the received message differs from the source. At best, the multimedia translation merely disambiguates a text—and that does change the text. One might ask whether this differs from what any reader does—but the role of the reader has received little attention in terms of this model (see Tompkins, 1980).

Third, what should the multimedia translation do with media-specific features? Oral features can be successfully encoded and decoded in written texts. The written text, however, adds its own features: the appearance of letters and words on a page; the addition of sentence, paragraph or chapter markings; the color of inks and papers; and the specific codes of writing. One must acknowledge that the Gutenberg press did something to the Bible. Should these secondary features be ignored or integrated in the translation? Can one separate them out with any degree of confidence? What of the kinds of oral resonances that a text could reproduce by cross-referencing (or a computer by hypertext links)? What happens on the other end—when the multimedia form has richer features than the original? Hypertext, after all, encompasses much more than oral resonance can. How can we determine fidelity of features non-existent in the source?

Fourth, how might one measure the fidelity of the multimedia rendering of episodes or pericopes? The very division of the text changes the flow of the narrative, yet the multimedia form—at least in the U.S. culture—presumes an episodic structuring. Granted that lectionary evidence indicates that the Church has long treated the Scriptures as episodic, the multimedia form still imposes its own structuring.

Fifth, can there be any kind of equivalence of non-narrative material in a multimedia format? For example, how could one (a) translate into multimedia an expository document like the *Letter to the Romans* and (b) evaluate the equivalence between source and receiver?

Typically and theoretically, from this perspective, multimedia translation depends on the same model of measuring equivalence between source and receiver as does linguistic translation—the judgment of a bilingual speaker, though in this case, we might say, the judgment of an informed media user. The key judgment is whether the message content remains functionally similar.

Communication as Semiotic System

A second, related, perspective drawn from communication studies, sees communication as a semiotic system. This view builds on the work of Ferdinand de Saussure (1959/1915), who described meaning—first in language and then more generally—in terms of the relation of signifier and signified, which makes up the sign. Others, including the American philosophers C. S. Peirce (1960-1966) and Charles W. Morris (1970/1938), also contributed to this perspective. That work emphasizes levels of signification as well as the process of reference. Virtually any meaning (or signification) system breaks down into signs with their component parts. Signs themselves relate to other signs in many ways but particularly by difference. That is, only signs that differ from one another become meaningful within a given system of signs. In typography, for example, the sign *a* differs from the sign *b* but not from the sign **a**. In addition sets of codes or rules describe how signs take on meaning, with different sign systems or codes following analogical rules—for example, one could describe a verbal code, a clothing code, a gestural code, and so on. Further, the signification process is recursive, so that a sign may take the role of a signifier to form a more complex sign made up of yet more signifieds. (See Figure 2.)

The semiotic system forms a descriptive tool in communication study. Scholars have applied it as a general theory of signs to linguistic or verbal systems (its primary application in de Saussure's writings) but also to graphic, visual, cinematic, cultural, and even culinary systems. Some, in

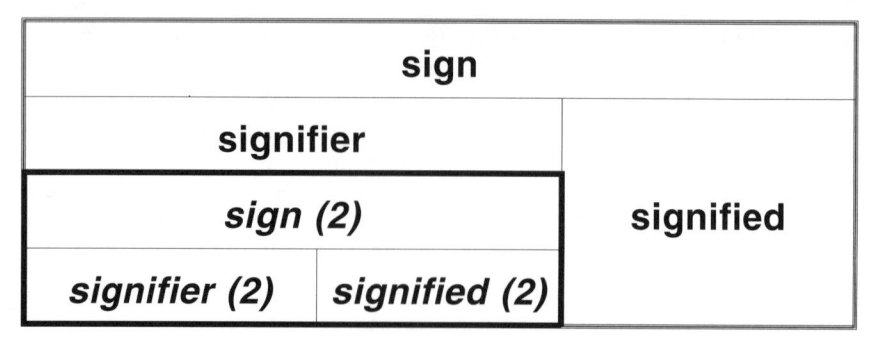

sign		
signifier		signified
sign (2)	
signifier (2)	*signified (2)*

Figure 2: Parts of a sign according to de Saussure's model, illustrating the recursive nature of signification, where a sign (2) becomes a signifier of another sign.

particular Roland Barthes (1972/1957), show great skill in describing one set of semiotic relations in terms of another (usually verbal) or in untangling the overlaid codes within a complex structure like the novel (1974/1970). Others, including Claude Lévi-Strauss (1969a/1967 & 1969b/1964) and Umberto Eco (1976), have found semiotics valuable to describe cultural and linguistic systems. (See the essays by Hodgson and Stecconi in this volume for additional discussion of the application of semiotics to communication study and translation.)

In this perspective translation might be described as a change of signifier. The resulting signs maintain reference to the same signifieds, but express those signifieds in different forms. If Barthes is correct, for example, clothing expresses cultural relations that could be translated into verbal descriptions. Lévi-Strauss attempts the same thing in terms of kinship relations (1969a/1967) and food preparation (1969b/1964). The resulting verbal description communicates the same information but in a different code. In a different, but somewhat related context, Ong (1997) points out that information (the code) is not communication. Information remains mechanical; people communicate only when they use the code to facilitate an interaction, to exchange meaning (p. 3), to influence another (p. 5). From a theoretical perspective, the translator, then, engages the semiotic code and moves it into communication.

We can also describe this process in terms of layers of structure and the codes (rules, conventions, norms) that give meaning to those structures. The translator determines a sub-surface structure of relations and expresses it in terms of a different set of relations. In semiotic terms, the signifieds and their relations (sub-structure) stay constant while the signifiers and their relations (surface structure) change, resulting in a different set of signs. The meaning and the reference stay the same. For example, one could encode the verbal reference, "I am angry," with a facial expression.

Here fidelity in translation refers to the identity of sub-surface structures and the codes that give them meaning. The decoding/encoding process needs to follow particular norms so that the surface structures in the two sign systems are equivalent. Theoretically, the process involves more work than that implied in the transport model, but remains essentially simple in description. (See Figure 3). Note, too, that the process of evaluation in this instance does not differ markedly from that involved in the transportation model. The test of fidelity is the recognition of equivalence of the sub-surface signifieds.

Just as with the transportation model, the semiotic model presents a number of challenges to multimedia translation, mostly because of what that translation attempts to do. Multimedia translation of the Bible moves from a verbal sign system to a more complex verbal and nonverbal one. This differs from other uses of semiotics in translation. Linguistic translation stays within at least analogously similar sign systems. Barthes's or Lévi-Strauss's translation work across differing systems takes a verbal system as its target. By moving in the other direction, multimedia work faces many of the same challenges identified above, but some others as well.

First, how do different sign systems work together to create complex systems of signification? While all of us negotiate such complexes in face-to-face interaction (verbal signs, nonverbal signs, tactile ones, and so forth), we do so unconsciously. In a multimedia translation, such decisions become conscious: should we value the visual over the verbal? What paralinguistic signs do we invoke? How does one sign system interact with another?

Second, multimedia translation must, in effect, create a new system of signification; one made up of visual, auditory, and interactive elements. Computer CD-ROM products have led the way here, but have not addressed the level of complexity required by the biblical text. This challenge, though, carries with it a very real benefit: the possibility of a much deeper understanding of the source material since a semiotic translation requires close analysis of the source and an understanding of the semiotic relations it contains.

Third, multimedia translation must discover and use readily accessible conventional signs. While sign systems can be (and indeed are) created, they need ready and wide acceptance in order to be effective. Is there a conventional multimedia "language," one that does not require a skilled reader like a Roland Barthes, a Roman Jakobson, or an Umberto Eco? The

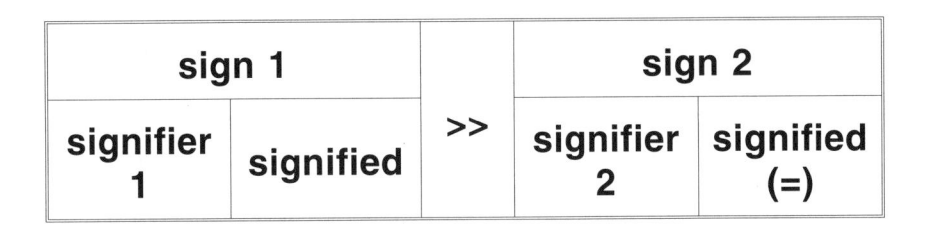

sign 1			sign 2	
signifier 1	signified	>>	signifier 2	signified (=)

Figure 3: Conversion of one sign system to another, retaining the same signified but altering signifiers and, consequently, signs.

availability of such a sign system would facilitate successful understanding of the translation, for if people cannot understand the "language" of multimedia, the translation will do them no good.

There is little precedent for measuring the equivalence of semiotic systems. But, if we regard translation as a kind of transport of meaning or transport of signification, from one language to another or from one medium to another, we can specify key elements in the process. The source (or source text) must in some way control the process; thus, part of the translator's task includes determining which elements contribute to the meaning, which elements constitute the core of the text. Both E.-A. Gutt (1992) and Patrick Cattrysse (1997) suggest ways to do this by examining key sign relations. Once one has identified such elements and created a target "text," one could devise a method of measuring the degree of success or degree of fidelity of the target.

Communication as Ritual

The second part of Carey's distinction describes communication as ritual. Communication, in this view, consists of something we do—a regular performance. Communication is less the transportation of information than the "construction and maintenance of an ordered, meaningful cultural world that can serve as a control and container for human action" (Carey, 1989/1975, pp. 18-19). Carey notes that such a view, though new to American communication study, actually predates the transport model, being listed in dictionaries as an "archaic" usage that links the definition of communication to "commonness," "community," or "sharing." He continues:

> A ritual view of communication is directed not toward the extension of messages in space but toward the maintenance of society in time; not the act of imparting information but the representation of shared beliefs.
>
> If the archetypal case of communication under a transmission view is the extension of messages across geography for the purpose of control, the archetypal case under a ritual view is the sacred ceremony that draws persons together in fellowship and commonality. (p. 18)

Ritual focuses attention on the uses of communication and the kinds of things that such uses accomplish. Carey's example of the newspaper under this view provides wonderful clarity: the ritual view "will, for example, view reading a newspaper less as sending or gaining information and more as attending a mass, a situation in which nothing new is learned but in which a particular view of the world is portrayed and confirmed" (p. 20).

Following this model, contemporary communication study envisions the entire process as a kind of participation or activity of communicators, with the receiver or audience holding significant power. The meaning of a given communication results from the process, with message creator and message receiver together evoking the meaning. Ong's clarifying distinction of information and communication works here, too. Communication, "the exchange of meanings...through a common system of signs" (1996, p. 3, quoting the *Encyclopedia Britanica*), or the influence exerted by one mind on another (p. 5), depends on ritual (the exchange) as much as on information (the encoded message). In other words, information forms a necessary, but not sufficient, condition for communication, as does ritual. And so, here too, the source message retains a measure of authority—within the ritual interplay of communicators, one cannot make a text mean whatever one wishes.

The task of the translator consists in providing the occasion for "portraying and confirming" a view of the world. The ritual experience of participating in the Bible follows from the translator's work. While such an assertion may beg the question of how translation works, it can clarify the goal of translation. Fidelity becomes the creation of similar use, of similar views of the world. Linguistic or semantic identity gives way to community identity and to a kind of inculturation. Ong again offers a helpful note when he remarks that thinking is an event stimulated by communication (1996, p. 5). The transportation or decoding of information is not communication, but only the occasion for it. Similarly, we could argue that the Bible is an event in the life of the believing community. The test of fidelity becomes the reality of that event.

Therefore, if we regard communication as a ritual, we must attend more closely to the role of the audience. How do they use the text? What role does it play in their lives? Their study? Their worship? From this perspective we have to recognize that the source text itself, while still maintaining authority, loses the centrality that it holds in the other two models. Instead the text takes on a variety of roles—and from those roles emerge the places that we could determine fidelity. Here a change in media could well have important consequences for fidelity.

Audience recognition—community adoption—plays a role here. Audiences and critics already make distinctions among translations; these form yet another focal point for an examination of the audience-source-fidelity interplay. For example, people seldom refer to a film or television work as a "translation"; instead they speak of a re-telling, a re-creation, an adaptation, an abridgement, a version, and so on. What differentiates these in the mind of an audience? How much do those terms indicate "adequacy" or fidelity? They do, however, indicate the audience's use of the experience provided by the encounter with the material.

And so, here too, multimedia translation faces some challenges posed by the communication model. The first, as I have just indicated, arises in the necessity to understand the audience (or the community) as it understands the source. How do individuals and communities understand when they participate in communication settings?

Second, how can we determine the ritual uses of this particular communication source material? Do they differ from one Christian community or denomination to another? Is the translation limited to Bible study or can it equally serve worship and prayer? Does it become a kind of spiritual support to something else? One might take a lead here by looking at other communication rituals—reading the newspaper, watching television, going to movies, and so on. Are these the same or merely analogous uses?

Third, a ritual view invites reflection on creating community as well as on the nature of that community. In asking what defines a Christian community, one should take care to avoid a para-social illusion of community, a situation where individuals mistake a pseudo-community for a real one, as happens for example in television talk shows or soap operas, where audience members feel as though they are part of a (fictional, though regularly meeting) group. James Beniger characterizes these as "superficially interpersonal relations that confuse personal with mass messages and increasingly include interactions with machines that write, speak, and even 'think' with success steadily approaching that of humans" (1987, p. 354). Only a true believing community could be the measure of ritual use of biblical material. In some ways this challenge is not new—it goes back to apostolic times, as both James 2.17 and 1 John 3.17 warn that faith must be accompanied by action lest one fall into the illusion of belief or of community.

Fourth, a ritual view demands another look at the nature of the source material. What status does the Bible hold for the Church? How are the two related? What best characterizes the ritual of the Bible? Clearly, these questions touching on ecclesiologies involve more than translation. But that is the nature of ritual.

This approach to communication study dramatically refocuses attention away from information towards activity. In this view communication maintains community and always takes place in the present, even if it should utilize older materials. In doing so, it recalls the status and the value of communication in an oral culture. As we more and more participate in what Ong terms "secondary orality" the challenge of the ritual view holds greater promise.

Communication as Conversation

A final model of communication takes the face-to-face interaction of people as its starting point. As the semiotic model qualified the transportation model, this conversation model specifies and clarifies the ritual approach to communication. Because it specifies things and because it lies closer to our day-to-day experience, most people find this model more accessible. Conversation consists of ritual behavior: the turn-taking that embodies a back-and-forth movement in which communicators create, sustain, and inhabit a world. It is a place of presence, of mutual disclosure, of interaction, and of a "fusion of horizons" (Gadamer, 1975/1960). We can represent the process itself as a circle through which the conversational partners

Figure 4: A conversational model of communication.

interact, the communication taking place not at any one moment, but throughout the ongoing conversation. (See Figure 4.)

From this perspective the translator becomes a conversational participant. Instead of the conversation occurring between two parties, three act together. Ideally the translator's role appears transparent, but the translator does mediate the source's part of the conversation. Textual translation (including biblical translation) poses an unusual situation for this model in that the translator mediates only one half the conversation. The situation also highlights the question of a "conversation" with a text, though Gadamer and others have explicated that somewhat analogous use of the term. In terms of the Bible, possible activities descriptive of such conversation include Bible study, preaching, prayer, and meditation.

Fidelity becomes an attribute of the conversation, of the act of exchange. Because, to use Gadamer's term, a fusion of horizons takes place, conversational partners must represent themselves honestly. Neither the (translational) source nor the "receiver" can claim absolute power over the interaction; nor can either disregard the other. Much of the work in reader-response criticism bears this truth out (Tompkins, 1980).

In multimedia translation the role of the translator takes on greater significance than that of the inter-linguistic translator. The multimedia group's role is larger and mediates different aspects of the Bible. The conversation more explicitly includes the translator; in other words, the very act of translation becomes opaque.

One test of fidelity results from the extent of engagement in the interaction. If the "receivers" interact in such a way as to recreate the biblical result (faith in the risen Lord, for example), then the translation manifests a degree of fidelity. Another measure of fidelity arises from the community and its formation around the Bible. Much like with the case of the ritual model, the measure of fidelity is the measure of "audience" acceptance. If people judge that the translation is a good one—if they accept it—then it is a good translation. Different Christian denominations will have their own mechanisms for such judgments—along a continuum from formal offices of doctrine to individual local church assemblies.

Like the other models, this one also identifies some challenges to multimedia translation. First, how can the multimedia material move the users, the participants towards conversation, to a heightened level of interactivity? Given the nature of the medium, multimedia users might be reduced to the role of a spectator or a passive receiver. This result, which can, of course, occur with written materials as well, may be mitigated by certain kinds of interactive designs.

Second, as multimedia translators include supporting materials, they face the temptation of allowing the receptor to lose sight of the priority of the biblical materials. Since the conversation includes the translator, the danger of confusing sources remains a possibility. (This was a criticism of the pre-Reformation Church where the clergy functioned as mediators of the Word.)

Third, any conversation must balance the interaction among the partners. How will a multimedia translation accomplish this? Should there be some kind of training in the use of multimedia translations beyond what might occur for Bible study?

The conversational approach heightens our appreciation of the interactive quality of communication and places the translator within that interaction. The measure of translation becomes a bit less certain since it is judged by community acceptance and use, by the quality of the interaction, or by personal conversation. This perspective clearly differs from the others in that communication scholars tend to focus on descriptive rather than prescriptive approaches.

Concluding Thoughts

Communication study provides a framework in which we can approach the question of fidelity; further, it helps to identify some of the key issues involved, though it may not in itself resolve them. Many of the challenges I have listed here point up those issues and, despite my attaching them to one or other perspective, describe problems that cut across all the approaches.

Each perspective on communication suggests a perspective on the Bible. The transportation or transmission model regards the Bible as valued information that must be delivered from one location to another. The semiotic model also regards the Bible as information, but as encoded information that exists in relation to other codes. Here we become aware of the Bible as part of a larger structure of relations. The ritual model sees the Bible as a container of shared beliefs, as an opportunity for sharing belief, and as a means of maintaining the believing community. The Bible does not exist apart from the community and any use of the Bible presumes the role of the community. Finally, the conversation model situates the Bible as a partner of the believer or community. It takes life only in the interaction; the Bible manifests the power of the Spirit who acts upon the believer.

The various perspectives also raise questions about translation and the role of the translator. Certainly, the transportation and the semiotic models treat multimedia or visual communication on the analogy of language. But, can we regard visual communication as a language? Is there a language of film? A language of television? Or a language of radio? Treating them as semiotic systems allows for a level of similarity in analysis, but does it suffice for a precise kind of translation? Is it enough for the translator to seek a semiotic equivalence?

Finally, what does a multimedia or "trans-media" translator do in terms of fidelity? Does the question of fidelity occur in comparison with an original or in terms of the use of the Bible? In other words, should we place the problem of fidelity at the beginning of the process or at the end? The former becomes an issue of preparation and the development of some norms or procedures. The latter suggests assessment, the development of some method to measure reception. After considering the communication models, it seems to me that the question of fidelity ultimately becomes one of acceptance by the believing community: an assessment issue. But to work towards this, we have to do an analysis of the procedures at the front end.

Multimedia translation focuses our attention not only on the question of fidelity but on the nature of the Bible itself. Does what translators do change the nature of the translated text? Historical studies show that the use of the Bible has changed over the centuries, as has the nature of the Bible—the manuscript Bible functioned differently from the oral tradition. The advent of the Gutenberg Bible (or, more generally, the printed Bible) similarly changed how people regarded the Bible and how people used the Bible. But these changes do not affect the Bible only; they are part of a larger sweep of cultural change marked out in communication patterns. Multimedia work has identified another phase change and can tell us much about the Bible and the Church in our own day, as well as about fidelity.

13

Semiotics, Fidelity, and New Media Translation

Robert Hodgson, Jr.

Overview and Introduction

Fidelity is a benchmark that print translators use to measure the success of their work. Fidelity is no less important to translators who work in new media, combining biblical text with sound and image in a variety of formats. Achieving fidelity in new media requires the same attention to careful exegesis as it does in print. The quest for fidelity, however, brings new media translators face to face with challenges that print translators need never deal with, for example, developing knowledge and skills for achieving and measuring fidelity in the realms of sound and image.

In this article, we develop the point that semiotics offers a body of theoretical and applied knowledge, providing, among other things, guidelines and principles that can help direct the efforts of Bible translators working in new media. We first indicate that new media fidelity requires attention to linguistic, paralinguistic, and extralinguistic factors. Next we point out some key semiotic axioms, definitions, and lead questions. Finally, four case studies illustrate a semiotic approach to fidelity.

Semiotics is the study of signs and of how signs signify or produce meaning. In semiotics, fidelity means preserving invariance within the informational core of a source text as that source text undergoes transformation (Toury, 1986).

Linguistic Fidelity

Producing fidelity (Louw, 1985) in new media translation begins where it does in print translation: with historical-critical exegesis that leads to the crafting of a text or a wordtrack. The purpose of a word track is to

---

This is a slightly revised version of a work originally published in the *Bulletin of the United Bible Societies: Current Trends in Scripture Translation, 182/183* (1997), 195-211. Reprinted with permission.

234   Robert Hodgson, Jr.

©United Bible Societies, reprinted with permission.
Figure 1: Frame from a United Bible Societies Scripture comic.

keep invariant under transformation the exegetical and linguistic component of an informational core. But even with an exegetically and linguistically sound wordtrack in hand, Bible translators are not assured of fidelity in the new media. After all, translators must move this information not just from a source to a target language, but also from one medium to another—from printed text to comics, audio cassettes, and videocassettes, not to mention CD-ROMs, digital video disks, and even World Wide Websites. As a word track is moved to a new medium, modifications are sometimes necessary.

H. A. Hatton (1985) illustrates the problem as it applies to Scripture comics, noting how this medium requires certain "adjustments and transformations" to the text. He mentions two: rendering narrative and reported speech as dialogue, song, or poetry, and selecting only a portion of a biblical text. Such moves are consistent with fidelity as long as they do not "distort the intent of the biblical text" (p. 432). (See Figure 1, From *Moses I Comic Book*, United Bible Societies Asia Pacific Region.)

Hatton explains how narrative turns into dialogue while still remaining faithful to the biblical message:

> The command by Pharaoh at the end of the balloon in bold lettering: "Get my war chariot ready! Call out the army" is a transformation of the narrative section in verse 6 which states (RSV): "So he made ready his chariot and took his army with him." It is implicit in this statement that Pharaoh orally commanded his servants to get the chariot ready and

call out the army. Therefore it is justifiable to transform this implicit command into speech in the comic. (p. 432)

Because new media are visual, oral, and aural, translators must also consider issues that go beyond adjusting a word track to fit the needs of a medium. They must also consider how the visual, oral, and aural capacities of new media add connotations above and beyond those already embedded in a word track. A narrator's voice on an audio cassette, the selection of font and typeface styles for a software program, or onscreen texts in a video all add subtle but real values and messages. In the above-mentioned Scripture comic, the command of Pharaoh is bolded, underscoring, visually, the authority of Pharaoh. What, for example, would the impact have been if Pharaoh's orders were set in italic or gothic? In such a case, Pharaoh might seem hesitant or even burdened about his orders, an attitude not consistent with the intent of the biblical text.

Linguistic fidelity in new media translating will combine theoretical principles that transcend all media (for example, adjustment and selection, closest natural equivalence, relevance) and pragmatic guidelines that are media specific and include such factors as audience point of view and audience participation in the making of meaning. (Soukup, 1997) This combination is a familiar one in print translation. Sensitivity to audience needs, for example, explains the Contemporary English Version (CEV) text of Matthew 1.23, which renders the Hebrew *ha-almah* (or Greek *parthenos*) of Isaiah 7.14 as "virgin," while placing in a footnote the alternative "young woman" (Bratcher, 1995).

Paralinguistic Fidelity

New media translators must identify the paralinguistic elements in an informational core and selectively transfer their meaning from one language and medium to another. These paralinguistic elements include the sounds and images (Thomas, 1994a, 1994b) that are invited by the biblical text as well as the historical, cultural, rhetorical, and performative knowledge that a biblical text assumes its audience knows. In print translations, paralinguistic elements show up as charts, notes, maps, and indices in study Bibles.

The invited images and sounds form the imagescape and soundscape, respectively, of a biblical text. A soundscape includes such elements as phonetics, colometrics, and accentuation, along with the music tradition inspired by a text across the centuries. A text's imagescape is comprised in part of its invited images, in part from the explicit visual, artistic, and even architectural traditions inspired by the text. One way of "seeing" a soundscape is to graph some of its phonetic elements. Figure 2 (The Phonetics of the Greek Language of the Two Sons) represents a quantitative phonetic analysis for the soundscape of the Parable of the Prodigal Son (Luke 15.11-32). Such a bar graph, properly interpreted, may reveal patterns and

The Phonetics of the Greek Language of the Two Sons

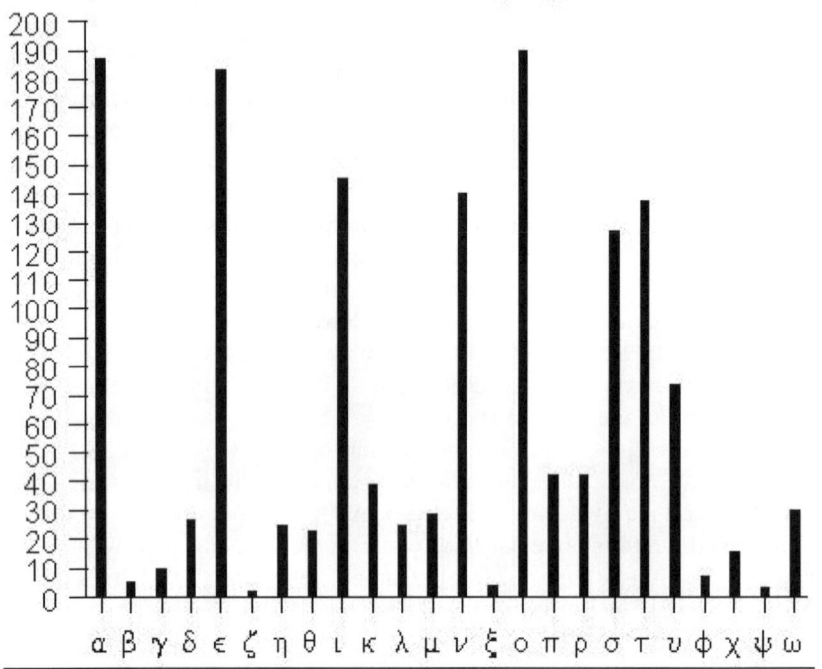

[Bar chart showing frequency of Greek letters α β γ δ ε ζ η θ ι κ λ μ ν ξ ο π ρ σ τ υ φ χ ψ ω on x-axis, with values from 0 to 200 on y-axis]

Figure 2: Phoetics of the Greek language in the Prodigal Son Parable (Luke 15.11-32).

associations with specific words and concepts in a text, leading us to ask: What values, messages, or meaning, if any, are communicated by this part of the soundscape? Do any of them belong to the informational core that must remain invariant under transformation?

To achieve paralinguistic fidelity, Bible translators in the new media apply the principle of closest natural equivalence. In its video translation *A Father and Two Sons* (Luke 15.11-32), the American Bible Society's (ABS) multimedia translation team used this principle to develop a symbolic structure or visual metaphor to help unify the film. Reasoning that a modern ranch was a natural equivalent for the farm or rural setting of the ancient parable, it shot many scenes on a working horse ranch. Similarly, when a unifying, visual metaphor was required for the CD-ROM version of the same parable, the team turned to a collage of modern malls and ancient market places as a natural *visual* equivalent for the public spaces in which Jesus and his first followers taught. Figure 3 shows a CD-ROM screen displaying one example of this collage.

Fidelity in new media translation does not require that the meaning of every paralinguistic element be transferred. Fidelity may in fact direct us toward selection and compression, rather like the procedures mentioned above in connection with Scripture comics. We cite an example from outside the

Semiotics, Fidelity, and New Media Translation 237

©American Bible Society, reprinted with permission
Figure 3: Screen from the CD-ROM *A Father and Two Sons*.

field of translation to illustrate the point that certain media only support a selection of paralinguistic elements: George Balanchine's ballet *The Prodigal Son*. According to a recent essay (Keen, 1997), Balanchine drew on two sources for the ballet: the biblical text of Luke 15.11-32 and Pushkin's short story *The Postmaster*. Knowing that he could not choreograph for all the words and movements in the parable, Balanchine selected and compressed. He focused on the actions of the father and Prodigal Son, eliminated the older brother, and added a Siren who seduces and brings the Prodigal Son to ruin. But even the actions of the Prodigal Son could not be danced in their entirety, so Balanchine eliminated the Son's tenure as a swineherd.

New media Bible translation selects and compresses paralinguistic elements because modern audiences and media do not require an image or sound for every word in a word track. Acting on this principle, the ABS team that produced the video translations for Mark 5.1-20 (*Out of the Tombs*) and Luke 15.11-32 (*A Father and Two Sons*) determined that the script did not need to *visually* represent the pigs in either story. The decision was justified on the grounds that in North American culture there is no close natural visual equivalent that offers all of the negative connotations that pigs held for Jewish people in the biblical world. To have visually included the pigs with their modern and wholesome connotations would have, paradoxically enough, conflicted with the intent of the ancient biblical story.

Extralinguistic Fidelity

By definition, extralinguistic elements lie outside source and target texts. Still, their presence affects the meaning of a text. Another name for such elements is "modeling systems," (Cattrysse, 1997) a term related to what semiotics calls codes. Some modeling systems are source modeling systems, consisting of general cultural norms, rules, and conditions that affect the meaning of a source text's informational core. For example, a patriarchal worldview shapes the meaning of the *Haustafeln* at Ephesians 5.21-6.9 and 1 Peter 2.18-3.7. Bible translators working in new media, having once identified such a source modeling system, must then ask if fidelity requires a functional equivalent in word, sound, or image.

Other modeling systems are target modeling systems, and their rules, norms and conventions affect the meaning of target texts. In modern media culture, there are many modeling systems that affect meaning. Television, for example, creates meaning by forcing images onto a rectangular screen and by using the sound bite and the cut as editorial tools. Terms such as "new media ecology," "millennial shift," "paradigm shift," and "secondary orality" describe collectively these systems. The "millennial shift," for instance, stands for a communications modeling system in transition from print to digital technology. Caught in transition, this system combines norms and rules from both print and digital culture.

How do extralinguistic factors, so-called modeling systems, affect fidelity? Or, putting the question in semiotic terms, how do such factors affect the invariance of an informational core under transformation? Using three recent videos based on the Parable of the Prodigal Son (Luke 15.11-32), we can see various modeling systems at work, and how each affects fidelity. All three videos retell the parable for modern audiences. In each case, the biblical text represents a starting point (we might say a "modeling system"), thus permitting us to use invariance with regard to a (actual or virtual) word track as one measurement of fidelity.

In the case of the Malawi Bible Society production, two modeling systems particularly stand out: television production rules and modern scripting conventions. The first determined that the film feature many indoor and medium close-up shots; the second added dialogue not present in the biblical text. In the case of the Bible Society of Thailand production, a contemporary social issue (child prostitution) provided a key modeling system that transformed a story about a father and two sons into a story about a mother and two daughters. In the ABS video, translation principles and guidelines provided a modeling system that allowed only the words of the word track to be spoken or sung. Genre was a modeling system that affected the outcome of all three productions. The ABS, for instance, opted for a music video in which an artist sings lyrics that follow a biblical word track. Its film runs about eight minutes. The Malawi Bible Society chose dramatic narrative, and its production lasts a good hour. (See essay by Sisley in this volume.)

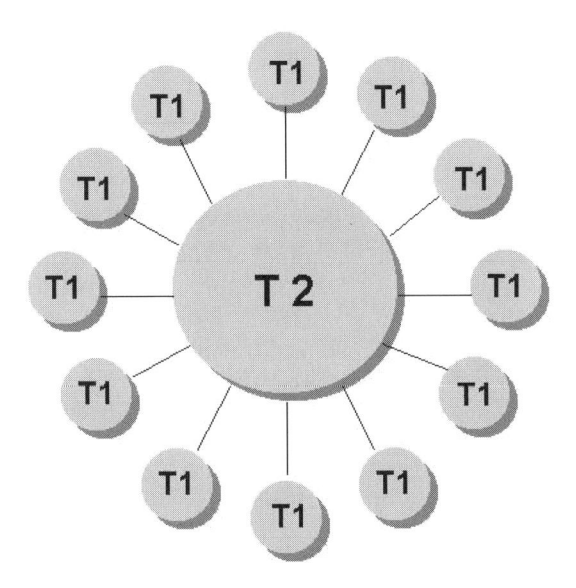

Figure 4: Star diagram of translation, modeled on Cattrysse, 1997.

In video and film production many modeling systems shape the final product and thus bear on the issue of fidelity. These systems include genre, acting and filming styles, scriptwriting conventions, and art direction, along with costume, makeup, lighting, and staging protocols. Not to be overlooked among the modeling systems are the structures and strictures set by budget and scheduling as well as by distribution, marketing, and testing.

Visualizing New Media Translation

A star diagram (Figure 4) (Cattrysse, 1997, p. 80) illustrates the process and product of new media translating. It also suggests an approach for evaluating new media fidelity. At the diagram's center is a circle labeled T2, which represents a finished target product—for the sake of the argument, we will call it the ABS video translation *A Father and Two Sons* (Luke 15.11-32). Surrounding the T-circle are smaller circles labeled T1, T1, T1, and so forth. They stand for all the linguistic, paralinguistic, and extralinguistic elements that contribute to a finished target translation. Each of these elements brings to the finished translation norms, rules, values, and messages. Thus, each affects the fidelity of a translation—even when we agree that fidelity is ultimately measured in terms of an exegetically sound word track that is translated from Greek or Hebrew and fully presented in either text or audio formats. During pre-production of *A Father and Two Sons,* the screenwriter-director suggested filming in black and white (a modeling system) because black and white films connote—among North

American teenagers at least—that a subject has "antiquity" and "classic value." On the other hand, the screenwriter-director originally scripted the film to include scene after scene with a horse (screen characters being a modeling system) that stood for the inheritance that the Prodigal Son squandered. Bible experts on the production team pointed out that the biblical narrative did not foreground the inheritance as prominently as the horse scenes threatened to do in the film. In short, fidelity was at stake. In the final version of the script, the horse lost many of its scenes.

The star diagram suggests some approaches that Bible translators can take as they put the Scriptures in new media, and do so with fidelity. For one thing, they will need to recognize that among the smaller circles pride of place goes to the one standing for a word track or biblical text (at least if a product wants to function as a translation). They will also seek a right priority and balance among the various, and sometimes competing linguistic, extralinguistic, and paralinguistic elements that make up a target product. They will also want to be informed about the active role that audiences play in screening a film or video, for example the capacity of an audience to make judgments about meaning and fidelity. As one wag put it, if you think that audiences don't participate in judgments about meaning and fidelity, then you have never seen a remote control device for a television set!

With respect to audiences, the star diagram shows that Bible translators and audiences will judge fidelity from different vantage points. Translators, for instance, will look at the circle representing a word track and use that circle as a litmus test to assess the fidelity of a target translation. Audiences, on the other hand, only see the big circle and are largely unaware of the smaller ones. What is more, an audience may well consider fidelity to a source text less important than other factors, for instance, the pageantry and film style of a Hollywood-style Bible epic.

The simplicity of the star diagram belies the many twists and turns that complicate an actual production, especially one that aims at fidelity. On the set of *A Father and Two Sons*, for example, the ABS team watched as a thunderstorm prevented a busload of African-American and Asian-American extras from showing up for a scene (see Luke 15.22-24) that had been researched and scripted as a multicultural feast and visual symbol for the Kingdom of God. When the film director insisted on rolling the cameras without the extras, the ABS team intervened and stopped the shooting until other extras could be found. It was pointed out to the director that without the extras the people in the feast/Kingdom of God scene would be all white, transforming the kingdom into an exclusive "whites-only" club and clearly violating the intent of the biblical text. (See the essay by Worth in this volume.)

Semiotics and Fidelity

Over the past decade, the search for principles and guidelines to promote fidelity in new media translating has scored solid progress, with important contributions to that search appearing in many places (Thomas, 1994a, 1994b; also Fry, 1987; Burke, 1993; Hagedorn, 1991). Though not specifically written with new media in mind, one contribution already pointed in the direction of a semiotic approach:

> Semiotics is the most all-embracing system for the analysis of signs,.... a sociosemiotic approach to the meaning of verbal signs always involves the total communication of an event with the social context; in other words, a text cannot be isolated from its context, despite the fact that some persons have tried to insist that texts have "an independent existence." (de Waard & Nida, 1986, p. 73)

What is Semiotics?

The founders of semiotics (Chandler, 1994; Seiter, 1992) are the American philosophers C. S. Peirce (pronounced "Purse" 1839-1914) and C.W. Morris (1901-1979) along with the Swiss linguist F. de Saussure (1857-1913). Modern semiotics has found many applications, not only to fields such as semantics, pragmatics, and syntactics, but also as a general theory of signs and signification for studies of literature, film, media, advertising, art, photography, and architecture.

The following are some basic semiotic axioms and definitions that can assist Bible translators working in new media.

Some Axioms and Definitions

1. *All cultural artifacts, including written texts, function as signs.*

According to Peirce's widely accepted definition, a sign is "something which stands to somebody for something in some respect or capacity." (Peirce, 1955, p. 99) A triangle (Figure 5, page 242) is often used to illustrate how signs and signification work.

At the left foot is that part of a sign called its signifier, for instance, the letters t-r-e-e, or the lines that make up a drawing of a tree. This is the "something" of Peirce's definition. At the right foot is the signified, the object, event, or relationship (for example, the object "tree") that corresponds to the signifier t-r-e-e. The signified corresponds to the "for something" of Peirce's definition. At the top of the triangle is the interpretant. The interpretant or meaning corresponds to the "in some respect or capacity" of Peirce's definition.

This triangular account of signification suggests that the distinction between meaning and signified object or event may be as important in new media translating as is the distinction in print translating between meaning and reference. A simple example will illustrate our point. The signifier H-

```
                    interpretant
                         B



        A                                    C
    signifier                             signified
```

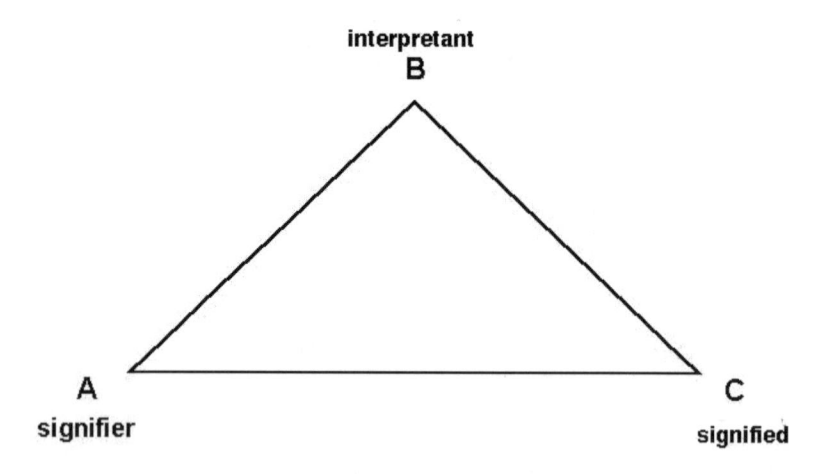

Figure 5: Semiotic triangle according to Peirce's model.

e-r-o-d occurs at Matthew 2.1. For the sake of the argument, we'll say that the interpretant is "a wicked king" and that the signified person is "son of Antipater and ruler of Judea from 37-4 B.C." Keeping in mind the distinction between meaning and signified object, person, or event, new media translators may opt for one of two *visual* depictions of the signifier H-e-r-o-d. The one would lay greater weight on reconstructing the signified person, perhaps leading to a Hollywood style Bible epic. The other, stressing the interpretant or meaning, would be free to use symbolic and abstract visual conventions to get the meaning across. Case Study 1 (see page 245) illustrates how to look at a biblical narrative from the vantage point of its signifiers, signifieds, and interpretants.

  2. *Signs may be classified in different ways. One such classification arranges signs as icons, indexes, and symbols.*

  Peirce divided signs into three classes (icons, indexes, and symbols), and many semiotic studies still work with this classification. It is a system based on the relationship that a sign's signifier has to its signified. Following Lyons (1977), we define an icon as a sign whose signifier is visually similar to the signified at which it points. Semioticians call such signs "motivated." Examples are maps, photographs, and statues. An index is a sign whose signifier has a known, assumed, or expressive connection with its signified. Smoke, for instance, signifies fire; a weather vane signifies wind direction. A symbol is a non-motivated sign. Here, the connection between signifier and signified is purely arbitrary, having been previously established by social convention. The red color and octagonal shape of a stop sign in the USA are arbitrary since there is no necessary connection between the signifier and the signified (driving behavior). Many verbal signs fall into this category.

Bible translators in new media can apply the distinction between icons, indexes, and symbols to verbal signs. By doing so, they uncover information about the relationships that obtain between a verbal sign's signifier and its signified. At the same time, they gain insight into appropriate visual and sonic functional equivalents for signifier and signified.

3. Codes bring together signifiers, signifieds, and interpretants in a process of signification or semiosis.

By themselves signifiers, signifieds, and interpretants cannot come together in a process of signification or semiosis. Codes are required.

Codes are like the rules that make up systems of spelling and grammar. For example, the letters t-r-e-e (signifier) don't lead us automatically to the signified "tree," nor to an interpretant for "tree." We require a code called English spelling rules to connect the signifier with its possible interpretants and signifieds. The code or set of rules that define Braille determine that raised dots positioned in the form of a backwards "L" (signifier) stand for the numeral 2 (signified). The code or rules that define Baroque art give a painting (signifier) its meaning (interpretant) and link it to some cultural or historical process (signified).

Codes comprise socially established rules, habits, and customs. They not only bring together the parts (signifier, signified, interpretant) of an individual sign, but they also connect groups of signs, forming texts (in the semiotic sense of any cultural artifact such as discourse, painting, opera, film). Codes also bring together groups of texts (again in the semiotic sense) to form culture. (Leeds-Hurwitz, 1993)

New media translators pay attention to codes for the same reason that print translators do: Codes impart meaning to the signs we translate. Additionally, analysis of the codes in a source text can reveal visual or even sonic functional equivalents that are required in the target translation. An important code in the biblical parable of the Prodigal Son (Luke 15.11-32) is inheritance law and custom. In the ABS video translation of that parable, *A Father and Two Sons,* this code is visually displayed in a horse that serves as a marker for the inheritance. Case Study 2 (page 246) illustrates the role of code analysis in new media work.

4. When a group of signs come together to form a text, structures or patterns are created that contribute to the meaning of the text.

When codes bring together signs to form a text (semiotic sense), they create structures. Patte, a New Testament expert, has referred to deep structure as "potentialities in quest of actualization" (1976, p. 22). His loom analogy illustrates the point nicely. A text's so-called deep structure may be compared to a weaver's loom with all the possibilities presented by the loom's threads, reeds, shuttles, and treadles. The surface structure is the actualization of some of those possibilities in the form of a text—a Persian rug, for instance.

Studying a text's deep and surface structures can pay handsome dividends to Bible translators working in the new media. For one thing, it opens up a rich storehouse of visual and sonic functional equivalents for the target translation. For another, it helps them more easily set limits on the meaning of a target text. Knowing the structural possibilities of a Gospel parable, for instance, we won't so easily create meanings in word, sound, or image that fly in the face of the parable's possibilities.

A recent structural analysis of the parable of the Good Samaritan determined that it involved a contrast between place—Jerusalem, Jericho, ditch, inn—and motion—journeying of bandits, priest, levite, Samaritan (Patte, 1976, pp. 80-81). The ABS team has used this contrast in pre-production studies of the parable with a view to treating it as a possible symbolic structure or visual metaphor for a projected video translation and CD-ROM study help of the Good Samaritan. Case Studies 3 and 4 (pages 246 and 247) show the role of structural analysis in new media work.

5. *Some semiotic questions for Bible translators working in new media.*

The following questions provide some guidelines for Bible translators who wish to apply semiotics to their new media work, particularly to the production of faithful translations.

a. What are key verbal signs, or groups of verbal signs that make up a source text? Are any of them icons, indexes, or symbols?

b. What are their signifiers, signifieds, and interpretants?

c. What are key linguistic, extralinguistic, and paralinguistic elements among those signs?

d. What functional equivalents are available in word, sound, or image for these key elements?

e. What are the key codes (rules, conventions, norms) operating in the signs that make up the source text?

f. What functional equivalents are available in word, sound, or image for these codes?

g. What structure or structures does a text reveal?

h. What functional equivalents are available in word, sound, or image for the structure?

i. What audience(s) will a target translation reach? How will the audiences participate in making meaning and judging fidelity? Will they, for example, have preferred or canonical readings?

k. Will a translation reproduce chiefly a text's signified or interpretant (its meaning or reference), or some combination of both?

l. What are the modeling systems that make up the target translation? What priority and balance is needed among the modeling systems to achieve a faithful translation?

Case Studies

In the following case studies we show some applications of semiotics to achieving and evaluating fidelity in new media Bible translations.

Case Study 1. This case illustrates the general point that biblical texts may be treated as systems of signs for the purpose of achieving and measuring fidelity in new media translation; or, to use Kenneth Thomas's words, for faithfully opening up "the perspective and the depths of the text" (1994a, p. 41). The case background, described by Hagedorn in this volume, is the research and production of the ABS video translation *Out of the Tombs* (Mark 5.1-20). An early problem facing the ABS team involved creating an overall visual story line that was faithful to the word track. The solution came as the ABS team and the scriptwriter determined that one of the key verbal signs in Greek was the signifier *h-e t-h-a-l-a-s-s-a* (vv. 1,13; translated "the sea" in the word track). One interpretant (an invited image) was "an inland body of water," the physical signified being the actual Sea of Galilee. Exploring this rich verbal sign, the ABS team and the scriptwriter found not only important linguistic elements but also important paralinguistic elements, the latter consisting of implied images and sounds of the sea. Accordingly, they transferred the meaning of these paralinguistic elements into images and sounds of the sea—shots of a beach and a seascape. But there was even more to be done with the linguistic and paralinguistic elements of this key verbal/visual sign. It connoted so much for the meaning of the story as a whole ("danger," "storm," "destruction," as well as "new life," "rebirth," "liberation," and "cleansing") that the ABS team and the scriptwriter wove these connotations into a rich tapestry of visual signs for *he thalassa* ("Sea of Galilee"). The end result (see Figure 6) was an

©American Bible Society, reprinted with permission
Figure 6: Brighton Beach in the ABS video translation, *Out of the Tombs*.

overarching visual symbol or metaphor that faithfully conveyed linguistic and paralinguistic elements of this key verbal sign (Goethals, 1997).

Case Study 2. This case points to the importance of understanding codes. Specifically, it shows that translators must sometimes transfer the meaning of underlying codes from source to target in order to faithfully render the meaning of a text. The case background is the research and production of the ABS video translation *A Father and Two Sons* (Luke 15.11-32).

Biblical experts have long recognized that honor and shame are among the most pervasive social codes in Mediterranean antiquity, honor being defined as a claim to worth, and shame as the loss of that claim. When the ABS research team realized that this code played an important role in the Lucan parable, it determined to exploit this finding in its video translation. It found, for example, that already at v. 12 the meaning of the text depended on an honor and shame code.

In the parable, the Prodigal Son asks his father for a share of the family property, and once granted the son squanders his inheritance in wild living. In v. 12, the son frames his request as *Pater, dos moi to epiballon meros tes ousias* ("Father, give me my share of the property"). This apparently simple request (signifier) actually violates the honor of the father. After all, in Mediterranean antiquity, families generally distributed an inheritance only after a father had died (code of inheritance). The son in effect treats his father as if he were already dead (signified).

New media translating can transfer the meaning of this code in a variety of ways, for example by scripting v. 12 as a scene that visually and sonically displays the moral ambiguity of the younger son's request. This approach to v. 12 was in fact taken in the ABS video translation of Luke 15.11-32, *A Father and Two Sons*. For one thing, the ABS word track and lyrics for v. 12 articulate this code by displaying the insolence of the son and his violation of the father's honor. It does so by translating the side-by-side occurrence of the dative *to patri* and the vocative *pater* as "...said to his father, 'Father...'" The intent was to retain in the word track a redundancy of the Greek text (signifier) that in light of the honor code marked a sham display of respect and esteem (signified). For another, as the lyrics of v. 12 are sung, close-up shots of the younger son show him alternating between grim looks and broad grins.

Case Study 3. This case shows that familiarity with a text's structure is an important step toward paralinguistic fidelity. Research and production for the ABS video translation A Father and Two Sons (Luke 15.11-32) provide background for this case. The problem stemmed from the discovery of a key structural element in the story and a desire to find an equivalent sonic sign for this structural element.

Drafting a wordtrack for this parable, the ABS team remarked that one prominent structural feature in the text stood out above all others: redundancy or the recurrence of phrases and lines. These included *ton moschon ton siteuton* ("the fatted calf") at vv 23, 27, 30; some variation of *hemarton eis ton ouranon kai enhopion sou, ouketi eimi axios klethenai huios sou; poieson me hos hena ton misthion sou* ("I have sinned against heaven and against you; I am not worthy to be called your son; treat me as one of your workers") at vv. 18, 21; and some variation of *ho huios mou nekros en kai anezesen, en apololos kai heurethe* ("my son was dead and is now alive; he was lost and now is found") at vv. 24, 32.

Since the medium for this translation was a music video, a question arose: Is there in music a sonic equivalent for this narrative redundancy? The answer was yes, in the "refrain type" musical tradition—a tradition that includes such genres as the *chant fabula*, ballad, and a modern expression of the ballad form known in the USA as Delta Blues. The production team then settled on the Delta Blues ballad form as the music style for the video translation of Luke 15.11-32, *A Father and Two Sons* (Werner, 1997).

Case Study 4. In this study, the point is again made that a text's structure contains important clues for achieving fidelity in new media translating. One element of structure is the explicit binary oppositions in a text, for example, human-animal; light-dark; good-evil, male-female; rich-poor; urban-rural. Sometimes these oppositions are only implied,

©American Bible Society, reprinted with permission

Figure 7: Nautilus image from CD-ROM *The Visit*.

showing up in the presence of one oppositional element and in the absence of the other. Such an implied opposition provided a key structural element for the ABS video translation The Visit (Luke 1.39-56). The ABS team found that one of the primary oppositions in the story turned on the presence of two explicitly foregrounded women (Mary and Elizabeth) and in the absence and consequent backgrounding of their husbands (Joseph and Zechariah). It is, in fact, this opposition that gives the story of Mary and Elizabeth part of its cachet in the New Testament. After all, it is one of the few stories in the entire Bible that foregrounds women, not because they are the wives of well-known men, or because they excel in masculine virtues, but because they are pregnant.

With this structural element in mind, the team sought a visual equivalent that could capture the essentials of the opposition as represented by Mary and Elizabeth: womanhood, (pro)creation, motherhood. The answer came in the form of a nautilus image (signifier) whose signifieds provided just these womanly values. The nautilus thus became the overall visual symbol for the video translation and its companion CD-ROM study help. (See Figure 7.)

Conclusion

New media translators need all the tools they can lay their hands on if they are to achieve fidelity in their work. Semiotics provides one chest from which they can draw such tools with the purpose of applying them as principles and guidelines in new media translating. Whatever the direction of new media translating, semiotics belongs in its workshop.

14

Peirce's Semiotics for Translation

Ubaldo Stecconi

Introduction

> In retrospect, the general disinterest in linguistics for the issues of translation can easily be recognized as a consequence of widespread theoretical precepts and ambitions. Among the most important were those which maintained that only coincidences generated by the system are significant and relevant; and that the major type of coincidence is the one between forms rather than between meanings or contexts. (de Beaugrande, 1991, p. 27)

This verdict comes at the end of an overview of the ideas about translation—or lack thereof—among the most influential linguists of our century; a similar overview conducted on the most influential translation scholars would certainly lead to the same conclusions. In the 1970s the crisis of linguistic-based approaches—ultimately aimed at a "science" of translation—produced an alternative movement. Originally based in the Low Countries, the movement gained followers throughout Europe and in Israel and when a now famous anthology came out with the title *The Manipulation of Literature* (Hermans, 1985) it also gained the provisional label of Manipulation School. The Manipulation School has the historical merit of having challenged the obsessive focus on language and the methodological aspiration of breaking the code that would allow people and—arguably—machines alike to translate between languages. However, both as a reaction to such scientific style of inquiry and as a consequence of their interest in literary studies, these authors seem to have overlooked the specific and "technical" core of translating. In short, investigation of the cultural significance of translation has left a dark spot at its focal point: how an image of a text from a different language and culture is produced.

Towards the end of the 1980s, two authors offered a different criticism of the systemic and formal tradition of translation studies: Mary Snell-Hornby (1988), who attacked and redefined the "rock bottom" notion of equivalence (see Stecconi, 1991a), and Dinda Gorlée (1989), who ventured

---

Originally published in *Koiné: Annali della Scuola Superiore per Interpreti e Traduttori*, 4 (1994), pp. 161-180. Reprinted with permission.

into a fresh investigation into the core of translation processes using insights from Wittgenstein and Peirce. These two studies, although vastly less ambitious than the loosely-knit project of the "manipulators," threw new light on the dark spot. Gorlée's attempt to provide an account of translating in semiotic terms seems particularly promising. To my knowledge, the earliest explicit link between translation and semiotics was established by Roman Jakobson in 1959 when the Russian linguist dubbed Charles Sanders Peirce "the deepest inquirer into the essence of signs" (Jakobson, 1959, p. 233; see Fisch, 1986, pp. 344-355 for a historical survey of early studies on Peirce); but his lead would not be followed for many years. More recently, apart from Gorlée's studies (Gorlée, 1994), some timid steps into the semiotics of translation have been taken by Pym (1993, esp. pp. 80-99) and Barnstone (1993, pp. 114-116), while an essay from José Lambert and Clem Robyns is forthcoming. All these authors have left the door ajar for introducing semiotics into the systematic study of translation; in this paper, I will try to open it wider by describing some aspects of translation processes in the light of Peirce's theory.

Translations are Never Final

The opening part of this study will discuss the rather commonplace remark that no translation is ever final. Practicing translators know it well when they revise their drafts or have them checked by editors; the more scrupulous never seem to be satisfied. For translation historians the remark is validated by the series of versions of one and the same text over time. Sacred texts offer good examples: the Bible has at least 21 translations in English between 1380 and 1975 (Barnstone, 1993, pp. 279-281) while in 1993-94 it received 623 translations globally (Buzzetti, 1995). As to non-sacred texts, Bogliolo (1991) counted 18 versions of Baudelaire's *Les fleurs du mal* into Italian—complete and partial—in less than a century, while the same Barnstone found it amazing that Homer was recently translated in English three times by Lattimore, R. Fitzgerald and Fagles "in scarcely three generations" (1993, p. 231). Why are translations so much more unstable than originals? It may be that a text's "afterlife" can erase the status of replica from sacred translations to raise them to authorized originals: when the people in power change, new versions are needed. A complementary explanation can be looked for in the genealogy of translation in the West: Latin authors translated extensively from their Greek masters to expand Latin lexicon and improve their style (Nergaard, 1993, pp. 26-28; Folena, 1991, pp. 3-9). The logic is clear: if translations are exercises, in principle you should never be satisfied with them—practice makes perfect, but since perfection is unattainable, practice is endless.

The Semiotic Chain of Translation

There are some more senses in which translations are never final. Before discussing this fact in semiotic terms, a premise is in order. According to Peirce, human beings have no direct apperception of the outer world nor intuition of the inner world (5.213-263; references to the *Collected Papers* of C. S. Peirce, 1960-1966, are hereafter made using only conventional two-part numbers); anything that can be known and said of both "worlds" is known and said through intermediate layers of signs; moreover all signs—whether they be a perception, a thought or something we intend for communicative purposes—establish a relation with the real-world object they stand for via other signs. Consequently, one of the principles of semiosis is that all signs are interpretations of previous signs and they are always amenable of interpretation by means of further signs.

It follows that, if the whole of the source text is regarded as just one sign, and the whole of the target text as another individual sign, it is easy to see that translations are signs interpreting their respective originals in strictly semiotic fashion, and that they can always be further interpreted by other texts, including other translations.

ORIGINAL — TRANSLATION 1 — TRANSLATION 2 — TRANSLATION ... — TRANSLATION n →

Figure 1: Translation as a semiotic chain.

Figure 1 may represent the sequence of translations of *Les fleurs du mal,* Homer or the Bible. The series is a simplification of the entangled network which any investigation into the intertextual relations of a translated work would reveal. However, what is important here is that, following our premise, source texts are also signs that interpret other signs; consequently, originals and translations are essentially alike in semiotic terms. Translations always stand for their originals, which are their objects; likewise, originals always stand for some other text-sign, and only through them for the objects in the real world.

This picture represents the "semiotic chain of translation," a line that extends endlessly towards both ends; if there is no end to the chain, there must be no beginning either.

> Before Hesiod there was Homer. Before the "blind" poet there were other bards. Even the birds, who were presumably the singer's first source for song, learned melodies in the parliament of earlier birds. (Barnstone 1993, p. 92)

← text -n ⊢ text ... ⊢ text -1 ⊢ orig. ⊢ trans. 1 ⊢ trans. .. ⊢ trans. n →

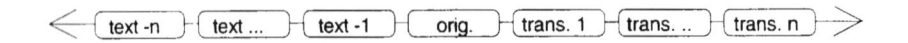

Figure 2: The distinction between original and translation.

Figure 2 also shows that the distinction between originals and translations is arbitrary; it derives from considerations that have little or nothing to do with the nature of writing and translating. Why do the texts left of the original still bear negative values, then? It has been said that every writer generates his own precursors; in the same way, translations generate their own originals: *Il nome della rosa* was not an original before—say—William Weaver wrote *The Name of the Rose*. Therefore, although the distinction between originals and translations is not of a semiotic character, it is undeniable that the two classes of text are perceived as different. How? I will leave this line of inquiry for future research: the links that bind Chaucer to his Italian and French sources, Cervantes to his "original" author Cid Hamete, De La Motte to Homer, Edward Fitzgerald to Omar Khayyam, and William Weaver to Umberto Eco are just some notorious spots across the spectrum.

For Whom the Wheel Rolls

The absence of a starting point has important consequences for each text along the chain. I am referring to the problem of how to define, locate and look for the meaning of source texts, that shadowy thing that translators are expected to carry over into their new texts. This issue has been famously dealt with by Derrida (1974) who argues that there is no stable meaning behind or before the text, a meaning that can be revealed and translated by patiently decoding the original. The claim destabilizes the translating practice of all who regard their originals as "sacred" either because they are holy Scriptures, or because *"[a]ll originals are sacred* in the eyes of the translators" (Barnstone, 1993, p. 81; emphasis in the original). Derrida's writings on translation (1985) point to a hermeneutical stalemate that threatens to paralyze translators for good. In the next section I will take up the gauntlet thrown by Derrida to try and develop the potentially liberating insights contained in his views.

If meaning is not *before* the text, then I propose that it be looked *after it;* meaning in translation would then result from a co-operation between author, original text, original readers and translator, not to speak of the eventual audience, the target readers. Such co-operation is regulated by conventions largely dependent on historically-determined social, ideological and cultural features. Recently, a radical position has been taken by Richard Rorty who advocates that texts have no internal coherence and that they should be granted whatever shape they take at the last roll of the semiotic wheel (1992, p. 97). Shall we follow Rorty along his slippery and subversive slope? It all depends for whom the wheel rolls. If a reader turns the wheel for his or her whim, why should anybody else be interested in what shape is given to the text? If a text really has no internal coherence, I can use it to make it say what I like—all readings would become misreadings, as the saying goes. If this was the case, how could I say that intertextual relations exist between a given text and any other, including the very special intertextual relations that link a translation to its original? Indeed, how could I say that a text *is* a translation in the first place? The very existence of translations, or better, the (admittedly unstable) social and cultural agreement that there are such texts called "translations," would make many eyebrows rise against Rorty's radical view. In fact, this is the crux of the matter: texts roll on the semiotic wheel for a definite community of interpreters in a definite historical setting. Translators squeeze meaning out of their originals in a way that would convince or persuade their readers, and that both readers and translation critics would find acceptable or reasonable. Only then does an interpretation and subsequent translation of the original become relevant, and therefore meaningful.

The Three Relations of Translation

A Description

The "community of interpreters" is one of the centerpieces of Peirce's thought (see Smith, 1989; Rosenthal, 1983). Although it is never easy to establish orderly series in Peirce's system, I would argue that the notion ultimately derives from Peirce's foundational definition of the sign.

> Now a sign has, as such, three references: first, it is a sign *to* some thought which interprets it; second, it is a sign *for* some object to which in that thought it is equivalent; third, it is a sign *in* some respect or quality, which brings it into connection with its object. (5.283)

Moreover, Peirce often insisted that in genuine signs no relation can ever be reduced to the other two. If translations are signs that interpret other signs, the above general definition could be re-written as follows. A translation is:

i) a text connected *in some respect* to its original;

ii) a text that *stands for* an original which is equivalent to it for certain readers; and

iii) a translation *to* those same readers who interpret it.

In genuine translations, none of these relations can be reduced to, or fully accounted for, by the other two. (See Figure 3, next page.)

I would like to draw your attention on the term "equivalent" in the second relation, which has become almost a taboo word in translation studies. Let me specify that translation is equivalent to its original only *under*

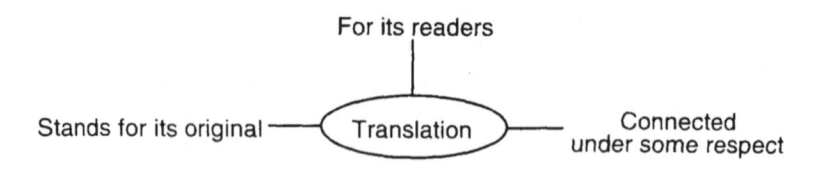

```
                        For its readers
                              |
Stands for its original ──( Translation )── Connected
                                             under some respect
```

Figure 3: Translation as a semiotic process.

some respect and *for its readers*. Therefore it should not be likened to mathematical equivalence; it is rather like the outcome of a bargaining process the translation carries out with the original and the readers. The transformation of Peirce's "thought" or "interpretant" into the notion of "readers" also requires some clarification, which I will give, following Fisch (1986, pp. 343-344 and pp. 359-360). In a letter of 1908 Peirce wrote:

> I define a Sign as anything which is so determined by something else, called its Object, and so determines an effect upon a person, which effect I call its Interpretant, that the latter is thereby mediately determined by the former. My insertion of "upon a person" is a sop to Cerberus, because I despair of making my own broader conception understood. (1977, pp. 80-81)

In the "broader conception," both sender and receiver of the sign would be described as *Quasi-utterer and Quasi-interpreter* (4.551). This implies a distinction between thinking and thought: The former is carried out by persons and belongs with psychology while the latter does not require any individual mind and belongs with logic or semiotics. In the last analysis, it is a matter of generality: My problem here is providing a workable description of real-life translated texts which are produced by flesh-and-blood translators for a definite group of readers. The more general level of analysis in which utterer and interpreter are "welded" into the sign (4.551) is here merely understood and gives validity to my level of description in which "readers" are a community of people who interpret the target text and give a response to it. (Discussions of the notion of interpretant and interpreters can be found in Eco, 1981, esp. chs. 1-2; Bonfantini, 1980, 1984, and 1987; and Proni, 1990, who also attempts a general systematization.)

At any rate, the main point in this approach is that translating requires interpretive work in all its stages. The following section will discuss a general semiotic model of it; for now, I wish to point out that the interrelation of the three features rules out all forms of reckless interpretation. Since interpretation always contains elements of invention, a translation re-creates its original, but (i) it does so according to a given and *knowable* respect; (ii) it re-creates *that* original and not any other text, and (iii) it is directed to a *definite* community of readers. Even the great misreader de la Motte, who claimed to have improved Homer by erasing all unsightly descriptions of

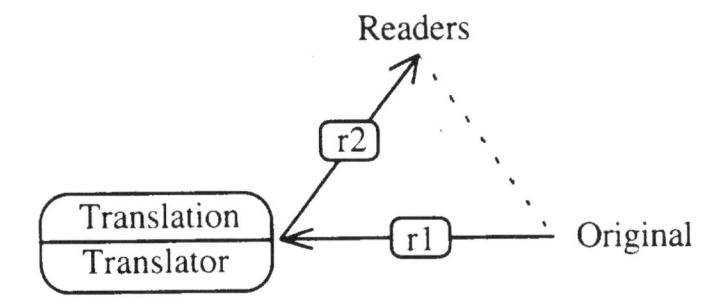

Figure 4: Translation mediates between an original and the readers.

wounds from the *Iliad*, had a community of interpreters in mind who wouldn't have stomached all that Greek blood (cf. Lefevere 1990, p. 27).

The Product

Natural readers do not need to be told by a semiotician that a translation stands for and says the same thing as its original; although these beliefs are in no way universal and change through time and across cultures, it is a fact that translators are surrounded by special expectations that do not concern—say—historians, anthologists, literary critics, and editors (see Lefevere, 1992, V-VI). Paraphrasing Peirce (2.303; see Bonfantini, 1980, XXXV for a discussion), it can be said that translation determines its readers to refer to an original to which the translation itself refers *in the same way*. (See Figure 4.)

This is a viable definition of the product of translation and accounts for its ethic: translators interpret and re-write the original to make sure that r1=r2 so that the readers' expectations are met. But this is still a naive picture; we need to know how translators turn source texts into target texts, and how r1 can be "the same" as r2. The next two sections will tackle these problems in order.

The Process

> Semiosis in the language-game of translation means that the interpreter —i.e. the translator—interprets and translates in fact his/her own interpretants. (Gorlée, 1989, p. 83)

In this section I will try to analyze this insight in strictly Peircian terms, but a short semiotic discussion is required first. Please observe Figure 5 on the following page..

The figure shows some aspects of Peirce's theory of the interpretant that are relevant for us. The two thicker lines going clockwise from the object to the interpretant through the sign indicate the first function of the interpretant, that is to "understand" the object thanks to the mediation of the

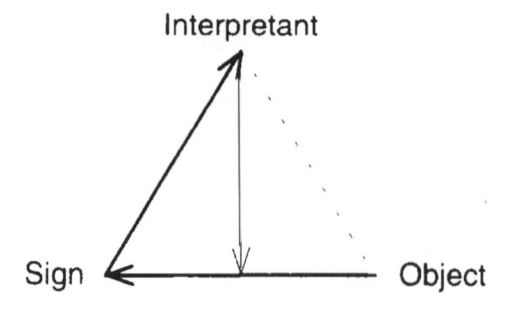

Figure 5: The semiotic triangle, according to Peirce.

sign. The dotted line falling from the top corner onto the base indicates the second function of the interpretant, that is to understand in which *way* the sign stands for its object. What the figure does not explain is that interpretants are also signs themselves, therefore they are always amenable of being further developed into other signs, an "interpretant [becomes] in turn a sign, and so on *ad infinitum*" (2.303). Thus we run the risk of falling into an abyss of regression; fortunately, Peirce gave us a ladder to climb down into the abyss: he said that interpretants come temporarily to rest when the interpreter reaches a state called "habit" (see 5.464-496).

The two functions of the interpretant are always at work together; for the sake of clarity, though, I will discuss how they function during the translation act as if they were two separate modes which, in keeping with Peirce's terminology, I will call Object-oriented mode and Relation-oriented mode. The following discussion draws on Proni (1990, esp., pp. 234-238).

(1) Object-oriented mode

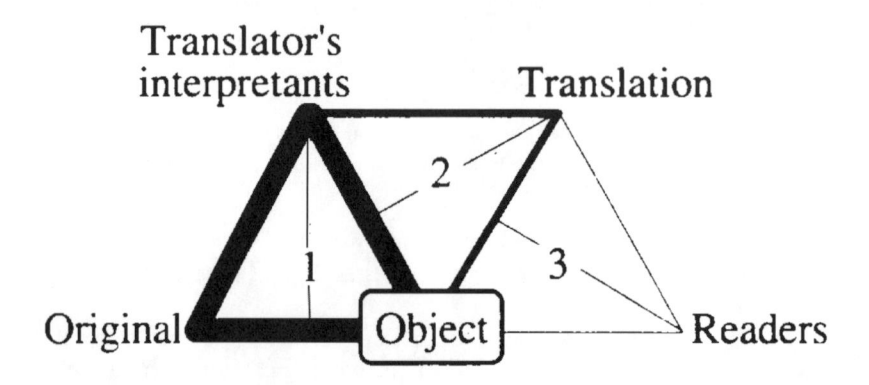

Figure 6: The object-oriented mode of translation.

(See Figure 6.) In triad number 1, the Original is a sign that interprets some real-world object (referent, content, topic...). The Original is already a representation—obviously through other signs that I have omitted—of a portion of the world that can be a natural object or event, or a cultural artifact. This sign-text is developed by the Translator into her own Interpretants —eg, she has a feeling that she understood its sense, she has a reaction to it, and she eventually develops a general translating strategy. Above all, she makes sure that she gets the *respect* under which the Original represents its Object. In triad number 2, the Translator's Interpretants have become a "sign" and the Translation sits in the top corner; it means that the translated text is a semiotic development of the translator's interpretive conclusions or habits. Triad number 3 represents the Translation as a sign in the hands of its Readers who believe that they are reading a text about the same object as the one represented by the Original. The Readers' response is again a semiotic development of the translated text, this is why the Readers hold the position of interpretant in the triad.

(2) Relation-oriented mode

(See Figure 7.) This mode represents the second function of the interpretant. Here the interpretant seeks to understand the way in which the "signs" stand for their respective objects here labelled O1, O2 and O3. Let me clarify that, as in Figure 6, the position of interpretant is held by the Translator's Interpretants, the Translation and the Readers in their respective triads. I will exemplify the figure with an imaginary literary translation. In the first triad the translator notices that the language of her original is heavily defamiliarized to attain certain effects of sense; consequently, she will not concentrate on the original's object (O1) but on the relation

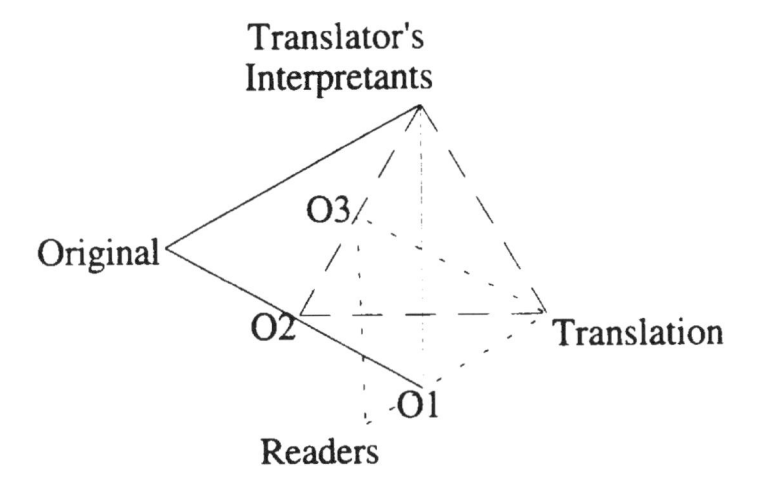

Figure 7: The relation-oriented mode of translation.

between the Original and O1. Her new object (O2) includes—say—the rhetorical devices employed by the original to attain such effects of sense, which she will analyze before looking for devices with matching effects in her own tongue and literary tradition. This interpretive work is then reflected in her own text, represented in triad number two: the Translation will obviously represent the *way* in which our translator found her literary solutions, here called O3. The Translation eventually becomes the sign that reaches the target Readers.

Several translation theorists have already dealt with similar distinctions: Peter Newmark, for instance, has written extensively about communicative vs. semantic translation, with an eye to the transfer of culturally loaded terms (see, 1991, pp. 10-11 and *passim);* from a very distant viewpoint, Barnstone (1993, pp. 33-41 and *passim)* distinguishes between information transfer and literary translation. My semiotic figures are both similar to and different from these distinctions. The main difference is that the Object- and Relation-oriented modes are in no way mutually exclusive, they are not two sides of a dichotomy: a purely object-oriented translation is impossible; even the most literal interlinear version is already the product of relation-oriented strategies. Likewise, a purely relation-oriented strategy is equally impossible: Translations always stand for their originals that, in turn, stand for their objects. The two modes of sign production are in fact complementary and always at work together in real-life translating: the former assures continuity of *reference* while the latter makes room for the generation of *new information* in the target text.

From Equivalence to Inference

I will now turn to the moot point of contemporary translation theory —the notion of equivalence. In most western cultures today, equivalence is that unique intertextual relation that only translations, among all conceivable text types, are expected to show. Let us see, therefore, what becomes of the notion of equivalence in a semiotic account of translation. The form of interpretation here proposed as the core of translating practices is a reflection of the kind called abduction or "explanatory hypothesis" (see 5.180-212, esp. 5.189). For translators, abduction is a form of hypothetical reasoning in which the translator places an interpretive bet on a sign which is later tested using deduction and induction. Following Peirce's cognitive theory —which is based on the identity of signs and thoughts—the signs translators interpret may be either existing texts or steps in the immaterial translation process. If the interpretive bet is confirmed by later testing, the guess can be adopted as a good enough interpretant. This mental procedure is constantly employed by translators in all the stages of their work: for instance, we use it to assess the likely reception our text is going to have in our cultural system; to understand the general topic of our original and of its components;

to arrange the units of our target text; to figure out stylistic and rhetorical features; and finally to make decisions on the physical appearance of the text (see Stecconi, 1991b on these divisions). In what follows I will focus only on the relation between abduction and equivalence.

Equivalence can be represented by the formula A=B; where A is an element in the original and B is its equivalent in the translation. In most studies, A and B are (usually formal) elements of the linguistic, cultural or literary structures of the source and target worlds respectively, therefore it is assumed that both exist before the time in which the translation gets written. Most authors also seem to imply that A and B are already equivalent; the task of the translator, then, consists in unveiling the meaning of A and spotting the correct B among the innumerable elements of her cultural world. It follows that there exists one B equal to A such that any other option—although admissible—is second-best. To use an analogy, translators are seen as looking for their textual elements as we would look for a spare part when our car breaks down during our holidays abroad: "There must be a garage with original parts!" Two conclusions can be drawn: if you believe in linguistic or anthropological universals (Nida, 1959, 1969) or if your metaphysics tells you that all languages are already imperfect translations of the language of God (Benjamin, 1992), then different worlds can be equivalent, and individual translations are possible; if, on the contrary, you believe that any two cultures are irreducible to each other (Croce, 1993), then you must conclude that translation is impossible. In a milder version of the second position, only some special expressions are deemed untranslatable; which is what Robert Frost probably had in mind when he said that "poetry is what gets lost in translation."

The truth is that translators adopt problem-solving strategies following what Peirce called our "natural light," which Bonfantini renamed "cultural light" (1987, p. 73ff.). After stabilizing our interpretant for A, we *guess* at a B; then, we conduct relentless mental experiments to test it against A itself, against our overall translation strategies, against the likely response of our readers, against the respect under which A meant whatever it meant, against what we want to mean by B, etc. Only at the end of this series of inferences do we normally reach a satisfactory solution. Another analogy: Translating is rather like furnishing your new house; you know that there is something missing on that wall, you need a picture that would go well together with your favorite picture, which is already hanging on the opposite wall. You look for a matching picture, and you normally find a satisfactory one—end of the analogy. B is still part of an existing structure—although at times you literally have to invent it as you may decide to paint your new picture yourself—but a translator's job consists in picking up B in her culture and language and concluding that it is equivalent to A. B had never been equivalent to A before it appeared in a translation: Using inferences of the abductive kind, the translator *makes* the two elements equivalent. In sum, our old formula A=B becomes A$\Rightarrow$B—if A then B—in the presence of factors x, y and z which account for the translation historical and cultural setting. (I thank Anthony Pym for this suggestion, personal communication, November 24, 1994.)

Notes on Inference

The formula for inference differs from that for equivalence in many respects. Most importantly, it stresses the fact that translating implies a problem-solving procedure more than the knowledge of a double structure of reference. In A=B, the elements of the equation usually represented formal elements of two languages while the process of their search was left in the background. On the contrary, in A⇒B, and more generally in the semiotic approach, the elements are signs in which A is a problem and B a solution. More specifically, A is a "surprising fact" (5.189) which raises a doubt whose presence spurs the translator into guessing hypotheses, testing them and eventually adopting one as a habit. The solution B is merely the action determined by such habit. A couple of examples will illustrate this process.

Some years ago I coordinated a team that was translating into Italian the manuals for a software package called Project. The original—written in the U.S.—extensively used the example of Project being used by an engineering firm in the construction of a golf course. During the preliminary stages of our work we had to decide whether the same fiction would work in an Italian context. We were undecided; among the many hypotheses tested, we even thought of using the construction of a football stadium as our example (we were near the football world cup finals held in Italy in 1990). Then we realized that golfing was becoming popular in Italy, especially among the class of people who were likely to purchase Project. When we discovered that they were actually constructing a new golf course a few miles away from our own town, the question was settled: We would retain the fiction. The second example is drawn from the same source. Towards the beginning of the general manual, a section gave advice on how to use the mouse—still a rather exotic beast in computing at the time. One of the tips read as follows (I am quoting from memory): "If, dragging the mouse on your table, you reach the edge, you should lift the mouse from the surface, move it towards the center of your working area, and resume dragging"—a surprising fact indeed. Our doubt was "do we want to tell our readers such a platitude?" This time the possible hypotheses were fewer: either keeping the tip in Italian or erasing it altogether. After an amusing debate we concluded we would rather drop it. That became our habit; the *absence* of the passage from the Italian manuals was our eventual solution.

Apart from giving substance to Peirce's views, these examples are meant to show that the theory here proposed goes hand in hand with the practice of translating. (I thank Yves Gambier for this suggestion, personal communication, Misano Adriatico, Italy, September, 1994.) Although practical examples do not abound in this paper, the theory here presented is close to practice because it ultimately rests on pragmatism (or "pragmaticism" as Peirce would have said). The fundamental argument can be sketched as follows: "the action of thought is excited by the irritation of doubt and ceases when belief is attained; so that the production of belief is the sole function of thought" (5.394). But beliefs produce habits which, in turn, are guidelines for action; this is why "there is no distinction of meaning so fine as to consist in something but a possible difference of practice" (5.400). The argument is crucial for us. Again referring to our second example above, when we reached the belief that the passage about the mouse should be dropped, a translation habit was immediately established. A few months later we were assigned the translation of a second set of manuals by the same company; when we found the passage again, we already knew what to do because we had already developed a habit. We simply had to exercise our volition and we quickly dropped the passage again: it was no longer a problem for us, no surprising fact, not much thinking. This makes the work of the translator feasible because we don't have to always establish unprecedented equivalences; more often than not, we are content with our old solutions.

This also means that translation inferences tend to form a system of equivalences over time; in formulaic terms: A$\Rightarrow$B tends to become A=B. However, this does not affect the primacy of inference; an analogy found in Wittgenstein (1969, p. 152; cit. in Frongia, 1983, p. 225) can illustrate the point. The position of stabilized equivalences in relation to inferential processes is similar to that of a geometrical axis around which a solid revolves. The axis is fixed not because of some intrinsic features, but rather because of the very movement of the solid around it; it is fixed only in relation to the spinning solid. Likewise, equivalences are only apparently central in the system, in fact they are historically constituted by inferential processes and can be altered or subverted any time by further inferences as soon as the need arises.

References

Achtemeier, P. J. (1990). Omne verbum sonat. *Journal of Biblical Literature, 109,* 3-27.

Allen, W. S. (1987). *Vox gracae: The pronunciation of classic Greek* (3rd ed.). Cambridge, UK: Cambridge University Press.

American Bible Society. (1886). *The sampler Bible.* Columbia, SC: Bell & Parsons.

American Bible Society Archives. (1989, April). Appendix to letter of agreement between the American Bible Society and Fern Lee Hagedorn.

American Bible Society Board of Trustees. (1990, December). Minutes of the board meeting.

Angles, H. (1954). Latin chant before St. Gregory. In A. Hughes (Ed.), *Early medieval music up to 1300* (Vol. 2, The New Oxford History of Music; pp. 58-90). New York: Oxford University Press.

Apel, W. (1958). *Gregorian chant.* Bloomington, IN: Indiana University Press.

Attridge, H. W. (1989). *The epistle to the Hebrews.* Philadelphia: Fortress Press.

Avenary, H. (1963). *Studies in the Hebrew, Syrian, and Greek liturgical recitative.* Tel-Aviv: Israel Music Institute.

Bahr, G. J. (1965). The use of the Lord's prayer in the primitive church. *Journal of Biblical Literature, 84,* 153-159.

Baker, M. (1992). *In other words: A coursebook on translation.* London & New York: Routledge.

Balogh, J. (1926). "*Voces paginarum*": Beiträge zur Geschichte des lauten Lesens und Schreibens. *Philologus, 82,* 84-109, 202-240.

Barnstone, W. (1993). *The poetics of translation: History, theory and practice.* New Haven: Yale University Press.

Barthes, R. (1972). *Mythologies.* (A. Lavers, Ed. and Trans.). New York: Hill and Wang. (Original work published 1957)

Barthes, R. (1974). *S/Z.* (R. Miller, Trans.). New York: Hill and Wang. (Original work published 1970)

Baugh, L. (1997). *Imaging the divine: Christ figures in film.* Kansas City, MO: Sheed & Ward.

Beaugrande, R. de. (1991). Coincidence in translation: Glory and misery again. *Target III,* 1.

Beniger, J. R. (1987). Personalization of mass media and the growth of pseudo-community. *Communication Research, 14,* 352-371.

Benjamin, W. (1992). The task of the translator, (H. Zohn, Trans.). In R. Schultze & J. Biguenet (Eds.). *Theories of translation: An anthology from Dryden to Derrida* (pp. 23-46). Chicago: University of Chicago Press.

Betz, H. D. (1995). *The Sermon on the Mount.* Minneapolis, MN: Fortress Press.

Black, M. H. (1963). The printed Bible. In S. L. Greenslade (Ed.), *Cambridge history of the Bible, Vol. 3. The West from the Reformation to the present day* (pp. 408-475). Cambridge, UK: Cambridge University Press.

Bloch, R. (1978). Midrash (M. Howard Callaway, Trans.). In W.S. Green (Ed.), *Approaches to ancient Judaism: Theory and practice.* Brown Judaic Studies 1 (pp. 29-50). Missoula, MT: Scholars Press.

Bogliolo, G. (1991). Qualche riflessione in margine alle traduzioni italiane delle *Fleurs du mal. Koiné 1,* 1.

Bolter, J. D. (1991). *Writing space: The computer, hypertext, and the history of writing.* Hllsdale, NJ: Lawrence Erlbaum Associates.

Bonfantini, M. A. (1980). Introduzione, in Charles Sanders Peirce, *Semiotica,* Turin: Einaudi.

Bonfantini, M. A. (1984). Introduzione, in Charles Sanders Peirce, Le leggi dell' ipotesi (pp. Xx-xx). Milan: Bompiani.

Bonfantini, M. A. (1987). *La semiosi e l'abduzione.* Milan: Bompiani.

Botha, P. J. (1992). Greco-Roman literacy as setting for New Testament writings. *Neotestamentica, 26,* 195-215.

Bratcher, R. G. (1995). Current trends in Bible translation in English. *Practical Papers for the Bible Translator, 46*(4), 439-444.

Brown, R. E. (1970). *The gospel according to John (xiii-xxi).* Garden City, NJ: Doubleday.

Brueggemann, W. (1982). *Genesis.* Atlanta: John Knox Press.

Buck, C. D. (1955). *Comparative grammar of Greek and Latin.* Chicago: The University of Chicago Press.

Bultmann, R. (1971). *The Gospel of John: A commentary* (G.R. Beasley-Murray, R.W.N. Hoare, J.K. Riches, Trans.). Philadelphia: Westminster. (Original work published 1964)

Burke, D. G. (1993). Translating Scripture into electronic media. *Technical Papers for the Bible Translator, 44*(3), 101-111.

Buzzetti, C. (1995). Da una traduzione all'altra: Confronto di modelli complementari o alternativi. *Koiné, V.*

Caldwell, J. (1978). *Medieval music.* Bloomington, IN: Indiana University Press.

Carey, J. W. (1989). A cultural approach to communication. In J. W. Carey, *Communication as culture: Essays on media and society* (pp. 13-36). Boston: Unwin Hyman. (Original work published 1975)

Carruthers, M. J. (1990). *The book of memory.* Cambridge, UK: Cambridge University Press.

Caruso, D. (1996, November 18). Technology. *New York Times*, p. D9.
Cassuto, V. (1978). *A commentary on the book of Genesis, Part 1*. (I. Abrahams, Trans.). Jerusalem: The Magness Press. (Original work published 1944)
Cattrysse, P. (1992). Film (adaptation) as translation: Some methodological proposals. *Target, 4*(1), 53-70.
Cattrysse, P. (1997). Audiovisual translation and new media. In R. Hodgson & P. A. Soukup, S. J. (Eds.), *From one medium to another: Basic issues for communicating the Scriptures in new media* (pp. 67-89). Kansas City: Sheed & Ward.
Chandler, D. (1994). Semiotics for beginners. Web document, available at http://www.argyroneta.com/s4b. Accessed July 28, 1998.
Clark, W. P. (1930-31). Ancient reading. *Classical Journal, 26,* 698-700.
Clarke, W. K. (1959) *Liturgy and worship*. London: S.P.C.K.
Clines, D.J.A. (1995). *Interested parties: The ideology of writers and readers of the Hebrew Bible*. London: Sheffield Academic Press.
Cohen, N. J. (1992, April). [Midrash]. Notes taken at a lecture at Temple Israel, Dayton, OH.
Cole, T. (1836). Essay on American scenery. *The American Monthly Magazine, Mag I, N.S.*, 4-5.
Cole, T. (Unpublished notes). Cole Papers: "lecture" (on the "arts of design") and "Pictures in Churches." Albany, NY: New York State Library.
Croce, B. (1993). Indivisibilità dell'espressione in modi o gradi e critica della retorica. In S. Nergaard (Ed.), *La teoria della traduzione nella storia*. Milan: Bompiani. [First published in *Estetica come scienza dell'espressione e linguistica generale*. Bari: Laterza, 1928 (1902), cap. IX, pp. 75-82.]
Cronin, M. (1996). *Translating Ireland*. Cork: Cork University Press.
Crystal, D. (1980). *A first dictionary of linguistics and phonetics*. Boulder, CO: Westview Press.
de Waard, J., & Nida, E. A. (1986). *From one language to another: Functional equivalence in Bible translating*. Nashville: Nelson Publishers.
Dean, M. E. (1996). The grammar of sound in Greek texts: Toward a method for mapping the echoes of speech in writing. *Australian Biblical Review, 44,* 53-70.
Derrida, J. (1974). *Of grammatology*. Baltimore: Johns Hopkins University Press.
Derrida, J. (1985). Des tours de Babel. In J. F. Graham (Trans., Ed.), *Difference in translation* (pp. 165-207). Ithaca: Cornell University Press.
Detweiler, R. (1985). What is a sacred text? *Semeia, 31,* 213-30.
Dickens, A. G. (1974). *The German nation and Martin Luther*. New York: Harper & Row.
Eco, U. (1976). *A theory of semiotics*. Bloomington: Indiana University Press.

Eco, U. (1981). *The role of the reader*. London: Hutchinson. (Original work published 1979)
Eco, U. (1984). *Semiotics and the philosophy of language*. Basingstoke: The Macmillan Press Ltd.
Eco, U. (1986). *Art and beauty in the middle ages*. (H. Bredin, Trans.). New Haven, CT: Yale University Press. (Original work published 1959)
Edwards, M. U. (1994). *Printing, propaganda, and Martin Luther*. Berkeley: University of California Press.
Eisenstein, E. L. (1979). *The printing press as an agent of change: Communications and cultural transformations in early modern Europe*. New York: Cambridge University Press.
Evans, E. (Trans., Ed.) (1953). *De Oratione Liber* (Tertullian's Tract on the Prayer). London: S.P.C.K.
Fanning, B. M. (1990). *Verbal aspect in New Testament Greek*. Oxford: Clarendon Press.
Faulkner, W. & Ford, R. (1959). *Requiem for a nun: A play from the novel*. New York: Random House.
Fenster, M. (1989). Genre & form: The development of the country music video. In S. Frith, A. Goodwin & L. Grossberg, (Eds.), *The music video reader* (pp. 109-128). London: Routledge.
Fisch, M. (1986). *Peirce, semeiotic and pragmatism: Essays*. (K. L. Ketner & C. Kloesel, Eds.). Bloomington: Indiana University Press.
Fish, S. (1980). *Is there a text in this class? The authority of interpretive communities*. Cambridge, MA: Harvard University Press.
Fishbane, M. (1985). *Biblical interpretation in ancient Israel*. Oxford: Clarendon Press.
Flagg, J. B. (1969). *Life and letters of Washington Allston*. New York: Scribner's Sons. (Original work published 1892)
Folena, G. (1991). *Volgarizzare e tradurre*. Turin: Einaudi.
Foley, J. M. (1995). *The singer of tales in performance*. Bloomington: Indiana University Press.
From O. J. to Diana. (1997, September 3). *The Wall Street Journal*, p. A20.
Frongia, G. (1983). *Wittgenstein, regole e sistema*. Milan: Franco Angeli.
Fry, E. McG. (1987). Faithfulness—A wider perspective. *United Bible Societies Bulletin, 148/149,* 41-60.
Gadamer, H-G. (1975). *Truth and method*. (G. Barden & J. Cumming, Trans.). New York: Seabury Press. (Original work published 1960)
Gilliard, F. D. (1993). More silent reading in antiquity: *Non omne verbum sonabat*. *Journal of Biblical Literature, 112*, 689-694.
Goethals, G. (1997). Multimedia images: Plato's cave revisited. In R. Hodgson & P. A. Soukup, S. J. (Eds.), *From one medium to another: Basic issues for communicating the Scriptures in new media* (pp. 229-248). Kansas City: Sheed & Ward.
Gorlée, D. (1989). Wittgenstein, translation, and semiotics. In *Target 1*, 69-94.

Gorlée, D. (1994). *Semiotics and the problem of translation.* Amsterdam: Rodopi.

Gutt, E.-A. (1992). *Relevance theory: A guide to successful communication in translation.* New York: United Bible Societies.

Hadas, M. (1954). *Ancilla to classical reading.* New York: Columbia University Press.

Hagedorn, F. L. (1989, May 2). Memorandum from Fern Lee Hagedorn to David Burke, Re: April report on audiovisual research project. American Bible Society Archives.

Hagedorn, F. L. (1990a). Faithfulness—a wider perspective: A synthesis of responses to the article by Euan McG. Fry (2/14/90). American Bible Society Archives.

Hagedorn, F. L. (1990b). Preliminary draft, provisional guiding principles, audiovisual translations (2/15/90). American Bible Society Archives.

Hagedorn, F. L. (1990c). Year-end report, "audiovisual translations" research project, 1 April 1989 - 30 March 1990 (4/1/90). American Bible Society Archives.

Hagedorn, F. L. (1991). Why multimedia translations? An American Bible Society perspective. *United Bible Societies Bulletin, 160/161,* 20-26.

Harris, W. V. (1989). *Ancient literacy.* Cambridge, MA: Harvard University Press.

Hatton, H. A. (1985). Translating Scripture in the comic medium. *Practical Papers for the Bible Translator, 36*(2), 430-437.

Hawking, S. W. (1988). *A brief history of time: From the big bang to black holes.* Toronto and New York: Bantam Books.

Hendrickson, G. L. (1929-30). Ancient Reading. *Classical Journal, 25,* 182-196.

Hermans, T. (Ed.). (1985). *The manipulation of literature: Studies in literary translation.* Beckenham, UK: Croom Helm.

Hertz, J. (1985). *The authorized daily prayer book,* (Rev. ed.). New York: Block Publishing Co.

Hinks, R. (1962). *Carolingian art: A study of early medieval painting and sculpture in western Europe.* Ann Arbor: University of Michigan Press.

Hodgson, R. & Soukup, P. A. (Eds.). (1997). *From one medium to another: Basic issues for communicating the Scriptures in new media.* Kansas City: Sheed & Ward.

Holborn, L. (1942). Printing and the growth of a Protestant movement in Germany from 1517 to 1524. *Church History, 11,* 123-117.

Iser, W. (1974). *The implied reader: Patterns of communication in prose fiction from Bunyan to Beckett.* Baltimore: The Johns Hopkins University Press.

Iser, W. (1978). *The act of reading: A theory of aesthetic response.* Baltimore: The Johns Hopkins University Press.

Ivins, W., Jr. (1968). *Prints and visual communication.* Cambridge, MA: MIT Press.
Jaeger, W. (1986). *Paideia: The ideals of Greek culture: Vol. 1 Archaic Greece, The mind of Athens.* (Gilbert Highet, Trans.). Oxford University Press. (Originl work published 1933)
Jakobson, R. (1959). On linguistic aspects of translation. In R. Brower (Ed.) *On translation.* Cambridge, Mass: Harvard University Press.
Jasper, D. (1995). *Readings in the canon of scripture.* New York: St. Martin's Press.
Josipovici, G. (1988). *The book of God.* New Haven, CT: Yale University Press.
Jungmann, J. A. (1959). *The mass of the Roman rite.* New York: Benzinger Brothers.
Keen, E. (1997). Telling the story in dance. In R. Hodgson & P. A. Soukup, (Eds.), *From one medium to another: Basic issues for communicating the Scriptures in new media* (pp. 151-180). Kansas City: Sheed & Ward.
Kelly, K. & Wilson, C. (1997, June 25). A wedding album from Walt Disney World. *USA Today*, p. 8D.
Kennedy, G. A. (1963). *The art of persuasion in Greece.* Princeton: Princeton University Press.
Kennedy, G. A. (1969). *Quintilian.* New York: Twayne.
Kennedy, G. A. (1991). *Aristotle on rhetoric: A theory of civic discourse* (Newly translated with Introduction, Notes, and Appendixes). New York: Oxford University Press.
Knox, B. M. W. (1968). Silent reading in antiquity. *Greek, Roman, and Byzantine Studies, 9,* 421-435.
Kraeling, K. (1967). *The Christian building.* New Haven, CT: Dura-Europos Publications.
Lake, K. (Trans.) (1977). Didache, or teaching of the twelve Apostles. In *The apostolic fathers* (Vol. 1; pp. 303-333). Cambridge, MA: Harvard University Press.
Lakoff, G., & Johnson, M. (1980). *Metaphors we live by.* Chicago: University of Chicago Press.
Lambert, J. (1997). Problems and challenges of translation in an age of new media and competing models. In R. Hodgson & P. Soukup (Eds.), *From one medium to another: Basic issues for communicating the Scriptures in new media* (pp. 51-65). Kansas City and New York: Sheed & Ward and The American Bible Society.
LaRue, J. (1970). *Guidelines for style analysis.* New York: W.W. Norton.
Leeds-Hurwitz, W. (1993). *Semiotics and communication: Signs, codes, cultures.* Hillsdale, NJ: Erlbaum.
Lefevere, A. (1990). Translation: Its genealogy in the West. In S. Bassnett & A. Lefevere (Eds.), *Translation, history, and culture* (pp. 14-28). London: Pinter.

Lefevere, A. (1992). *Translation, re-writing and manipulation of literary fame.* London: Routledge.

Leibowitz, N. (1974). *Studies in bereshit* (Genesis). Jerusalem: Publishing Department of the Jewish Agency at Haomanim Press.

Lentz, T. (1989). *Orality and literacy in hellenic Greece.* Carbondale, IL: Southern Illinois University Press.

Leupold, U. S. (1965). Introduction to the German Mass and order of service. In U. S. Leupold, (Ed.) *Liturgy and Hymns* (pp. 53-60), Vol. 53 of *Luther's works.* (H. T. Lehmann, General Ed.). Philadelphia: Fortress Press.

Levi-Strauss, C. (1969a). *The elementary structures of kinship.* (J. H. Bell, J. R. von Sturmer, & R. Needham, Trans.). Rev. ed. Boston: Beacon Press. (Original work published 1967)

Levi-Strauss, C. (1969b). *The raw and the cooked.* (J. Weightman & D. Weightman, Trans.). New York: Harper & Row. (Original work published 1964)

Liber Usualis. (1961). New York: Descle.

Lindars, B. (1972). *The Gospel of John.* London: Oliphants.

Long, L. (1995). *Well and truly translated.* Unpublished Ph.D. Thesis, University of Warwick, UK.

Louw, J. P. (1985). A semiotic approach to discourse analysis with reference to translation theory. *Technical Papers for The Bible Translator, 36*(3), 101-107.

Lyons, J. L. (1977). *Semantics.* 2 vols. Cambridge, UK: Cambridge University Press.

Manguel, A. (1996). *A history of reading.* New York: Viking.

Marbeck, J. (1980). *The book of common prayer noted*, with an introduction by R. A. Leaver. Oxford: Sutton Courtnay Press.

McDannell, C. (1995). *Material Christianity: Religion and popular culture in America.* New Haven and London: Yale University Press.

McKnight, G. H. (1956). *The evolution of the English language.* New York: Dover Publications.

McLuhan, M. (1964). *Understanding media: The extensions of man.* New York: McGraw-Hill.

McLuhan, M. (1967). *The medium is the message.* New York: Bantam Books.

Metzger, B. M. (1971). *A textual commentary on the Greek New Testament.* New York: United Bible Societies.

Millgram, A. E. (1971). *Jewish worship.* Philadelphia: The Jewish Publications Society of America.

Missale Romanum. (1956). 5th ed. Cincinnati, OH: Benzinger Bros.

Mocquereau, A. (1989). *A study of gregorian musical rhythm*, Vol. 1. (A. Tone, Trans.). Sable-sûr-Sarthe, France: Solesmes. (Original work published 1908-1927)

Morris, C. W. (1970). *Foundations of the theory of signs.* Chicago: University of Chicago Press. (Original work published 1938)
Multimedia Translations Research Team. (1991). Minutes, March 5-6. American Bible Society Archives.
Multimedia Translations Research Team. (1991). Minutes, April 24. American Bible Society Archives.
Neale, S. (1995). Questions of genre. In Grant, B. K. (Ed.), *Film genre reader II* (pp. 159-183). Austin: University of Texas Press.
Nergaard, S. (1993). Introduzione. In S. Nergaard (Ed.), *La teoria della traduzione nella storia* (pp. 1-49). Milan: Bompiani.
Newmark, P. (1991). *About translation.* Clevedon, UK: Multilingual Matters.
Nida, E. A. (1959). Principles of translation as exemplified by Bible translating. In R. Brower (Ed.), *On translation* (pp. 11-31). Cambridge, MA: Harvard University Press.
Nida, E. A. (1964). *Toward a science of translating with special reference to principles and procedures involved in Bible translating.* Leiden: E.J. Brill.
Nida, E. A. (1984) *Signs, sense, translation.* Capetown, South Africa: Bible Society of South Africa.
Nida, E. A. & Reyburn, W.D. (1981). *Meaning across cultures.* (American Society of Missiology Series, NO. 4). Maryknoll, NY: Orbis Books.
Nida, E. A. & Taber, C. (1969). *The theory and practice of translation.* Leiden: Brill.
Noble, L. L. (1964). *The life and works of Thomas Cole.* Cambridge, MA: The Belknap Press of Harvard University.
Nord, C. (1997). *Translating as a purposeful activity: Functionalist approaches explained.* Manchester: St. Jerome Publishing.
Nordenfalk, C. (1995). *Book illumination: Early middle ages.* Switzerland: Bookking. (Original work published 1957)
Ong, W. J. (1996). Information and/or communication: Interactions. *Communication Research Trends, 16*(3): 3-17.
Patte, D. (1976). *What is structural exegesis?* Philadelphia: Fortress Press.
Peirce, C. S. (1955). In J. Buchler (Ed.), *The philosophical papers of Peirce.* New York: Dover Press.
Peirce, C. S. (1960-1966). *Collected papers.* (C. Hartshorne & P. Weiss, Eds., vols. 1-6; A. W. Burks, Ed., vols. 7-8). Cambridge, MA: Belknap Press of Harvard University Press.
Peirce, C. S. (1977). *Semiotics and significs: The correspondence between Charles S. Peirce and Victoria Lady Welby.* C. Hardwick, (Ed.). Bloomington: Indiana University Press.
Pettus, R. (1997). Programming issues in multimedia design. In R. Hodgson & P. A. Soukup, (Eds.), *From one medium to another: Basic issues for communicating the Scriptures in new media* (pp. 249-257). Kansas City: Sheed & Ward.

Porter, S. E. (1989). *Verbal aspect in the Greek of the New Testament, with reference to tense and mood*. New York: Peter Lang.

Postman, N. (1985). *Amusing ourselves to death: Public discourse in the age of show business*. New York: Penguin Books.

Postman, N. (1992). *Technopoly: The surrender of culture to technology*. New York: Vantage Books.

Proni, G. (1990). *Introduzione a Peirce*. Milan: Bompiani.

Pym, A. (1993). *Epistemological problems in translation and its teaching*. Calaceit, Spain: Caminade.

Rebera, B. (1994). *Report given to the United Bible Societies' Video Consultation 28 February-4 March 1994*. Reading, UK: UBS World Service Center.

Revell, E. J. (1971). The oldest evidence for the Hebrew accent system. *Bulletin of the John Rylands Library, 54*, pp. 214-222.

Revell, E. J. (1979). Hebrew accents and Greek ekphonetic neumes. In Wellesz, E. & Velmirovic, M. (Eds.), *Studies in eastern chant* (Vol. 4, pp. 140-170). London: Oxford University Press.

Robbins, V. K. (1993). Progymnastic rhetorical composition and pre-Gospel traditions: A new approach. In C. Focant (Eds.), *The synoptic gospels: Source criticism and the new literary criticism* (pp. 111-147). Leuven: Leuven University Press.

Rorty, R. (1992). The pragmatist's progress. In S. Collini (Ed.), *Interpretation and overinterpretation* (pp. 89-108). Cambridge, UK: Cambridge University Press.

Roschke, R. W. (1992, May). Scholarly reaction to the Gerasene demoniac. American Bible Society Archives.

Rosenthal, S. B. (1983). Meaning as habit: Some implications. In E. Freeman (Ed.), *The Relevance of Charles Peirce* (pp. 312-327). La Salle, IL: The Hegeler Institute.

Saussure, F. de. (1959). *Course in general linguistics*. (C. Bally & A. Reidlinger, Eds., W. Baskin, Trans.). New York: Philosophical Library. (Original work published 1915)

Schnackenburg, R. (1982). *The Gospel according to St. John* (David Smith, G.A. Kon, Trans.). New York: Crossroad. (Original work published 1965)

Scott, B. B. (1994). *Hollywood dreams and biblical stories*. Minneapolis: Fortress Press.

Seiter, E. (1992). Semiotics, structuralism, and television. In R. C. Allen, (Ed.), *Channels of discourse, reassembled,* (pp. 31-66). Chapel Hill: University of North Carolina Press.

Shannon, C. & Weaver, W. (1949). *The mathematical theory of communication*. Urbana: University of Illinois Press.

Simson, O. von. (1948). *Sacred fortress: Byzantine art and state craft in Ravenna*. Chicago: University of Chicago Press.

Smith, J. E. (1983). Community and reality. In E. Freeman (Ed.), *The Relevance of Charles Peirce* (pp. 38-58). La Salle, IL: The Hegeler Institute.

Smyth, H. W. (1984). *Greek grammar.* Cambridge, MA: Harvard University Press.

Snell-Hornby, M. (1988). *Translation studies: An integrated approach.* Amsterdam: John Benjamins.

Snyder, G. (1985). *Ante pacem: Archaeological evidence of church life before Constantine.* Beaumont, TX: SeedSowers.

Soukup, P. A. (1997). Understanding audience understanding. In R. Hodgson & P. A. Soukup, (Eds.), *From one medium to another: Basic issues for communicating the Scriptures in new media* (pp. 91-107). Kansas City: Sheed & Ward.

Speiser, E. A. (1964). *Genesis.* Garden City, NY: Doubleday.

Staeblein, B. (1962). Pater noster. In F. Blume (Ed.). *Die Musik in Geschichte und Gegenwart,* (Vol 10; pp. 944-950). Kassel, Germany: Bharenreiter-Verlag.

Stanford, W. B. (1967). *The sound of Greek: Studies in the Greek theory and practice of euphony.* Berkeley, CA: University of California Press.

Stecconi, U. (1991a). Mary Snell-Hornby: un approccio integrato. *Koiné, 1*(1), 169-175.

Stecconi, U. (1991b). Una retorica per la traduzione. *Koiné, 1,* 127-139.

Steiner, R. (1980). Lord's prayer. In S. Sadie, (Ed.). *The new Grove dictionary of music & musicians.* (vol. 11, pp. 229-230). London: MacMillan Publishers, Ltd.

Stubbs, M. (1980). *Language and literacy: The sociolinguistics of reading and writing.* London: Routledge and Kegan Paul.

Thomas, K. J. (1994a). Can a youth be faithful to a 2000-year old spouse? *Bulletin of the United Bible Societies: Current Trends in Scripture Translation, 170/171,* 37-42.

Thomas, K. J. (1994b). Criteria for faithfulness in multimedia translation (and related audio components). *Bulletin of the United Bible Societies: Current Trends in Scripture Transaltion, 170/171,* 43-48.

Tompkins, J. P. (Ed.). (1980). *Reader-response criticism: From formalism to post-structuralism.* Baltimore: The Johns Hopkins University Press.

Toury, G. (1986). Translation: A cultural-semiotic perspective. In T. A. Seboek, (Ed.) *Encyclopedic dictionary of semiotics/2.* (p. 1113). Berlin-New York-Amsterdam: Mouton-de Gruyter.

Trible, P. (1994). *Rhetorical criticism: Context, method and the book of Jonah.* Minneapolis: Fortress Press.

van Wolde, E. (1991). The story of Cain and Abel: A narrative study. *Journal for the Study of the Old Testament, 52,* pp. 27-35.

Vatican Working Group for the Final Revision for the *Lectionary for Mass.* (1997). Commentary on the revision of the *Lectionary for Mass.* Na-

tional Conference of Catholic Bishops Committee on the Liturgy Newsletter, 33, 25-32.

Venuti, L. (1995). *The translator's invisibility.* London: Routledge.

Vogt Marketing Services, Inc. (1992, April). A contemporary video translation of the Gerasene demoniac: A qualitative study. American Bible Society Archives.

Waltke, E. & O'Connor, M. (1990). *An introduction to biblical Hebrew syntax.* Winona Lake, IN: Eisenbrauns.

Wenham, G. J. (1987). *Genesis: Word biblical commentary.* Vol. 1. Waco, Texas: Word Books Publishers.

Werner, E. (1984). *The sacred bridge,* (Vol. 2). New York: KTAV Publishing House, Inc.

Werner, J. R. (1997). Musical *mimesis* for modern media. In R. Hodgson & P. A. Soukup, (Eds.), *From one medium to another: Basic issues for communicating the Scriptures in new media* (pp. 221-227). Kansas City: Sheed & Ward.

Westermann, C. (1984). *Genesis 1-11: A commentary.* Vol. 1. (J. J. Scullion, Trans.). Minneapolis: Augsburg Publishing House. (Original work published 1974)

White, H. C. (1991). *Narrative and discourse in the book of Genesis.* New York: Cambridge University Press.

Wittgenstein, L. (1969). *Über Gewissheit/On Certainty.* (G. E. M. Anscombe & G. H. von Wright, Eds.; D. Paul & G. E. M. Anscombe, Trans.). Oxford: Blackwell.

Working Group for the Final Revision of the Lectionary for Mass. (1997). Commentary on the revision of the *Lectionary for Mass. National Conference of Catholic Bishops Committee on the Liturgy newsletter, 33*, 25-32.

Index

A Father and Two Sons 29, 70-72, 82, 85, 122, 125-127, 215-217, 236-240, 243, 246, 247
ABOUT US: The Dignity of Children 67-70
ABS (American Bible Society) 4, 5, 29-35, 38-40, 42-45, 56, 60, 65, 70-72, 75, 82, 89, 119, 122, 127, 134, 135, 151, 152, 154, 169, 173, 174, 197, 202, 205, 215, 216, 219, 236-240, 243-246, 248
accuracy 45, 59, 174, 177-179, 207
Achtemeier, P. J. 106
Adam and Eve 96, 98, 100, 120, 136, 150
adaptation 16, 42, 175, 204, 227
Against the Heavenly Prophets 179
allegory 71, 214
Allen, W. S. 181, 182, 184
Allston, Washington 149-151, 162
Amidah 188
Angles, H. 187
Anglican Church 192
Animated Stories, The 214
Apel, W. 190
Aristophanes of Byzantium 181
Aristotle 106, 108, 112, 117, 182
Aristoxenus 182, 184
art
    contemporary religious 163-166
    early Christian 135-139
    manuscript 139-148
    medieval 139-148
    nineteenth century 149-163
Attridge, H. 116

audience 1-5, 10-16, 18-26, 30, 32, 35-37, 40, 42, 44, 49, 51, 54, 55, 57, 58, 60, 61, 81, 82, 86, 89, 100, 116, 118, 123, 125, 126, 128, 129, 133, 149, 150, 170, 171, 201, 203-206, 208, 210, 212-214, 217, 219, 226-228, 235, 240, 244, 252
audiovisual 8, 30-33, 59, 206
Augustine 107
authority 38, 44, 53, 115, 116, 145, 193, 201, 203, 204, 206-209, 211, 217, 221, 227, 235
Avenary, H. 178, 180

background information 17, 77, 83, 123-125, 127, 128
Bahr, G. J. 188
Baker, Mona 5, 75, 88
Balogh, J. 105, 106
baptism 37, 120
baptistry 136-138
Barthes, R. 224, 225
Beniger, J. R. 228
Betz, H. D. 180, 181, 184, 185, 189
Bible
    comic series, Asia Pacific 17
    Hebrew 93, 105, 175, 176, 179
    King James Version (KJV) 44, 77, 80-82, 84-86, 193, 209
    new media 60-63
    New Revised Standard Version 77, 166, 184
    Societies 4, 7, 9, 12, 13, 17, 22, 24, 33, 42-45, 75, 76, 119, 124, 129, 130, 166, 173, 205-207, 234

275

Biblenet, Inc. 215
Biblia Pauperum 147, 148
Black, M. H. 102
Bloch, R. 175-177
Block, Rory 70
Boesak, A. 95
Bolter, J. D. 105
Book of Common Prayer 192-195, 197
Book of Kells 143-145, 147, 169
Botha, P. J. 106
Brown, R. E. 117
Buck, C. D. 182, 187, 194
Bultmann, R. 116
Burke, David 29, 30, 180, 241

Cain and Abel story 95-100
Caldwell, J. 186, 187
Calvin, John 134, 148, 149
canon 12, 50, 119, 152, 160-162, 185, 188, 208
Carey, J. W. 220, 226
Carruthers, M. J. 107, 108
Catacomb of Priscilla 136
Contemporary English Version (CEV) 80, 84, 85, 86, 124, 140, 143, 156, 235
Chagall, Mark 162
Chartres Cathedral 139
Chiang Mai 13
China 121
chirography 107
Church of England 209
cinema 36, 40, 208, 212, 213, 215
Clark, W. P. 106
Clarke, W. K. 191, 193, 194
Codex Vaticanus 107
Cohen, N. J. 175, 176
coherence 11, 213, 214, 252, 253
Cole, Thomas 149-151, 162
Coleridge, Samuel T. 149
colon 111, 112, 115, 117, 181, 183
comics 17, 49, 166, 169, 171, 234, 235

(*see also* Bible comics, and Scripture comics)
communication
   as a semiotic system 219, 223
   as conversation 219, 228
   as ritual 219, 220, 226
   as transportation 219, 220
   study 201, 219, 220, 223, 224, 226, 228, 230
Confessions 107, 211
content
   theological 23, 24
conversation 60, 98, 133, 169, 201, 219, 228-231
Cramner, Archbishop 192-195
Cronin, M. 87
Crystal, D. 181
Cubicle of the Velatio 136
Cultural Studies 212, 213
culture 15, 36, 42, 47, 49, 50, 53, 56, 57, 60, 102, 105, 111, 116, 119, 121, 129, 134, 135, 139, 148, 149, 163, 170, 203, 216, 221, 228, 237, 238, 243, 249, 259
   minority 53

Daniel, William 87
Danish Bible Society 163
Darlington, Gilbert 119
De Mille 161, 215
de Waard, Jan 15, 174, 178, 181, 241
Dean, M. E. 106, 108, 111
Decalogue 175 (*see also* Ten Commandments)
decoding 201, 204, 224, 227, 252
Demetrius 112
Detweiler, R. 204, 208
Deuteronomy 98, 175
dialogue 17, 22, 60, 95, 96, 100, 134, 169, 175, 176, 234, 238
Dickens, A. G. 102
digital
   technologies 45

technology 56, 238
world 4, 47, 50, 55
Dionysius of Halicarnassus 182
discourse 8, 9, 11, 12, 14, 16, 18, 25, 26, 213, 243
  direct 14
  oral 14
  setting 9, 11
  speech 17
  structure 11
  unit 11, 25
distortion 14, 19, 21, 23, 24, 220
Doré, Gustave 152, 154, 156, 158, 160-162
drama 17, 49, 67, 120, 145, 209, 215
dramatization 11, 16, 17, 24, 31, 36
Dunlop, William 149
Dura-Europos 136-138
Durand 149
dynamic equivalence 207

Eco, Umberto 171, 205, 206, 224, 225, 252, 254
Edwards, M. U. 102
Eighteen Benedictions 188
Eisenstein, E. L. 102, 103, 107
Emperor Domitian 116
encoding 201, 204, 222, 224
episodes 10, 76, 138, 223
epistemology 101, 103
equivalence 7, 8, 15, 17, 19, 32, 37, 41, 80, 85, 141, 174, 178, 187, 188, 201, 202, 204-207, 221-223, 225, 226, 231, 235, 236, 249, 254, 258-260
evangelism 208, 209
Evans, E. 180, 188, 190
Eve 96, 98, 100, 120, 136, 150

faithfulness 3-5, 7-12, 14, 17-26, 32, 39, 60, 65, 134, 171, 173, 201, 204-209, 214 (*see also* fidelity)
  to biblical author 10

Fanning 116
Fenster, M.. 215
fidelity 3-5, 32, 38, 39, 43, 45, 47, 51, 53-56, 59, 60, 63, 93-95, 101, 104, 110, 118, 122, 133, 134, 139, 141, 143, 147, 152, 161, 170, 173, 174, 177-179, 201, 202, 204-208, 211-215, 219, 221-227, 229-231, 233-236, 238-241, 244-248
  and access 47-63
  and aesthetics 133-171
  and literary analysis 95-100
  and midrash 175-177
  and new media 122-130
  extralinguistic 238-239
  in translation 7-27
  linguistic 233, 235
  paralinguistic 235-237
film 3, 8, 11, 29, 30, 33, 35-40, 42, 44, 65-68, 70-72, 133, 134, 152, 161, 162, 201, 203-205, 212, 214, 227, 231, 236, 238-241, 243
  adaptation 42
  theory 204
Fish, S. 208, 212
Fishbane, M. 175, 178
Foley, J. M. 111
Fry, E. McG. 4, 5, 7, 31, 173, 174, 177, 178, 241
functional equivalence 1-3, 7, 8, 15, 19, 32, 37, 41, 174, 178, 221, 222
fusion of horizons 229

Gadamer, H.-G. 228, 229
Gallican liturgy 188
Genesis 4.1-16 95, 96
genre analysis 212-213
Gerasene Demoniac 4, 29, 35, 40, 41, 65
German hymnody 179
Gilliard, F. D. 106, 107

Goethals, Gregor 34, 94, 120, 133, 169, 208, 246
Good News New Testament 119
Good Samaritan 110, 122, 159, 244
Good Shepherd 136
Gorlée, D. 249
Gospel
    John 24, 34, 88, 112, 116, 117, 119, 121, 128, 130, 134, 140, 148, 149, 159, 166, 191, 193, 195, 228
    Luke 29, 62, 76, 81, 84, 110, 119, 122, 159, 188, 210, 235-240, 243, 246-248
Great Britain 121, 209
Greek
    education 106
    New Testament 93, 105, 107
Gregorian Psalm Tone 179
Gutenberg 4, 50, 52, 53, 59, 63, 94, 101, 222, 231
    press 222
    world 50, 59
Gutt, E.-A. 226

Hadas, M. 106
Hagedorn, Fern Lee 4, 5, 29, 31-33, 169, 241, 245
Harris, W. V. 106, 108
Hendrickson, G. L. 106
Hertz, J. 188
historical imagination 65-73
history
    oral 214, 215
Hodgson, Robert 3, 202, 219, 224, 233
Holborn, L. 102
Hollywood Jesus 36

icon 47, 53, 71, 134, 145, 242
ideology 207, 208, 212, 214
imagescape 235
integrity of the biblical text 26
intended audience 10, 13, 14, 16, 19, 21, 44, 123, 128, 205

intent/intention
    of biblical author 9, 10, 12, 17, 18, 23, 26, 72, 221, 234, 235, 237, 240, 246
interactive software 29
Internet 50, 57, 62, 75
interpretant 202, 241-245, 254-259
interpretation 12, 23, 24, 26, 32, 35, 71, 100, 102, 107, 108, 110-112, 121, 126, 130, 136, 137, 173, 190, 203, 204, 206-208, 211, 212, 214, 216, 217, 222, 251, 253, 254, 258
    biblical 203
    theological 23, 26

interpretive community 207-209, 228-230, 253, 255
irony 99, 100
Iser, W. 105
Ivins, W., Jr. 133

Jackson, W. 160
Jaeger, W. 112
Jakobson, R. 225, 250
Jasper, D. 208
Jeremiah 210
Jesus 29, 34-38, 114-118, 120-122, 125-128, 130, 133, 137, 140, 141, 145, 147, 156, 157, 159, 160, 163, 165, 166, 175-177, 184, 185, 201, 236
Jesus Christ Superstar 122
John the Baptist 128
Johnson, M. 103
Jordan, Clarence 130
Josipovici, G. 211
Jungmann, J. A. 187, 188

Kennedy, G. A. 105, 108, 109, 112, 117
King David 121
Knox, B. 105-107
Kraeling, K. 137
Kristensen, E. H. 163, 165, 166

Lake, K. 188
Lakoff, G. 103
language
    receptor 7, 9, 14, 32, 103, 121, 129, 207, 230
    source 221
    target 89, 221, 234
LaRue, J. 185
Last Supper 140, 141, 165, 166
Latin Vulgate 190
Law and Prophets 176
lectionary 3, 62, 120, 223
Lefevere, A. 204, 255
Leibniz, Gottfried 88
Lentz, T. 106-108
Leupold, U. S. 179
Lévi-Strauss, Claude 224
Lindars, B. 117
literacy v, 15, 93, 106, 107, 203
Long, L. 203
Lord's Prayer, musical settings 180-197
    Marbeck setting 191-195
    medieval setting 188-191
    Mozarabic setting 186-188
Lost But Found 209-212, 215
Luke 15.11-32 29, 122, 235-239, 243, 246, 247
Luther, Martin 54, 95, 101, 119, 179, 180, 195
Luther German text 119

Magnificat 127
Malawi Bible Society (MBS) 209, 215, 238
Manguel, Alberto 147, 148
Manipulation School 249
Marbeck, John 191, 193-195
Mark 4 37
Mark 5.1-20 4, 29, 35, 122, 237, 245
marriage 63, 120, 152
Martinez, Maria 30
mass audience 51, 60
Matisse, H. 164
McDannell, Colleen 151, 170
McLuhan, Marshall 18, 44, 52, 101, 104
media
    new 3-5, 29, 31, 32, 38, 40, 43-45, 51, 54, 56, 57, 59-63, 70, 75, 93-95, 99, 100, 104, 119, 121-124, 126, 127, 129-131, 133, 134, 169, 173-175, 177, 178, 180, 187, 195, 196, 201-203, 219, 233-248
    new media Bible 60-62, 93, 237, 244
    New Media Translations Program 4, 29, 45, 94
    new media translator 94
    personal 47, 54, 57, 59, 60
    shift 49, 50, 54, 59, 104
melodic figures 179, 182, 190
memoria 107
Menius, Justus 179
meter 112
Metzger, Bruce 117
midrash 94, 173, 175-177, 185, 195
millennium 50, 101, 178
Millgram, A. E. 185, 188
Mishnah 176
Missale Romanum 189
Mocquereau, A. 175
Morris, C. W. 223, 241
mosaic 138, 141, 166
music 20, 21, 33, 35, 36, 41, 42, 47, 49, 65, 70, 94, 108, 122, 130, 169, 171, 173-175, 178-182, 186, 193, 194, 196, 197, 205, 215-217, 235, 238, 247
    in translation 20-24, 178-180
    pop 49
    video 35, 36, 205, 215-217, 238, 247
myth 214, 216

narrative
    structure 99, 100

style 100
National Academy of Design 149
Neale, Stephen 213
new translations 14, 16, 195, 207
New York Times i, 104
Newman, Barclay 33
Newton, Issac 88, 89
Nida, Eugene 3, 15, 94, 103, 110, 119, 141, 174, 178, 181, 184, 220, 221, 241, 259
Nirvana 121
Nord, Christiane 86

Old Testament 119, 123, 148, 214
Ong, W. J. 224, 227, 228
Out of the Tombs 29-45, 122, 124-126, 131, 205, 206, 237, 245

parable 110, 121-123, 125, 128, 159, 209-212, 215, 216, 235-238, 243, 244, 246
Pater Noster 186-188, 190
Paul, the Apostle 160, 165, 166, 169, 201, 211, 219
Peace of Constantine 135-137
Peirce, C. S. 202, 223, 241, 242, 250, 251, 253-256, 259, 260
Philo 95
Plato 108, 120
Plutarch 108
poetry 72, 78, 97, 100, 102, 109, 112, 174, 234
Pope Gregory the Great 188
Porter, S. E. 116
post-colonial modernity 212
Postman, N. 101
postmodern age 101
pragmatism 260
Presbyterian 120
printing 4, 45, 57, 93, 102, 104, 107, 134, 135, 148, 151, 152, 161, 174, 175, 203
Prodigal Son 65, 209-212, 215, 216, 235, 237, 238, 240, 243, 246
Protestantism 102, 151

Psalm 141, 143, 179, 190, 191

radio 8, 14, 49, 51, 52, 133, 231
rap 122, 124-127
Ravenna 138
reading
    aloud 14, 105-107
    silent 93, 102, 105, 107-111
realism 104, 159, 170, 213, 214, 216
Rebera, B. 206, 222
Reformation(s) 94, 102, 134, 135, 139, 148, 175, 179, 185, 191-193, 195, 230
restructuring 13-17, 24, 26, 173
revelation 206
Revell, E. J. 179
Reyburn, W. D. 220, 221
Reynolds, Sir J. 154
rhetoric 98, 105, 106, 112, 117, 182, 208, 212
rhythms 20, 52, 143
ritual 120, 135, 137-139, 151, 169, 201, 219, 220, 226-230
Robbins, V. K. 105
Romans 211, 223
Rossano Gospels 140, 141, 143, 147
Rouault, George 162
Rule of St. Benedict 107
Ryder, Albert P. 162

Sampler Bible 154, 156, 160, 161
San Apollinare Nuovo 138, 139, 141
Sarum Rite 191
Saussure, Ferdinand de 102, 223, 241
Schnackenburg, R. 117
Scott, B. Brandon 93, 101, 103, 123, 222
scriptural authority 201, 203, 206
scriptural music 178-197
semiotic chain of translation 251
semiotic system 219, 223
semiotics 201, 202, 224, 225, 233, 238, 241, 244, 248-250, 254
Shahn, Ben 162

Shannon, Claude 220, 221
sign
   system 202, 225, 226
signification 206, 223, 225, 226, 241, 243
signified 102, 103, 110, 111, 118, 223, 241-246
signifier 102, 104, 110, 111, 223, 224, 241-243, 245, 246, 248
Simson, Otto von 138, 139
Sisley, Joy 201, 203, 238
Smyth, H. W. 181, 182, 189
Snell-Hornby, Mary 249
Snyder, Graydon 135-137
Solomon 154, 156
Soukup, Paul 3, 44, 55, 103, 105, 201, 219, 235
sound mapping 111, 112
soundscape 235, 236

Staeblein, B. 188
Stanford, W. B. 106, 181, 182
Steiner, R. 188
Stephanus 182, 184
Stubbs, Michael 102
Suetonius 117
synagogue 136, 137

television 8, 18, 36, 37, 42-44, 49-61, 104, 105, 134, 152, 201, 203, 204, 209, 212, 213, 215, 227, 228, 231, 238, 240
   cable 51, 52, 60
   personal 57-59
   traditional 52-54, 56, 59
Ten Commandments 208, 215
Tertullian 180, 187, 188, 190
testing and evaluation 40
text identification 17
text/reader relationship 203, 217
textual authority 204
The Drama House 209
The Visit 29, 76-82, 85, 122, 125, 126, 128, 248
theater 8

Theodoric 138
Thomas, Kenneth 33, 205, 216, 221, 235, 241
Tompkins, J. P. 105, 222, 229
Tractarian Movement 195
translation
   audiovisual 31, 32
   cultural context 121-122
   exercises 75-89
   multimedia 33, 94, 203-205, 207, 208, 217, 221-223, 225, 227, 229-231, 236
   multimedia program 173
   process 5, 14, 16, 29, 33, 39, 42, 84, 110, 258
   theory 42, 50, 51, 53, 258
   video 4, 29, 36-38, 41, 203, 205, 209, 212, 213, 236, 239, 243-248
Trumbull, John 149
typography 107, 108, 223

United Bible Society (UBS) 9, 11, 13, 20, 26, 29, 31, 33, 107, 166
USA Today 47, 104
Utrecht Psalter 141, 143, 147

VCR 52
Venuti, L. 207
video 3-5, 8, 10, 11, 29, 31, 33, 35-38, 40-43, 49, 50, 52, 54-56, 58, 65, 78, 123, 125-130, 173, 203-207, 209-217, 234-240, 243-248
voice
   tone of 14, 222
   tonus peregrinus 190

Wagner, Peter 186
Wagner, Richard 175
Waltke, E. 179
Weaver, William 220, 252
Welk, Lawrence 171
Werner, E. 190

Wittenberg Chapel 179
word track 233-235, 237-240, 245, 246
World Wide Web 55, 57, 62
Worth, Merle 4, 36, 65, 68, 211, 240, 246

Zechariah 119, 248
Zwingli, Ulrich 148

About the Authors

Mona Baker is Course Director of the M.Sc. in Translation Studies at University of Manchester Institute of Science and Technology, UK (UMIST). She lectures on translation theory and linguistics at UMIST and by invitation at various venues abroad and supervises a number of Ph.D. students in the area of translation studies. Apart from numerous papers in scholarly journals and collected volumes, she is author of *In Other Words: A Coursebook on Translation* (Routledge 1992; reprinted five times), co-editor of *Text and Technology: In honor of John Sinclair* (John Benjamins, 1993), General Editor of the *Encyclopedia of Translation Studies* (Routledge, 1998), and Editor of *The Translator: Studies in Intercultural Communication,* a refereed international journal published by St. Jerome. She is former Chair of the Education & Training Committee of the Institute of Translation & Interpreting, and currently serves on a number of translation committees and advisory boards, including the Translation Committee of the Arts Council of England. E-mail: MonaBaker@compuserve.com.

David G. Burke presently serves as the Associate Vice President of the Scripture Publications Area of the American Bible Society. He is concurrently also the Director of the Translations Department within the Scripture Publications Area. A specialist in Hebrew Bible and cognate literature, Burke holds a doctorate from the Johns Hopkins University, where he studied under Delbert Hillers. Prior to joining the staff of the American Bible Society, Burke held a senior post at the Lutheran World Federation-USA National Committee and before that, a university chaplaincy at Rutgers. His scholarly interests include the Book of Baruch, translation theory and practices, and Jewish-Christian relations. He presently serves on the editorial board of *Explorations*; a journal devoted to Jewish-Christian dialogue. Burke holds ordination in the Evangelical Lutheran Church in America. E-mail: dburke@americanbible.org.

Euan McG. Fry is a former United Bible Societies Translations Consultant, now serving in a part-time editing and writing capacity. Formerly a missionary with the Australian Methodist Church in Papua New Guinea and a full-time Bible translator, he served over the years from 1967 to 1988 as Translations Secretary for the Bible Society in Australia and as a UBS Translation Adviser in the South Pacific area. He had a particular interest during that time in the presentation of biblical text in the comic format and audiocassette media. He is currently the editor of *Practical Papers for the Bible Translator*, and co-author of the recently published *Handbook on Genesis* (in the UBS *Helps for Translators* series). E-mail: euanfry@ozemail.com.au.

Gregor Goethals is a graphic designer and art historian. Her academic interests in both Art History and Philosophy of Religion led to graduate work at Yale and later to a doctorate at Harvard. Following that, the Rhode Island School of Design in Providence became an immeasurably rich environment for over 20 years. There, she became Professor of Art History, serving as department head and later as dean of graduate studies. She has currently set up a design studio in Sonoma, California. Her books include *The TV Ritual: Worship at the Video Altar* (Boston: Beacon 1981) and *The Electronic Golden Calf: Images and the Making of Meaning* (Boston: Cowley 1991). Presently she is working on *Escape from Time: Ritual Dimensions of Popular Culture* and serving as art director for ABS's Multimedia Translations Program. E-mail: 75144.2226@compuserve.com.

Fern Lee Hagedorn was instrumental in the formation of the ABS Multimedia Translations Program (now the New Media Translations Program). Presently as one of its chief consultants, Hagedorn continues to oversee the work of producing the translations and companion study-helps. Working on the philosophy that the project must be content-driven (the Bible) while technology and audience-informed, she has worked on three award-winning music video translations and multimedia CD-ROM programs: *Out of the Tombs (Mark 5.1-20); A Father and Two Sons (Luke 15.11-32);* and *The Visit (Luke 1.39-56).* A fourth is entitled *The Neighbor, (Luke 10.25-37).* Hagedorn headed the ABS program from 1989-1997, held staff and board memberships within the national and international entities of the Lutheran Church, including Director of Communication for the Lutheran World Federation-USA where she produced the award-winning documentary *They Speak of Hope: The Church in El Salvador.* Hagedorn was a founding member of the Asian American Film Festival and was honored upon the festival's 15th anniversary in 1993. E-mail: FLHagedorn@ezaccess.net.

Bob Hodgson, Assistant Director in the Translations Department at the American Bible Society (ABS), presently manages the newly-formed ABS Research Center for Scripture and Media. He joined the ABS in 1991 as a print translator assigned to the Contemporary English Version project. In Spring of 1992, he became part of a team working on multimedia Bible translations and interactive Bible study helps. Prior to his service with the ABS, Hodgson held from 1980 to 1991 a professorship in the religious studies department at Southwest Missouri State University, Springfield, MO. From 1977 to 1980, he held a joint professorship at St. Andrew's Seminary, Quezon City, and in the Southeast Asia Graduate School of Theology. In Germany from 1967 to 1976 he began (Goettingen) and completed (Heidelberg) his doctoral studies. In addition to editing this volume, he published with Paul Soukup in 1997 *From One Medium to Another: Basic Issues for Communicating the Bible in New Media* (New York and Kansas City: American Bible Society and Sheed & Ward). E-mail: BHodgson@compuserve.com.

Eugene A. Nida, a linguist, anthropologist, and biblical scholar, began his association with ABS in 1943 and was an Executive Secretary for the Translations Department. His early projects included field surveys, research, training programs, and checking manuscripts of new translations. His work has taken him to more than 85 countries, where he has conferred with translators on linguistic problems involving more than 200 different languages. He has authored or co-authored more than 40 books and 250 articles on linguistics, cultural anthropology, translation theory and practice, and the science of meaning. His most recent volumes are *Language, Culture, and Translating, The Sociolinguistics of Interlingual Communications,* and *Understanding English* (soon to be published in English and Chinese).

Nida was also Translations Research Coordinator for UBS from 1970-1980. He has now retired from administrative responsibilities, but continues to consult with the Bible Societies, as well as broadening his areas of research and lecturing extensively in Europe and Asia.

Basil A. Rebera is the United Bible Societies Global Translation Services Coordinator, based at the American Bible Society, New York. He took linguistic studies at Australian National University and Mcquarie University in Sydney, Australia and received his Ph.D. degree in biblical studies from Mcquarie University. He has served as a UBS Translation Consultant in the Asia Pacific Region based in India, Thailand, and Singapore and then as Translation Consultant and Director of the Translation and Text Division of the Bible Society in Australia before moving to New York as UBS Translation Services Coordinator.

About the Authors

Lydia E. Lebrón-Rivera works as a Bible Studies Specialist for the Office of Spanish Scholarly Resources at ABS. She is an ordained minister of the United Methodist Church and has worked with Hispanic ministries in the U.S. for many years. She holds a M.Div. from the Seminario Evangelico de Puerto Rico, a STM from Union Theological Seminary in New York, and currently pursues a Ph.D. in biblical studies from the same institution.

Gary R. Rowe is president of Rowe, Inc. and of inSITElearning, Inc. Rowe's focus is the opportunity to create integrated television-based experiences by combining text, graphics, audio, data and images through digital production and distribution solutions.

Rowe's presentation for the White House Conference on Library and Information Services was published in *The Information Society Journal,* "Multimedia Technology as the Catalyst for a New Form of Literacy," in 1992. "Education in the Emerging Media Democracy" was published in the journal *Educational Technology* in 1994. In 1997, his article, "Publishing Words and Images: Schools and Learning in the Millennial Shift," appeared in *From One Medium to Another: Basic Issues for Communicating the Scriptures in New Media,* published by The American Bible Society and Sheed & Ward. In 1992, Rowe received a George Foster Peabody Award for his work with CNN during his service as Senior Vice President of Turner Educational Services, Inc. E-mail: growe@rowemedia.com.

Bernard Brandon Scott is the Darbeth Distinguished Professor of New Testament at the Phillips Theological Seminary on the campus of the University of Tulsa. He has been a Visiting Professor at Yale Divinity School and previously taught for 17 years at St. Meinard School of Theology, St.

Meinard, IN. Scott serves on the editorial board of *Biblical Theology Review, Religion, Semeia,* and *The Catholic Biblical Quarterly.* He is a member of the Society of Biblical Literature, Catholic Biblical Association, American Academy of Religion, Societas Novi Testamenti Studiorum, and the Westar Institute. He is also a consultant for ABS's Multimedia Translations Project.

Scott is the author of many books and articles on the New Testament. He has just published *Hollywood Dreams and Biblical Stories* (Fortress, 1994) which brings into conversation modern American movies and the New Testament. His *Hear Then the Parables* (Fortress, 1989) has been critically acclaimed. E-mail: sem_bbs@centum.utulsa.edu.

Joy Sisley was born in Rwanda where her parents served as educationists with the Rwanda Mission for 35 years. She worked in Nairobi and Brussels with the United Bible Societies as Assistant to the Regional Secretary from 1974-1979. In 1979, she moved to England to study for a B.A. in culture, communication and media studies at Leeds University. She has worked as a film and television editor before she began teaching drama and television at King Alfred's College in the U.K. She is currently engaged in Ph.D. research at the University of Warwick into translation strategy and genre choice in multimedia translations of biblical texts. She serves as an advisor to the United Bible Societies on their video translation program.

Paul A. Soukup, SJ, has explored the connections between communication and theology since 1982. His publications include *Communication and Theology* (London: WACC 1983); *Christian Communication: A Bibliographical*

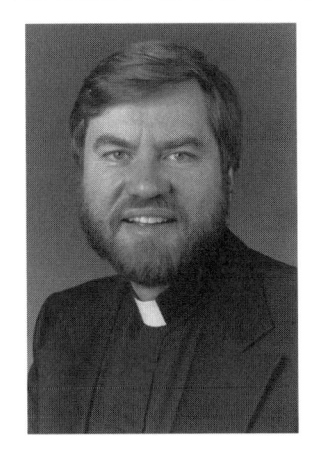

Survey (New York: Greenwood 1989), and *Mass Media and the Moral Imagination* with Philip J. Rossi (Kansas City, MO: Sheed & Ward 1994), and *From One Medium to Another* with Robert Hodgson (Kansas City and New York: Sheed & Ward and ABS, 1997). In addition, he and Thomas J. Farrell have edited three volumes of the collected works of Walter J. Ong, SJ, *Faith and Contexts* (Atlanta: Scholars Press 1992-1995). This later work has led him to examine more closely how orality-literacy studies can contribute to an understanding of theological expression. A graduate of the University of Texas at Austin (Ph.D., 1985), Soukup teaches in the Communication Department at Santa Clara University. E-mail: psoukup@mailer.scu.edu.

Ubaldo Stecconi was born in Ancona, Italy. He received a degree in translation from the University of Trieste. He helped found the School for Translators and Interpreters San Pellegrino at Misano Adriatico Rimini, where he taught for five years. From 1992-1998, he served as assistant professor at the University of the Philippines and Ateneo de Manila University in Manila, as well as cultural advisor to the local Italian Embassy. His publications include: Peirce's Semiotics for Translation (*Koiné, V*, 1998), Transgression and Circumvention through Translation in the Philippines, with Maria Luisa Torres Reyes, in Snell-Hornby, Jettmarava, & Kaindl (eds.), *Translation as Intercultural Communication* (John Benjamins, 1997). With Carmina Bautista, he edited and translated into Italian: *Daydreams and Nightmares: A Fearless Anthology of Italian Short Stories* (Anvil, 1997), and *Balikbayan*, a selection of Philippine short stories (Aracne, 1998). Since 1996 he has been review editor of the journal *Pen & Ink: the Philippine Literary Quarterly*.

J. Ritter Werner is music director of the New Media Translations Project for the American Bible Society. He also composed the settings for the art/chant version of *The Visit* and *A Father and Two Sons*. He received a Doctor of Musical Arts from the College Conservatory of Music at the University of Cincinnati where he majored in organ and minored in musicology and music theory. Postdoctoral work took him to Canterbury Cathedral, England, to study under Allen Wicks. After returning to Ohio in 1974, he divided his professional time between church work and university teaching. In his free time he earned an M.A. in biblical studies from United Theological Seminary. Werner teaches organ at Wright State University, and lectures at his new alma mater, United Theological Seminary. E-mail: jwerner@desire.wright. edu.

Merle Worth has served as a director, producer, and editor for nearly every major network and cable television station. Her work crosses all boundaries, from music videos to theatrical shorts and documentaries. As president of Worth Associates, Inc., this Emmy-award winner has won over 30 film festivals for her work with the Beatles and Ravi Shankar in RAGA, the theatrical short *The Kite, CBS Reports* with Bill Moyers, and her two-hour prime time ABC Special, *"The Dignity of Children."* Her dramatic long-form music videos won her a Best Interactive Media Award. Her films are profiled in *First Cut,* published by the University of California Press. Worth scripted and directed the video translations *Out of the Tombs, A Father and Two Sons, The Visit,* and *The Neighbor.*

Sheed & Ward
Books of Related Interest
available at your favorite bookstore

From One Medium to Another
Communicating the Bible Through Multimedia
ed. Paul A. Soukup, Robert Hodgson
A sign of our times is an increased awareness of the ways in which culture, theology, and communications interact. We have come to see this interaction particularly at the places where the Church transfers its theological content between cultures in forms such as electronic and screen technologies. In this collection, eighteen experts from a wide variety of academic and professional fields engage key question in a series of thought-provoking essays that define the emerging field of new media Bible translating.
P 382 pp 1-55612-968-8 *$24.95*

New Image of Religious Film
ed. John R. May
This collection brings together contributors from richly diverse backgrounds — literature, art history, sociology, philosophy, theology — to explore a wide range of issues concerning religion and film. May also analyzes the changing "religious" language of feature films, and reflects on the theology and spirituality found in contemporary movies. This book suggests how cinema can be a worthy ally for evangelization and in faith's search for understanding.
P 288 pp 1-55612-761-8 *$24.95*

Imaging the Divine
Jesus and Christ-Figures in Film
Lloyd Baugh, S.J.
Specifically focused on several recent and prize-winning films, this book creates a complex and challenging approach to religious film and how it deals with the metaphor of the Christ-event. Offering a new approach and criteria for the appreciation and judgment of these films, this is a necessary aid in understanding the dialogue between Christian theology and film.
P 350 pp   1-55612-863-0   *$24.95*

Media, Culture and Catholicism
ed. Paul A. Soukup, S.J.
Contributors represent pastoral and academic fields. Concerns include the "levelling" effect of television's compressed form of communication, the electronic transmission of the Word, preparing church leaders for a technological age, and preaching the Gospel in a video culture. How far has the MediaChurch impacted your parish? Your preaching and presiding style? Your prayer?
P 240 pp   1-55612-769-3   *$24.95*

SHEED & WARD
An Apostolate of the Priests of the Sacred Heart
7373 South Lovers Lan Road
Franklin Wisconsin   53132

Email sheed@execpc.com   *Phone* 1 800 558 0580 or *Fax* 1 800 369 4448